CAUGHT IN THE UNDERTOW

CAUGHT IN THE UNDERTOW

Escaping the Grip of Childhood Abuse

JEFFREY GOLDSTEIN

CEDAR FORGE

Copyright © 2014 by Jeffrey Goldstein
All rights reserved. No part of this publication may be reproduced, distributed, or transmitted in any form or by any means, including photocopying, recording, digital scanning, or other electronic or mechanical methods, without the prior written permission of the publisher, except in the case of brief quotations embodied in critical reviews and certain other noncommercial uses permitted by copyright law.

For permission requests, please address
Cedar Forge Press
PO Box 2222
Poulsbo, WA 98370

Published 2014 by Cedar Forge Press
Printed in the United States of America
18 17 16 15 14   1 2 3 4 5
ISBN 978-1-936672-75-2
Library of Congress Control Number: 2014937195

Net proceeds from the sale of this book will be donated to agencies that provide assistance to abused children and their families.

I value your comments. Please feel free to give feedback:
jeff.goldstein51@gmail.com.

Names of the people in this book, other than family members, have been changed to protect their privacy.

For Gretchen,
You have made everything possible!

Author's Notes

I WRITE THIS AS A RECORD of my experiences being caught in the undertow, and my journey to a better place. This is not meant as an indictment of anyone. I have long ago forgiven any people who purposely or inadvertently harmed me.

Prologue

I WAS ONLY SEVEN YEARS OLD. But I awoke that morning with a feeling of anguish. An angst. A profound emptiness gnawing through my insides that was unbearable. I was lost. I felt numb. I walked around the house, and realized that it was cold. No one else was there. I got dressed, ate some cereal, and walked through my back yard. I took my usual route through the bushes and the yard on the next block, to the big field behind Shore Road Elementary School. A group of kids were already there. They stared at me. They whispered. They looked away when I looked back. Finally, I saw my friend. He came up to me, and he told me.

"NO! IT'S NOT TRUE!" I punched him in the face. Mrs. Garelock, our teacher came running towards us, and I was scared. But instead of yelling, she hugged me. And I ran away. I ran as fast as I could. If I could only run fast enough, none of this would be true. My lungs were burning. I gasped for air. I ran harder.

I burst through my front door. My Grandma was vacuuming the floor. She was crying. My Grandpa was collapsed in a chair. He was shaking and crying so loud that ... I knew. I knew that my sister Sheryl was dead. I buried my face in my pillow. I was dazed. And I knew. I knew that nothing would ever be the same.

Part One
BROOKLYN

Being born leaves no time for rehearsal
A slap, a cry
And we're on our way

Jeffrey Goldstein

One

I WAS BORN IN BROOKLYN, IN 1951, at the Brooklyn Woman's Hospital." I'm a boy! How could I be born in a woman's hospital?" I used to ask. And Mom and Dad would laugh. I didn't know why they laughed, but I enjoyed making them laugh. We lived at 228 New York Avenue, in an apartment building with a big stoop. To the left of the stoop were cement steps that went down to a big steel door that opened into a dark basement. A monster lived in that basement. A monster that was able to come up through our bathtub drain and drag you down.

The door to our apartment opened into a long hall. To the left, at the far end of the hall, was a tiny kitchen, and the opening to a small living room. At the other end of the hall there was a toy chest, a bedroom, and our little bathroom. My Mom and Dad slept in the big bed. My sister Sheryl, who was two years younger, slept on a small bed on one side of the room. I slept on a bed with cowboy sheets on the other side of the room. Sometimes we'd all get in the big bed.

The monster could come up from the basement through the bathtub drain, even though we were on the third floor. That made me afraid to go to the bathroom alone. I did not want him to pull me down the drain. So when I had to go, I would chant in a sing-song voice, loud enough for all to hear, "I have to go to the bathroom. Sit on the toy chest!" I would chant until an adult obliged me. I hoped that this was before I wet my pants. But I would not go into that bathroom alone. And I would always go with the door open.

One day Mom and some of her lady friends were playing mahjong in the living room. They did this each week. I was sitting on the toilet, and someone had been sitting on the toy chest. But when I looked up, no one was there. I ran out of the bathroom, down the hall, and into the living room with my pants around my ankles. Mom was not very happy about this. I liked exposing myself to her lady friends. I had discovered that if I had my pajama bottoms on, and I moved my hips back and forth, the bottoms would fall down. I enjoyed taking the opportunity to do this.

My Dad was in the Navy during World War II. He had a duffel bag full of his Navy stuff in the back of a closet. I heard stories about how he was the bombardier on a plane that flew in the South Pacific. His plane took off from a big aircraft carrier. He usually was friendly, pleasant, and loved to sing, but sometimes he suddenly exploded. He would throw me across the room, and then hug me and tell me how much he loved me. I never saw him touch my Mom or Sheryl. He was a big muscular man, and I craved his love and attention.

Dad worked in the children's clothes industry, and Sheryl and I always had brand new fancy clothes. All four of us would walk down the street, Dad holding my hand, and Mom pushing Sheryl in a baby carriage. I'd be wearing black and white shiny shoes, red shorts, a plaid jacket, and a red cap. Everyone seemed to know my Dad. "How ya doing, Eli. What's going on, Eli. Beautiful family, Eli." I felt like royalty.

Walking was a way of life in Brooklyn. We'd stride down the different blocks with different types of people, different smells, and hear different languages. I always felt safe. I was holding my Dad's hand. Once a dog was running at us, and in a split second, Dad lifted me up in the air over his head. I imagined that I was in an airplane flying over the ocean. But no one could shoot *me* down. Dad yelled at the dog and it ran away." Lift me up again, Daddy."

The most fun was when we walked a few blocks over to

Nostrand Avenue, where all the stores were. We'd pass food stores, clothing stores, toy stores, book stores and a store where Dad would buy his cigars. He was not allowed to smoke in the apartment, so he'd often walk down the street with a big cigar in his mouth. He'd seem even more important. And I felt even more protected.

Several nights a week we would have our bath ritual. When we were younger, Sheryl and I would take a bath together. When we got older, Sheryl would go first, be dried off, and then I would have to bathe in her dirty water. An adult sat on the toilet and read while I was in the tub. This gave me protection from the monster. I had little boats and rubber toys that I played with, but the most fun that I had was with my hair. I loved my mops of curly dark brown hair. Using the shampoo, I would shape my hair into two horns, or one big horn like a unicorn, or maybe spikes like the Statue of Liberty. Sometimes I tried to make all my hair flat like a big version of Dad's flat top haircut. Then I could put little toy airplanes on it and pretend that they were on an air craft carrier.

Dad didn't share my positive feelings toward my curls. When I was a year old my hair was so long and thick that Dad took me to one of those Italian barbers. I allegedly kicked and screamed and cried so much that the barber refused to finish the haircut. I went home with the sides all shaven and all the hair on the top untouched. I was a baby with a Mohawk.

Another part of the bath ritual was having our hair and scalp cleaned. I imagined it was to get rid of any cooties. This would be done by my Dad. He would drag a sharp little white comb through our hair. It hurt. We would scream, "Oh No, Not the Fine Tooth Comb!" He told us that when he was in the Navy there was a man on the ship who smelled because he didn't clean himself or his hair properly. The rest of the men felt compelled to drag him into the shower and to clean his body and his head with steel wool. As we resisted, Dad yelled, "Stop crying or I'll give you something to really cry about."

After Sheryl and I were clean, we went into the bedroom and sat down next to Mom on the big bed. Mom read to us every night, mostly from little Golden Books. The books had colorful covers, and gold tape on the spines, speckled with black dots. We loved those books. There was a Golden Book with a clock on it. I used it to teach myself how to tell time when I was just three years old. I then got one of my most prized possessions ever, my own Mickey Mouse wrist watch. I would ask every one that I met, "Do you want to know what time it is?" And I would tell them.

Bed time came after we were read to. We were both tucked into our beds and Dad would kiss us goodnight and rub the stubble on his unshaven face on our smooth baby faces. After the lights were out and the door was closed, Sheryl and I always played for a while. We played hide and seek or one of a myriad of games that we made up using our vivid imaginations. Sometimes, after we were finally in bed, we would hear Mom and Dad fighting. I always told Sheryl that everything was alright. But I was not so sure.

Jeffrey, age 3, and Sheryl, age 1

Jeffrey age 4, Sheryl age 2

Two

My GRANDMA, BORN ROSE DRESSLER, and Grandpa, born Max Wegbreit, lived a few blocks away, on Montgomery Street. They were my Mom's parents and we spent a lot of time together. We hardly ever saw my Dad's parents, who were referred to as, "the other grandparents." They also lived somewhere in Brooklyn.

My Grandma was a very warm, nurturing woman. And she was very athletic. She could swim in the ocean. She would play catch with me, with a baseball, without using a glove. She drank a glass of borscht every day. I thought that it was blood and that drinking it made her strong. I was always happy to see her. My Grandpa was very scary. He had strange nervous tics, and would make snoring type noises, even though he was awake. He once tried to kiss me on my lips, and I stabbed him on his forearm with a pencil. "That boy is evil," he yelled. I was only trying to protect myself. He always seemed upset about something.

One of the things that upset Grandpa was the Brooklyn Dodgers. He used to go to many of the games at Ebbets Field, but said that I was too young and never took me along. Grandpa also would sometimes take me on long walks. We went down Nostrand Ave. and Pitkin Ave. past the many stores. Most of the stores had radios playing and they would all be tuned to the Dodger games. Grandpa told me that the announcer was named Red Barber. When there was a game, Red Barber's voice was everywhere. Grandpa would listen to the game as if he was in a trance. He would be ecstatically happy or inconsolably sad, depending on how the game was going. I began to realize that baseball was a very important thing. Grandpa cried when the Dodgers moved to Los Angeles.

Grandma and Grandpa were both born in Poland and came to America when they were teenagers. Grandpa came from Warsaw, and Grandma came from a city called, Lodz. Grandma pronounced it, "Ludge". She had two sisters and two brothers, and they lived on the second floor in a two bedroom apartment in the Jewish section of Lodz. They lived very primitively. There was no refrigerator or ice box, so they had to shop for food each day. There was no bathroom, only an outhouse in the backyard. There was no running water. A man came each day with a yoke on his shoulders that had buckets of water hanging from each end. The family would fill pails of water from the buckets and use that water for drinking and washing.

Grandma's mother, my Great Grandmother, had the English name, Sarah Rebecca. My sister Sheryl Robin is named after her. Great Grandmother would have to shop, cook and clean every day. Grandma's father, my Great Grandfather, had the English name, Jakeal. I am named after him. He was a tailor and he made the family's clothes. The family could all speak Polish, Russian, German, and Yiddish, which they called speaking "Jewish". Yiddish was the only language that they spoke at home. Getting an education was very important to them, so they found a way to send all the children to school, even though they had to pay for the three girls.

Anti Semitism was prevalent in Poland, and the men would be harassed and have stones thrown at them on the way to temple, or *shul,* as they called it. Grandma's father would try to hit them back with his cane. Sigmund, the oldest son, eventually left to go to America. Then the second boy, Hymie, also left for America. They both were successful and were able to wire back enough money for their parents and three younger sisters to join them. The Dressler family sold all of their possessions, except for their clothes, and tearfully said good-bye to their relatives and friends. They took a train to Russia, took a boat to England, and boarded a ship for the trans-Atlantic voyage to

America. This was in June of 1912. They were all very frightened because they had all heard about the Titanic tragedy in April of 1912. But they were eager to join Sigmund and Hymie in Brooklyn.

Grandma was born in 1897, and was 15 years old when they settled in Brooklyn. This was too old to start going to public school, so her parents told everyone that she was born in 1900 and was 12. She was put into a class with other foreigners and learned English very quickly. For the rest of her life, she remained three years younger.

Grandma Rose Dressler and Grandpa Max Wegbreit's marriage was arranged by their mothers. Grandma did not want to get married. She was enjoying all the fun that she was having as a single woman. She liked Max, and thought that he was good looking, clean, or "immaculate," as she put it, and polite, but was not ready to marry him. However, you did not disobey your Mother, and they got married in June, 1924. Max and Rose had their only child in December, 1925, and named her Mildred. Mildred, nicknamed "Millie" as a girl, later took the name, "Micki". Micki grew up to become my Mom.

My Grandparents both wrote and spoke English very well, but spoke only Yiddish to each other. Yiddish words and expressions were sprinkled into their English. My Mom and my Grandparents would gossip about other relatives, friends and neighbors, and they would use very descriptive words. Grandma would refer to her wealthy older brother Sigmund as a *Shnorrer*, a cheapskate. Our neighbor Murray was a *Shlub*, a worthless, lazy jerk. The other Grandparents were *Meshugener*, or crazy. A cousin married a non Jewish girl, or a *Shikseh*. Cousin Shirley had a *Goyisher Kop*, or was stupid. When we left my Grandparent's apartment, they would say, *"Gai Gezunterhait,"* "Go in good health." They taught me Yiddish songs, and I loved the names of some of the entertainers they talked about, Ish Kabibble, Moisha Oysher, and Menasha Skulnick.

Curses and superstitions were a big part of my grandparent's language and culture. It was wrong to talk about your good fortune because that would cause something bad to happen.

Caught in the Undertow

They believed in the "evil eye," *Einhoreh*. They spoke colorful Yiddish curses, such as," *Gae kucken ahfen yam,*" "Go shit in the ocean," and *"Gai plats,"* "Go split your guts." When Grandma was around she would want to see my bowel movement after I went to the bathroom. She would always look at it and exclaim, *bubkas,* which meant, "nothing". In her mind, I never pooped a big enough amount to indicate that I was healthy.

Grandma and Grandpa had old 78 RPM records of Yiddish songs. They had albums and albums full of big, black, fragile records. Some of them used very obscene words and concepts. They let me listen to them and assumed that I wouldn't understand what they were saying. But I figured them out and knew at least 5 different ways to say penis by the time I was in Kindergarten.

Grandma also sang and chanted various verses in English. I was enchanted by the rhythms and cadence of the words. I enthusiastically followed her lead, as if she were a choral director, and crooned the following meaningless ditty:

Hello, hello, hello, sir. Meet me at the grocer. No sir! Why sir! Because I have a cold sir! Let me hear you sneeze, sir! Achoo! Achoo! Achoo!, Sir!

I felt connected to something indescribable that was bigger than we were when we sang together. Grandma was my link to a different time and a different place.

Grandma and Jeffrey, age 2

Three

Growing up in Brooklyn, there were countless other kids to play with. There was a big sidewalk in front of the buildings on my block, and that is where we played when the weather was nice. We played different versions of tag, red rover, spud, and hide and go seek, while groups of older girls played jump rope. We used the stoop in front of the building to play, "Go to the top of the class". We younger kids would all sit on the lowest step, and the older girls would ask us questions. If you answered one correctly, you got to move up a step. The kid who made it to the top first won. The street that ran down our block didn't have much traffic, so sometimes we got to play in the road. The older boys played stick ball, and we played a game called "skully". We would use chalk to draw a board with boxes and numbers in it on the road, and use bottle caps to shoot onto the board and to get points. The girls would use the chalk to draw boxes to play hopscotch with. The games would be interrupted temporarily when a car came by. Whoever saw the car first would have to shout, "Car, Car, C-A-R, stick your dick in a pickle jar!" Then we would all laugh and run onto the sidewalk. We were young kids, so our Moms were usually watching us. If they were listening we would shout, "Stick your head in a pickle jar," instead saying "dick".

Steven, who was fatter than the rest of us boys, was what my parents called a *schlimazel*. He was always stepping in dog poop, cutting himself on a piece of broken glass on the sidewalk, wetting his pants, or tripping over an untied shoelace. He got hit in the eye by a bottle cap when we were playing "skully," got a bloody nose from a ball that hit him when the older boys were playing stickball, started to cry when we were playing in the park because a bug had flown up his nose, and never made it higher than the first step when we played, "Go to the top of the class". The girls would purposely ask him harder questions. I imagined that one day his dick really would get stuck in a pickle jar.

My parents called my friend Willy a *shvartza*, the Yiddish word for a black person. He lived with what seemed like dozens of siblings. They lived in one of the few single family houses in our neighborhood. He actually had a yard around his house, and a pet dog that would lick my face when I visited. I loved spending time at his house. They had the first television set that I ever saw, and when we played hide and go seek in his house, there were more places to hide than there were outside. His older brothers had pictures of naked women, and a flip book that showed a man having sex with a woman. Willie's brothers seemed to think that it was their responsibility to teach me about sexual matters and female anatomy. I had no idea what they were talking about, but I thought that it was probably important to remember these things. They showed me a feminine napkin and explained their version of woman's monthly periods. Maybe this was the reason that my Grandma drank borscht.

Willie had seen a TV show where some men became "blood brothers". He told me about this and said that since we were such good friends, maybe we should become blood brothers. He took out a sewing needle and said that we had to prick our arms, make ourselves bleed, and then mix our blood. That way we would be blood brothers forever. We tried, but neither of us really wanted to make ourselves bleed. I then had a brilliant idea. I had some gum in my pocket. If we both chewed the same gum, our spit would mix, and that would make us blood brothers too. So we shook hands, shared our spit, and became secret brothers.

In September, 1956, I started Kindergarten. Parents would take turns walking a group of us kids a few blocks to P.S. 161,

Caught in the Undertow

which stood for Public School 161. In Brooklyn, the elementary schools had numbers instead of names. I would carry my little school bag loaded with a lunch in a brown bag, my milk card, pencils, crayons, and a notebook. We would pass Willie's house, with his dog in the yard that wanted to lick my face, and other houses that also had dogs in the yard. One big dog had a bunch of little puppies suckling under her, and I thought about what Willie's brothers had taught me about "tits".

I definitely felt ready for school. I had already learned how to tell time, was proudly wearing my Mickey Mouse watch, and I had learned how to read a little. I thought about how I usually won when we played, "Go to the top of the class". I was excited and I felt like I definitely knew enough to be allowed to go to school.

P.S. 161 was a big brick building. There were many intimidating looking older kids also walking into the building. I went into a big classroom, with old wooden desks, a piano and a smiling, welcoming teacher named, Mrs. Halley. There was one bathroom in the back of the room, a row of hooks on the back wall to hang our coats, and shelves under the hooks to put our boots. I felt very safe and special there, and always looked forward to going to school. I thought that I knew more than the other kids, and that Mrs. Halley liked me more. I also felt like I wore the nicest clothes.

My hook on the back wall, and my desk were next to a boy named Richard. Richard would always poke you or punch you when you were near him. He would hide your school bag, or put garbage in your boots or coat pockets when you weren't looking. When we lined up to go to another room, if Richard was behind you, he would tickle you. When you told him to stop, he would laugh at you and call you a baby. "Baby, baby, stick your head in gravy, wrap it up in bubble gum, and send it to the navy." He was also a poet.

Joy Worth was a ragged, smelly, odd looking little girl who wore thick glasses that always had a broken bow. We called her Joy Wart, and in our class, cooties weren't contagious, you got "Joy Bugs" instead. Mrs. Halley played the piano everyday and we sang different songs. Joy was apparently tone deaf because when she sang, every note of every song came out the same.

Around Easter time the class was learning to sing, "Here Comes Peter Cottontail". After school, I gathered a group of boys together and told them that when we get to the part that goes, "Bringing every girl and boy, A Basket full of Easter Joy," we should all stand up and point at Joy Bug at the same time that we sang the word, Joy. I laughed to myself all the way home that day thinking about how funny this would be. The next day we all gathered around the piano and Mrs. Halley started the song. The boys all looked at each other and grinned. Right on cue, we all stood up and pointed at Joy at the same time that everybody sang, "Joy". My magic moment was ruined by Joy bursting into tears and running out of the room. Mrs. Halley was very angry and lectured us about how we should treat everyone with respect. I felt so guilty that I thought the monster was going to pull me down the drain that night.

It was while I was in Kindergarten that Sheryl and I were told that Mom was pregnant. We were very excited at the prospect of having a younger brother or sister, even though there didn't seem to be enough room for another person in our apartment. Thanks to Willie's brothers, I felt that I had a pretty good understanding of how Mom got pregnant, but resisted the urge to explain it to Sheryl. Sheryl was very precocious, and we did have deep conversations. We had an elderly relative who lived in Philadelphia and who died when I was in Kindergarten. We all drove down there for the funeral and Sheryl and I had many questions about the topic of death. For example, if you went to heaven after you died, why did they bury you in the ground? We never received any appropriate answers, but we continued to discuss these issues. Sheryl and I saw our first cemetery on that trip.

The week before my Mom gave birth, my parents asked Sheryl and me if there were any names that we liked for the new baby. Sheryl and I both agreed that it should be Karen if it is a girl, and Cubby if it is a boy. Those were the names of our two favorite characters on the Mickey Mouse Club TV

Caught in the Undertow

show. Both names were rejected, and on January 23, 1957, we had a new baby brother named Keith Brian. We all agreed that Keith Brian was a nice name also. Keith slept in a crib that was added to our already crowded bedroom. So, it was decided that we would all move to a house on Long Island, or "Long Guy Land," as it was pronounced with our Brooklyn accents. Many of our neighbors had already moved there.

Our days in Brooklyn were going to come to an end. I studied Mom's face as she filled the suitcases. I watched Dad as he paced around our apartment. I stared at Grandma as she scrubbed the kitchen sink. Sheryl was sitting on the couch and playing with her dolls. I shuddered as the image of the cemetery vaguely intruded and then faded away.

Jeffrey, age 5

*Jeffrey, Sheryl (2nd from the right), and cousins
in Brooklyn, Oct., 1956*

Part Two
LONG ISLAND

Naïve, exuberant, joyous, and young
Close to the wild heart of life
Willful and wild-hearted
Cheeks aflame and body aglow
Striding on and on, on and on, on and on
Singing, shouting, fiercely crying to the sea

Halting suddenly, the sound of pounding heartbeat
In the quiet

The tide turns and the day is on the wane
A few last figures appear in distant pools

Jeffrey Goldstein

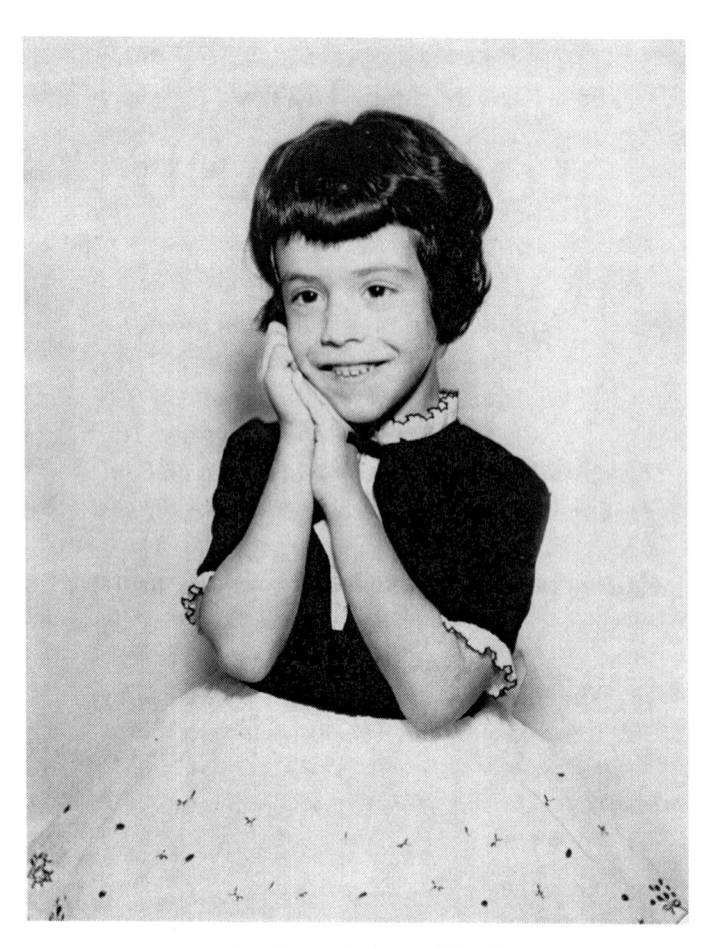

Sheryl, age 4, Long Island

Four

DAD DROVE A BIG, BLUE CHEVY with big tail fins. I sat in a car seat, with a toy steering wheel, in the middle of the front seat. Mom held Keith on her lap and sat next to me, and Sheryl was in a car seat in the back. Sometimes Grandma and Grandpa would sit in the back next to Sheryl. The best thing about going out for drives was the car radio. Dad loved to play music and to sing along. I knew many of the songs by heart and especially liked a song called, *True Love*. Sometimes he would put on a station that played Elvis and we would sing and bounce up and down on our seats. I knew Elvis songs because there was a character on "The Howdy Doody TV Show" called, "Elvis Pretzel," who would sing rock and roll songs. I also had a "Howdy Doody" record player and had records of songs such as, *Mairzy Doats*, and *How Much is that Doggie in the Window*. I would get so excited when songs that I knew had came on the radio. On weekends we would take rides out to Long Island to look at model houses. The music, and Mom and Dad's good moods, made the rides fun.

Dad would also get extremely angry when he was driving. If another car cut us off, he would scream, "If I didn't have my kids in the car, I would ram right into you!" If anyone honked their horn, he would yell out the window, "Shove that horn up your ass!" In between songs, Mom would yell at him that he was driving too fast and he would yell back with me sitting in the middle. Dad had tried to teach Mom to drive, but they would always come home screaming at each other. Mom eventually took driving lessons from a professional teacher so that she could drive after we moved to the suburbs. I got very frightened at the level of their emotions when they fought with each other. Being in a car seemed to bring out the best and the worst in them, but everything seemed good as long as the music was playing.

During the summer of 1957, the Goldstein family moved to a brand new three bedroom split level house on the newly built street called Navy Place, in a village called Bellmore. Bellmore was on the south shore of Long Island, right near the ocean. The south part of Bellmore, where we lived, was mostly built on land created by filling in the marshes and wetlands. There was a street named Army Place, then came Navy Place, and it ended with Marine Place. Soon more of the marshes were filled in and about another quarter mile of streets and houses were created. A new elementary school called Shore Road School was built on the corner of Marine Place and Shore Road for all the new children that were moving in. It opened a year after we arrived, when I was in second grade. Everything was growing and everyone seemed happy.

There seemed to be kids living in every house. The first kid my age that I met lived three houses down the block to the right. His name was Harry Vinkovitch. Actually he was two years older but only one grade ahead of me because he had to repeat a year. Harry was the skinniest boy that I had ever seen. People would jest that Vinny was so thin that if he stood sideways and stuck out his tongue, he would look a zipper. I called him, Skinny Vinny, and the name stuck. When we played outside together, he proved to be unbelievably fast, and also had the nickname, The Flying Vinny. He eventually was called Vinny preceded by whatever adjective fit that day. At various times he was Lazy Vinny, Crazy Vinny, Cheapskate Vinny, Silly Vinny, Bucktooth Vinny, and Rin Tin Vinny. We also would replace two syllable words in songs with his name. *My Vinny lies over the ocean. Black is black, I want my Vinny back. You ain't nothing but a Vinny, Crying all the time.*

Vinny and I shared a love of sports. He and I, and various other neighborhood kids, would play baseball, football, running bases, and other games that we made up. Vinny had the biggest yard and we mostly played there. Vinny's parents would never let anyone into their house through the front door, which led to an untouchable living room. I only saw it once and there were couches and chairs that were covered with plastic, and a carpet on the floor that looked like no one had ever walked on it. The room also had a covered up piano that no one was allowed to play. So, to get to Vinny, I had to go around the side of the house to the back door that entered into their downstairs den. Going through their side yard was not easy. The side yard of the neighboring house, which was directly adjacent to Vinny's, had a fenced in area that contained a humungous brown and black Doberman named Hunter.

If Hunter was outside at the time, he would jump up on the side of his fence and bark and growl and bang on the fence until you were out of sight. It seemed like he was at least a foot taller than I was when he stood up. We knew that Hunter was a "he" because when he stood up he displayed the biggest genitals that anyone had ever seen. His fenced in area was full of big piles of dog poop that emitted incredible odors. At least once a week, Hunter was able to jump over his fence, and chase down us kids. We would all run in different directions screaming, "Hunter's loose, Hunter's loose!" Hunter would then catch one of us, knock us over, pin us to the ground and growl in our face. Whoever was caught would have to lie there sobbing and shaking until one of the adults who owned him rescued us. "He's only playing with you," they would always say. We made sure that we targeted their house every Halloween.

When we first moved in, Navy Place was the last block of houses and behind our street were the wetlands that bordered on an inlet that attached to the Atlantic Ocean. Jones Beach was just a few miles away and you could easily see the Jones Beach tower from our house. They were filling in the wetlands and building new houses at a rapid rate, and there were bulldozers, cranes and other signs of construction everywhere you looked. Big mounds of dirt bordered our backyards. We turned this area into a playground. We used the dirt piles to act out thousands of versions of "King of the Hill," and we formed teams and waged wars. We made "dirt bombs" out of the clumps of dirt and used then as weapons. If you were hit by one, you were dead until the war was over. The team with the last man standing won. Vinny couldn't throw very well, but we all wanted him on our team because his speed and his slender frame made him hard to hit. A boy named Paul always cried when he was hit, so it was an unwritten rule that we hit him first. Sometimes we all threw at him at the same time, including the members of his own team. By the time fall had arrived and we were back in school, Marine Place had been completed and our war zone was gone.

That summer before first grade, Grandma and Grandpa would visit for a few days each week. Grandpa, as he did in Brooklyn, would take long walks. Grandpa told us about a 98 year old man that he had become friendly with on Army Place. The man was from Germany and his last name was Frankenstein. Mr. Frankenstein had a great grandson who was my age, named Albert. Albert Frankenstein already had a reputation. Everyone said that he was a genius.

My parents and grandparents told me that I also was very smart. I could read and write, I learned to tell time when I was three, I was good at arithmetic, and I had learned to play chess. Dad had taught me and we played a few times a week. "Maybe you should meet Albert and spend time with him instead of playing in the dirt all day with Skinny Vinny," Dad decreed. So the next day, Grandpa took my hand and we took the walk to the end of the block, around the corner to Shore Road, and down Shore Road to Army Place.

Albert Frankenstein was about my height. I stared hard at him wanting to see what a genius looked like. I was surprised to see his long stringy hair. We all had short crew cuts back then. He also had a very round face with very full lips. He shook my hand, something only adults had done with me, and said, "Pleased to make your acquaintance." I felt like I was talking to one of the rich boys from a Little Rascals movie. He talked nonstop. He told me that he was proud of his last name.

Frankenstein was the name of many famous doctors, scientists and inventors in Germany, where his grandparents were from. Albert said that he was going to be a scientist. We went up to his bedroom. He told me about the significance of numbers. Albert explained that if you woke up at night to go to the bathroom, you had to go an odd number of times. If you went an even number of times, 2, 4, or 6 times, you would not be able to fall asleep until you went once more. It was a scientific fact that your body reacted differently to odd or even numbers.

As he kept talking, my eyes searched his room for a baseball glove, or baseball card, or something that I could talk about to change the topic. He had dozens of books, but they all seemed to have scientific titles. I saw charts, and a diagram of the solar system. He had a telescope, a globe, and a microscope. At last, I noticed a chess set. "Do you play chess?" I asked. "Oh, yes," he replied, and he went on about famous chess players and chess strategies that I never heard of. "Do you want to play?" he asked. And we sat on his floor and began our battle.

Albert would take forever to make a move, but I eventually won. He did not like that, so we played again. I was feeling more confident, and defeated him quicker. "Let's make it the best of five matches," he said.

"That would be good because five is an odd number," I said. Albert frowned and frowned even harder when I won again. "We must do this again," he said, and I walked back home with Grandpa. When we got home Mom was with our next door neighbor, Claire.

"I beat Albert Frankenstein at chess three times in a row!" I glowed.

"Why are you so smart?" Claire asked.

"I was just born this way," I replied.

Towards the end of that summer, we met Steven Eckstein, or, The Eck, as we called him. He lived around the other corner on Legion Street, and was the same age as Skinny Vinny. He also loved sports and was the best athlete in our group. If we wanted another kid for our games, we had to wait for Eck to come to us. When we went to his house, no one would ever answer the door. Once, a group of us rang the front door bell while others knocked on the back door. We could see lights in the house and hear the TV. We kept this up for almost fifteen minutes, but no one came to the door. We never tried again.

Eck was very mean. He always had something insulting to say, and at times would unexpectedly get violent. During a ball game, he would purposely throw a ball at your head, throw his bat at the person standing on deck, spit in someone's face, or trip you as you ran by. One day we were all gathered in front of Vinny's house choosing up sides for a game. All of a sudden, Eck walked up to me and punched me in the face. I felt blood from my nose dripping into my mouth. I had never been in a fight before and felt enraged. I threw a punch at him, but missed and he punched me in the eye. I fell down, jumped up and tried to kick him, but he grabbed me by the ankle and pushed me back down. He then spit at me and laughed. Everyone else just stood and watched, and I ran home.

Dad had been doing yard work in front of our house and saw the whole thing. I was crying and expected sympathy. Instead, he put his hand around my neck, lifted me up off the ground, held me against the house, and put his face next to mine. I could smell his breath as he looked me in the eyes and told me that he was ashamed to be my father. I fought like a girl, he said, and deserved to be beat up. I felt unbelievably small and helpless. Later, Dad would spend time giving me boxing lessons, in matches that I could never win.

Five

OUR NEW HOUSE IN BELLMORE had three bedrooms on the third level, as opposed to the one bedroom that we all shared in Brooklyn. Mom and Dad slept in the big bedroom on the far end of the hall. Keith, at first, slept in a crib in their room. Sheryl had the middle bedroom, and I had the one on the other end of the hall. Sheryl's bed was next to the wall, and mine was next to the other side of the wall. Most of the time, Sheryl annoyed me. She wanted to tag along with me and my friends, or wanted me to play with her. We would play cards and board games. The one time that I wanted to be with her was when we talked at night. Sometimes, after everyone was asleep, she would knock on the wall between our beds. We would then meet in the hall and talk. The topics were mostly about things that we didn't understand, like death and heaven. We'd talk for a while, pose unanswerable questions, and then go back to bed.

In September of 1957, I started first grade. The kids in my neighborhood took a school bus to Winthrop Ave. Elementary School, which was about two miles away, in the old part of Bellmore. Merrick Road divided the two sections of Bellmore. South of Merrick Road, where we lived, there were the new houses and the new families, who mostly were Jewish, and who had moved from The City. North of Merrick Road were the old smaller houses, and the blue collar Catholic families who had lived there much longer. We were all mixed together in a big brick school that once was the high school. Directly north of the school, was Sunrise Highway, which separated the residential part of Bellmore from the commercial area. The Long Island Railroad had a station on Sunrise Highway in Bellmore. Many of the men in Bellmore, including my Dad, commuted to their jobs in The City on the Long Island Railroad.

My teacher's name was Mrs. Warner, and just like it was in Kindergarten, I had a teacher who played the piano and sang. This time there wasn't anybody named Joy in my class. Each day at the beginning of the class, we would all stand for the Pledge of Allegiance, and for the Lord's Prayer. Many of us were Jewish, and weren't familiar with the Lord's Prayer, but I memorized it pretty quickly. Then we would sing along with Mrs. Warner as she led us in her rendition of America the Beautiful. There was one bathroom in the back and we had to raise our hand and get permission to use it. The desks were big old wooden ones that still had empty ink wells in them. When I was bored, I would read all the names and graffiti that former students had carved in the desk. I tried to figure out how the students had been able to do this without getting caught. I daydreamed that I would carve Jeffrey Arlen Goldstein into my desk, and years from now when I was famous, people would come from all over the world to see my name. Mrs. Warner, no matter where she was in the room, seemed to know everything that was going on, so I never got the opportunity to follow through.

Every once in a while during the nice weather, a set of bells rang, and we all exited the building for a fire drill. On the way out, as we walked silently in single file, some of us would poke or pinch the kid in front of us. The goal was to get him or her make noise so that they would get into trouble. Often someone with sharp finger nails would be painfully pinching me on the way out. It would take every ounce of self control that I had to stay silent, but I never made a sound. Except for the one time that the girl in front of me, without even turning around, punched me in the balls and I yelped. I got yelled at, but didn't blame her. If you *did* "tattle" on someone, you were inviting the other kids to beat you up after school. Albert always tattled on other kids, but no one ever wanted to mess with him. He was, after all, a genius. I was, however, extremely impressed with the girl. First, that a girl would break the rules like that. Most of them never did anything wrong, and second, that she would hit me in the balls. Her name was Valerie, she lived on the other side of Merrick Road, and I was in love.

Every other week or so, for the whole school year, a siren went off and we had an air raid drill. These were much more serious. The teacher would yell, "Drop!," and we had to "duck and cover" as quickly as we could under our desks. This was so that we could protect ourselves if we had a nuclear war with Russia. In October, Russia had launched the first satellite into space, called Sputnik. We all were now afraid that Russia could drop nuclear bombs on us from space. Everyone believed that New York City was going to be a target, and we would be poisoned by the radiation. We all had to watch a government movie called, "Duck and Cover". We were taught the proper way to squat down under our desk with our hands over our heads. People were building fallout shelters in their houses, and we little kids were scared beyond words. Even though we were very young, we all knew that squatting underneath a desk was not going to do us much good if the bomb was dropped. I tried not to think about it, but we were all reminded each time we heard that siren.

Vinny and Eck were a grade ahead of me, and I would never see them at school. Every day after school, however, I would brave my way past Hunter and go to Vinny's backyard so that we could play ball. Across the street from Vinny's house, there was a cul-de-sac, shaped like a horseshoe, called Navy Court. Each house had at least one kid living there, and it became the area where we had our games. At the end of the school day I was restless and overflowing with energy, and was the one who wanted to play the most. We would have big baseball, football, kickball, or dodge ball games. I liked it as long as there was running and competition. We played all year round, no matter how hot or cold or rainy or snowy it was.

Sometimes there were only two or three of us. When there were just three, usually Vinny, Eck and I, we played one on one football. Eck would be the quarterback for each team. Vinny or I would be on offense, while the other person played defense. If the offensive player caught three passes in four downs, he earned a first down. If he got the ball past the telephone pole at the end of the cul-de-sac, it was a touchdown. We would play this for hours, taking turns on offense and defense. We all also had little two wheel bikes and would ride them at each other, trying to knock each other down, in a game called, "chicken". I wanted to have as much fun as possible before the bombs dropped.

My favorite time of the year became the spring. That's when baseball season began. I loved the smell of the new grass, the warm breezes, the baseball diamonds turning green, the sounds of the geese and the seagulls that filled the air in our neighborhood, and, I loved the New York Yankees. In first grade, I was introduced to baseball cards. We would excitedly ride our bikes almost a mile down Shore Road and then down Newbridge Road to the corner of Merrick Road. That was where our favorite place, Bart's Candy Store, was located. We paid five cents for a brand new package that contained five shiny baseball cards and a hard flat piece of bubble gum. The anticipation was unbearable. We'd eagerly rip open our packages to find out which player's cards were waiting for us. If you were lucky enough to find a Yankee, even an obscure one, it was like winning the lottery. But even if you didn't have a Yankee, you had a card with the picture of a major leaguer on the front, and their statistics on the back. We'd go and buy cards whenever we had any change. Then we learned about "flipping" cards. We competed in games called match 'em, leaners, closest to the wall, and topsies. The winner of each game would get all the cards for that round. We would only risk the cards that were doubles, and we'd keep the rest. They all were numbered and only a certain set of numbers were released at a time. The complete set wasn't all released until the summer. The goal was to get a complete set, or at least as many Yankees as you could.

Caught in the Undertow

One of the most exciting occurrences that year was buying my first new baseball glove. Before that, I had used an old hand me down glove that belonged to some kid who was the son of one of Dad's coworkers. Robin Hoods was a sports store on Sunrise Highway in Merrick, and they had a whole section with nothing but mitts. I had dreamed of going there for my own mitt, and now it was finally happening. Dad took me there on a Saturday morning, and I spent over thirty minutes trying on different, wonderfully smelling, brand new leather gloves with famous baseball player's names printed on them. They had first baseman's gloves, catcher's gloves, infielder's gloves, lefty gloves and all imaginable shapes and sizes. I wanted to be a centerfielder like Mickey Mantle, (saying his name was like saying the name of a god), so I concentrated on outfielder's gloves. Dad gave me a baseball and I threw it into different gloves to see how they felt. The sound, the feel, the smell, the excitement, I was in heaven.

Finally, I found it. It felt perfect. I wore it with my index finger out in the back like Mickey did. The great Willie Mays was the name printed on the side. I had to have it. Dad tried it on and approved. But then he looked at the price, $20.

"I don't know," he said, "that's more than I wanted to spend". Tears welled up in my eyes. I was devastated. I stared at the ground. I knew that it would do no good to argue with him. I could talk Mom into things, but not Dad. Finally he said that he would buy it, but don't dare ask for anything else this year.

When we got home, Dad showed me how to break it in. I had to form a pocket, and soften up the leather. So we put a little bit of olive oil on the pocket, put a baseball in it, tied some string around it to hold it in the right position, and placed it under my mattress. If I slept on it for a few days, it would be perfect and ready to use. A few days later, I had my first catch, using my new glove, with Vinny. "Throw it as hard as you can," I challenged. "I can catch anything." And I felt like I could.

The spring of first grade was when I first played in Little League. In first and second grade, you were in the division called the "farm system". If you did well enough at the tryouts, you could be in the "minor leagues" starting in second grade. After that, you had an opportunity to make the "major leagues". The tryouts were held by Winthrop Ave. School, and you batted and did fielding drills while all the coaches watched. I had played often with my friends, and I had my new mitt, so I felt very confident. I was told that I did very well, and I was assigned to a farm system team. The team had four different parents coaching, including my Dad. I admired the way Dad could be so charming and funny when interacting with the other adults. He tended to ignore the other kids, however, and spent all his time coaching me.

After the season started, Dad began practicing with me when he got home from work and on weekends. I loved playing catch. It felt like I was connecting with the other person on a primal level. It felt like the two of us were in harmony. The sound of the ball hitting the mitt was musical. The smell in the air, the breeze on your face, the warmth of the sun, and the feel of a baseball in my hand embodied everything that was the rebirth that occurred in the spring.

Dad seemed to look forward to playing catch with me, also. Most days, he would change his clothes as soon as he got home and we would go out onto our street. At first, he was very jovial and pleasant and I couldn't wait to play with him. He was a fantastic athlete, he would catch the ball wherever I threw it, and I felt loved being with him. He was the only father I would see playing catch on our block. Then as I got better, his monster side came out. He would throw the ball as hard as he could. If I dropped it, he would yell abusively. If the ball went over my head, he criticized me for being too short. If I didn't throw the ball directly at his mitt, he would stand still, let it go by, and make me chase after it. I eventually made sure that I wasn't home when he arrived from work. His actions, however, didn't diminish my love for baseball. Or for my Dad.

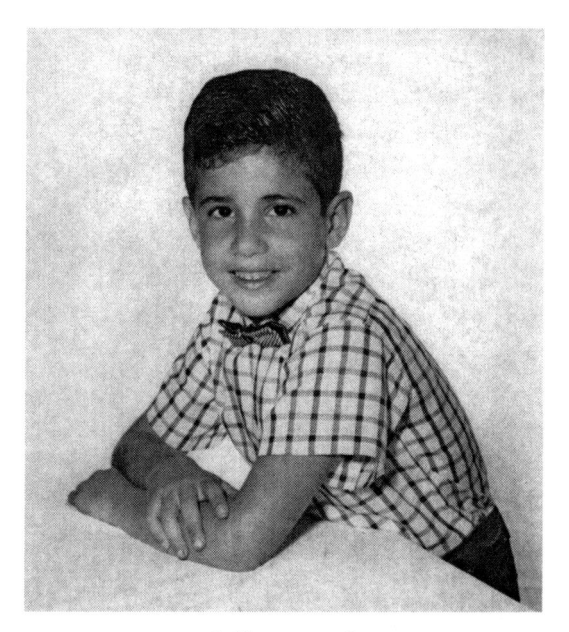

Jeffrey, age 6

Jeffrey and Sheryl (far right) at family birthday party

Grandma and Aunt Yetta

Mom and Dad on patio in Bellmore

Six

ON JULY 1, 1958, I turned 7 years old and was done with first grade. Later that month, we took the first one of our summer trips to the Catskill Mountains. Our destination was an area also known as the Jewish Alps, or the Borscht Belt. We drove north of the City, to route 17 and ended up in a resort area frequented by Jewish families from Long Island and the City. Ellenville was one of the towns famous for fancy resort hotels like the Concord, Grossingers, The Granit, Browns, and the Neville, and for comedians, singers and musicians such as Jerry Lewis, Rodney Dangerfield, Benny Goodman, and Barbra Streisand. Mom, Dad, Grandma, Grandpa, Sheryl, Keith, and I squeezed into our car and we were off for a week's vacation. The trip up included my favorite car activity, listening to music on the radio. If Dad was in a good mood, he would sing, and say silly expressions like, "Do you think the rain will hurt the rhubarb?" Sometimes we would listen to the Yankee game on the radio. Red Barber became a Yankee announcer instead of moving to Los Angeles with the Dodgers, and Grandpa liked him.

We stayed in a bungalow in Ellenville. We stayed with Mom's cousin Milton and his family. Milton Lichaw was Grandma's sister Yetta's son, and Mom was very close to him when they were growing up. Milton and his wife Shirley had 3 daughters. The oldest was named Jackie and she was 6 months older than I was. I enjoyed being with Jackie. I liked the idea of having a cousin. Dad had three sisters, and they had five children. They were my first cousins, but we hardly ever saw that side of the family.

Grandpa spent a great deal of time standing in the cascading waters from a stream that became a waterfall near our bungalow. He would almost ritualistically splash the fresh water on his face. I thought of how he also did the same thing with water back home in Bellmore. Often when he took us on a walk, Keith in a stroller and Sheryl and I at his side, he went to one of the inlets from the ocean. There he leaned over, and splashed the salt water on his face. No one that I asked had an explanation for this. I thought that maybe he did it because there were no bodies of water in Brooklyn.

At the bungalows, the kids were put into a day camp with other kids the same age. There were teenagers who acted as counselors. We played games, had contests, and went out on a lake in row boats. I was out on a row boat one very sunny day with other kids and two counselors. As the bright sun hit me, the female counselor noticed that I had some short, white, peach fuzz type hair growing on the side of my face. She looked at it and asked, "Does your father have a heavy beard?"

I answered, "He doesn't have any beard."

The two counselors laughed. It always felt good to make people laugh, even when I didn't understand the joke.

It was intriguing watching the male and female counselors interact. The male one in my boat had straight black hair that was piled high on his head like Elvis's. He would take a small white comb out of his pocket and comb it straight back. But when he moved, some of the hair would fall out of place. The females always seemed to be giggling around him and trying to get his attention. I tried to figure out why the girls were so drawn to him, and I came to the conclusion that it was his hair. When I got back to the bungalow that night, I combed mine straight back.

Every night we would go watch the entertainment in the main building. There were usually comedians. One of them said, "My doctor told me that I am in terrible shape. I told him that I want a second opinion. Okay, he said. You are ugly, too!" They were always insulting themselves, other people, or their wives. I thought that it was hilarious and tried to remember some good ones to use on my friends. After the first act, the kids were told to leave and go to bed. One night some of us snuck back, hid, and watched the adult entertainment. We were lucky enough to see a stripper. She had very talented breasts and I thought that she was even funnier than the comedian.

On the last day of our vacation, we were out on a boat with our counselors. It suddenly began to get dark and windy, and the teenager with the Elvis hair started to row as hard as he could. The water was splashing on my face, so I stood up and tried to move to another spot. I lost my balance as a strong wind blew me off the boat. I had no idea how to swim yet and felt myself sinking deeper and deeper into the water. Water went up my nose and into my mouth, but everything felt calm and peaceful. I saw different shades of white glimmering and unfolding. A feeling of warmth enveloped my body. "I must be dead," was my one thought. I was still sinking when I felt the Elvis counselor grabbing me and pulling me back up to the boat. I believed that I had experienced what death feels like.

The next day we drove back to Bellmore and I never told anyone about what had happened. Dad would say that it was all my fault.

Seven

I WAS PART OF THE FIRST GROUP of kids to attend the brand new Shore Road School, as I started second grade in September, 1958. The school was on the corner of Shore Road and Marine Place, and unlike Winthrop Ave. School, it was a modern, white brick, one story building. The school was on the next block, so I was able to walk through my backyard, through the yard of the house behind us on Marine Place, and make a right down Marine Place to the school. All of these new houses were built on the area that had consisted of the mounds of dirt that served as our play ground the previous summer. So, we created new play grounds. Behind the school there was a long rectangular cemented area that sat under an awning attached to the back of the gym. This became the place where we flipped baseball cards before school started, during recess, after school. On any given day, dozens of boys would divide into groups, usually by age, and attempt to win more cards.

My teacher's name was Mrs. Garelock, and I was again eager to go to school. This year, there was no piano in the room, but we had brand new desks, new books, big windows in the back of the room, and colorful charts and posters on the walls. On the first day of school, all the students in the school were asked to sign a scroll that was put into the cornerstone of the building. The cornerstone has a big 1958 carved on it, and my name inside of it. I was proud that Sheryl's name was also in it. That was the year that she and a group of her friends started Kindergarten. A group of parents took turns walking them to school, just like they did for me in Brooklyn. The Kindergarten was in a different wing of the school, but if I ever did see her during the day, I would make a funny face. I told Sheryl that I would protect her from anyone at school who might bully or pick on her. I was her older brother.

In class we were divided into three reading groups. Each group had a different teacher, a different book, and the name of a different animal. I was in the "bear" group, but we all knew who was in the smartest group and who was in the dumbest. Mrs. Garelock differentiated us even more by posting a list each week. She would rank the class from 1 to 23 based on our work and current test scores. The list would seldom change. Albert was always number 1, and I was invariably number 2. Rickie Donatuti, who lived in one of the few old houses that were south of Merrick Road, was always number 23.

A group of kids would make try to make fun of me each week by chanting, "You're not as smart as Albert, You're not as smart as Albert!" Other kids would chant, "Teacher's pet, teacher's pet!" It was no great honor to get good grades. But, Mom and Dad were very proud.

I started reading Hardy Boys books that year. Dad had some old books from when he was a boy, and new editions were coming out. When we visited Milton and Shirley at their house in Levittown, Mrs. Winkler, Shirley's mother, would always give me a new Hardy Boys book. I would devour the first few chapters in the car on the way home. Cousin Jackie read Nancy Drew books, and we compared the plots. I fantasized about being a detective and solving mysteries the way Frank and Joe Hardy did. The books were numbered, just like baseball cards, and I wanted the whole series. *The Tower Treasure* was number 1, and I had both the old and new version. Soon, I had all the books up to number 11, *While the Clock Ticked*. I had a children's dictionary, and looked up words from the books, such as "sinister," "sleuth," and "chum". I then attempted to use those words at school, mispronouncing many of them. I wanted to replace Albert as number 1, but never made it.

Paul Baldwin was usually number 3 in the class. He lived on Marine Place, one house away from the school yard. Grandma called him a *nebbish,* the Yiddish word for an awkward person. Paul tried to fit in, but nobody liked him. I made the mistake of being nice to him, and was rewarded by having him follow me around at school.

Paul began collecting baseball cards, and told me that he had a Mickey Mantle card, the most difficult one to get. We kids would kill for a Mickey Mantle. None of us had ever seen one, and it was rumored that only ten of them were even printed. Paul said that he might trade me for it if I would show him my Yankee cards. I brought him up to my room after school, showed him my most prized cards, which included a Yogi Berra, which I had doubles of, a Whitey Ford, and a Duke Snyder, the star center fielder for the Dodgers. But he didn't want to trade. Paul really did have a Mickey Mantle though, and I got to hold it.

Every day that week we flipped cards at school, as we normally did. When Paul would join us, he would lose all of his cards, but he never flipped any good ones. Other kids did flip their good ones and on Saturday morning I was sorting through all of the cards that I had won and went to put a few more Yankees in the drawer with my other prized cards. But they were gone! I looked under the bed and all over the room, but they weren't there! I went crazy. I yelled at everyone else in the house and wanted to know, "Who took my cards! You don't mess with someone's baseball cards!" Mom said that I was *meshugeneh.*

After I was convinced that no one in my family took them, I decided that I would be a detective and solve the mystery. I went outside and interrogated every kid that I could find. I then sat down and wrote down the names of anyone who had been in my room that week. I finally remembered Paul Baldwin. I ran to his house and rang the bell. His Mom, a person that was considered evil by the whole neighborhood, answered the door. She said that Paul wasn't home, and I said that I had left something in Paul's room and ran by her to the stairs. The

Caught in the Undertow

nebbish was sitting there. I looked him straight in the eyes and demanded my property back. He denied having it, so I grabbed him by his shirt, shook him, and said that if he wanted to live, I better get my property back right now. He still denied it. I threw him down, looked around his room, and saw my cards on his desk. Just as I grabbed them, his evil mom came at me. I ran around her, and out of the house feeling proud of the way I retrieved my possessions.

Saturday afternoon, a group of us were playing a baseball game called, "catch a fly is up" on the field behind the school. Suddenly, Paul and his evil mother came walking towards us demanding that I give Paul's cards back. Paul said that he would beat me up if I didn't. Everyone made a circle around us, and I told Paul that he is welcome to try. He threw a punch at me, I ducked and began using the boxing skills that Dad taught me. As soon as I landed the first punch, Paul covered up his face and started screaming, "You broke my nose! You broke my nose!" I put my fists down and walked over to look at him to see if he was all right. As soon as I got close enough, he uncovered his face, laughed, and started punching my face in a sneak attack. Someone taught him some skills, also.

I fell down and heard his evil mother screaming, "Kick him, Paul, kick him!" which he does, and continues to do with his evil mother encouraging him. He kept this up until another parent from down the block finally came over and ended it. I lost another fight, but Paul's and his evil mother's reputations were forever damaged. And we had another house to target on Halloween.

Eight

IN SECOND GRADE WE BEGAN having gym class. We were introduced to the gym teacher for all the boys at Shore Road School, Mr. Deluca. Three times a week all the second grade boys gathered in the gym. We were taught to stand at attention in perfectly straight lines, from shortest to tallest. He drilled us to correctly stand at ease, turn left face, right face and about face, and to march to different cadences. There was a draft, he barked at us, and all of us, except for the sissies, would be soldiers one day. We needed to be physically conditioned, disciplined, and able to follow orders. We were still having air raid drills, and we were being indoctrinated to hate communism and to hate and fear Russia. Mr. Deluca sure knew how to take all the fun out of being in gym.

Our first day of gym, Mr. Deluca told us that we all needed to purchase athletic supporters, or jock straps, and that we had to always be wearing them in class under a pair of gray gym shorts. If we came to class without one, we would be punished. Dad took me to Robin Hoods to buy one. I was so proud. I was going to wear a jock strap just like all the major leaguers. We also bought the gym shorts and the required gym t-shirts that made up our gym uniforms. Dad told me stories about how he was a great athlete in when he was in school. He said that he was the starting quarterback on his high school team, and that he wanted me to make him proud. I was just thinking about trying on my new jock strap. I had never actually seen one before.

The next week in gym, Mr. Deluca walked down each row and made us pull down the front of our shorts to show him our jock straps. We all wanted to be fathers someday, he said, and jock straps would protect our vital parts. Willie's brothers had never explained this part to me. Several kids did not have one on. They had to endure a punishment called, "milking the cow." First, you stuck both of your arms out to the sides in a straight line parallel to the ground. Then, you kept squeezing each hand in a fist like you were milking a cow. You had to keep your arms up and had to keep squeezing for five minutes. If you stopped squeezing or if you arms fell below parallel, he added an additional 2 minutes. After about a minute, your arms felt like they weighed a ton, and your shoulders were screaming in agony. The boys had to stand in the front of the class while the rest of us stood at attention with Mr. Deluca lecturing at us holding a stop watch. If any of us talked or deviated from the perfect attention stance, we had to join the boys milking the cow. We couldn't start the class activities until all the boys had fulfilled their punishment. Sometimes a boy's arms would keep dropping and we would have to spend the whole class standing at attention. We made sure that whoever it was felt the effect of our anger, too. All I learned was that I never wanted to be in the Army.

Besides the list of who was smartest in the classrooms, there were lists ranking us in gym class. We were tested on how many pull-ups, pushups, sit ups, and squat thrusts we could do. Roger Jackson was always number one in every category. His father was a life guard at Jones Beach, and Roger exercised with him each day. Roger never played baseball or football with us, but did gymnastics and took judo classes. He ran to and from school every day, even in the rain. I could do six pull-ups and was third in the class, way ahead of Albert and Paul who couldn't do any. Bobbie Blake could do eight. But Roger could do twenty-one pull-ups. Roger didn't talk much to the rest of us, and that just added to his mystique. He was considered to be on a different level physically and Mr. Deluca used Roger often as an example of someone who was the paragon of hard work and discipline. We could all do twenty-one pull-ups if we worked at it.

We also were ranked according to our running ability. We

all ran a 100 yard dash, with Mr. Deluca timing us. We would compete in groups of ten, with the winners competing against each other. Then we would race each other around the perimeter of the whole field, which was about one half of a mile. Several boys couldn't run that far, and would stop and walk or just stop and gasp for air. Mr. Deluca would become enraged and yell at them for being lazy, gutless and out of shape. "How are we going to beat the Russians with such disgracefully pathetic American boys?" he shrieked. Mr. Deluca was so abusive that we actually felt sorry for those boys. Only the meanest kids would make fun of them.

Getting praise from Mr. Deluca was like being blessed by the Pope, as my Catholic friends would say. When we all stood at attention at the beginning of class, he would talk about us, only referring to us by our last names. He would use this time to single out kids for criticism, and to praise others. Roger was the only kid who seemed to have a first name, and he was one of his main recipients of commendation. In the class after we had our running competitions, Mr. Deluca put the spotlight on me.

"Goldstein had the second best time for the 100 yard dash," he said, "and the third best time for the long run. It is very unusual to have both the ability to run fast for short distances and to have the stamina to run fast for long distances."

I turned around to smile at my friends, and ended up standing in front of the class milking the cow for not keeping my eyes straight ahead while at attention. But having just been anointed, it didn't hurt as bad.

Mr. Deluca was also the school disciplinarian for the boys. If two boys got in trouble for fighting or arguing, Mr. Deluca would have them settle it with a boxing match. During the next gym class, he would strap big, soft boxing gloves on the miscreant boys, have the rest of the class sit in a circle around them, and say, "Girls, let's see what you can do."

The rest of us hooted and cheered while they would fight until someone gave up, bled, or was knocked down. It was great entertainment, and his message always was, "If you are going to fight, do it right."

Our favorite part of the day, during the warm weather, was recess. We were basically on our own for twenty minutes. Everyone clustered together with their own group of friends. My group played baseball, flipped baseball cards, or played dodge ball. If Paul tried to join us, everyone was mean to him in an attempt to make him leave. I often felt sorry for kids who were picked on, but not for Paul.

Moving secretly amongst all of us were various rogue kids. You never knew what they were going to do. Ira, one day, appeared out of nowhere, punched me as hard as he could in the jaw, and disappeared. My jaw ached for days. Another time, Fred snuck up to me, kneed my nuts with tremendous force, and left as I fell to the ground in the worst pain that I had ever felt. I barely made it back into school after recess. David, who was immensely tall and fat, would walk up behind you, give you a bear hug, lift you high in the air, and drop you on the ground. When it was my turn, I landed on my back and had the air knocked out of me. We all just viewed these incidents as normal things that occur during recess.

At recess and during breaks in the school day, television was becoming a bigger topic. We had a TV in our den, but we were not allowed to watch it very much. Mom and Dad let us watch from 7:00 to 7:30, and we enjoyed children's shows like "Claude Kirschner and Terrytoon Circus," "Sandy Becker," or sometimes "Lassie" was on. We went to our rooms at 7:30 and I read and then went to bed. In November, there was a movie on, starting at 7:00, called, *Godzilla*. It seemed like everybody at school was talking about the monster, *Godzilla*, and how they couldn't wait to watch the movie. I pleaded, but they stood firm that I was not going to see it. I snuck down later and peered into the den, but they were watching something else. I knew that everyone would be talking about it at school, so when I first got there, I eavesdropped on other kid's conversations about the movie. I gathered enough information so that when someone asked me what my favorite part of the movie was, I answered as if I had really seen it. I wasn't ranked number two for nothing.

Nine

DURING CHRISTMAS VACATION THAT YEAR, we all drove to Brooklyn to visit Grandma and Grandpa. We would take the Meadowbrook Parkway to the Southern State Parkway through the 5 cent toll booths to the Belt Parkway and exit in Brooklyn. We had made that trip so many times I had all the landmarks memorized. After we arrived, Grandma, Mom, Sheryl and I went for a walk outside on Montgomery Street. All of a sudden, Sheryl passed out. She just fell to the ground. They took her to the family doctor, Dr. Epstein.

When they all got back, they said that Sheryl would need to have some tests done. But she probably was anemic. She needed to eat more iron, and that would fix the problem. Everyone seemed very concerned, but they always worried about things, so this time didn't seem to be any different.

Over the course of the next few months, everyone spent their time focusing on Sheryl. They had jars of powder which they tried to make Sheryl eat, but she would have no part of it. Mom and Grandma started to put the powder in applesauce to get Sheryl to eat it that way. Everyone was spending time with her, buying her things, and I felt totally left out. Whenever I asked if anything was wrong, I was told that it is anemia and she will be alright. Sheryl didn't seem to be herself, but I clung to what they said. She has anemia and she will be alright.

I was totally taken by surprise that April when I found out at school that my sister Sheryl had died. No one in the family had told me that she had been taken to the hospital. No one had told me that she had died. When I ran back from school that morning, all Grandma did was ask me if anyone had said anything to me. She didn't even stop vacuuming. Grandpa was crying so hard that he looked like he was having convulsions. He didn't notice that I was looking at him, and he didn't notice when I walked away.

I sat crying, alone in my room. Sheryl is dead. What does that mean? Where did she go? Will I see her again? Does it hurt? Is it like when I fell off the boat? All anyone had ever told me about death is that you go to heaven. Where is that? What is that? Then it hit me. Right in my gut. The deepest pain that I have ever felt. The most profound loneliness. Sheryl is gone. She is not coming home. I will never talk to her at night again. I never had the chance to say goodbye. I will never have the chance to say goodbye. I will never be able to tell her that I love her. That hurt the most. Does Sheryl know that I love her? Why wasn't I given the chance to tell her that I love her?

I was lying on my bed, crying, with my face buried in the pillow, when Mom burst into the room. She had the most pained, hurt look that I have ever seen. Her face was soaked with tears. Then, she ripped out my heart and threw it against the wall. She caused my whole world to collapse on top of me. There are no words to describe the anguish that I felt when she looked me in the eyes and shrieked, "You should have died instead of Sheryl! She was the good one. You are the bad one. I wish that you died instead!" Before I could even process her words, she was gone.

The next day was Sheryl's funeral. I was not allowed to attend. Nor was I at the burial. Then we began the process of mourning, Sitting Shiva. The mirrors were all covered, and the adults sat on small wooden stools for seven days. Many adults came into our house. A few touched me or put their hands on my shoulder, but no one talked to me. I felt evil. I ached. I ached to see Sheryl. I ached to tell Sheryl that I was sorry. I ached to have someone hug me. I ached to have someone tell me that I should be alive. I ached for someone to tell me that none of this was my fault. I ached to have my Mother love me again. I ached for my Father to love me. I ached for someone to tell me that everything was going to be alright. Mostly I just ached.

I felt so alone. I wanted to hold someone. I wanted to cry. I wanted to die. There were hands squeezing my neck. I couldn't breathe. I was in so much pain.

Before Sheryl had been born, I had been told, Grandpa suffered a heart attack. He was dying. Mom told him that she was pregnant and that he had to stay alive to see the baby. And he did. He stayed alive to meet Sheryl. He stayed alive to see her die. He never stopped crying. A little while later an ambulance came for him. I was sitting in my garage with Jackie. She looked at me and told me not to worry. He would be alright. But I knew. Sheryl died and now Grandpa would. And he did. And the mourning continued.

Ten

I KNOW THAT I WENT BACK to school, back to the second grade and to Mrs. Garelock's class. Back to gym with Mr. Deluca. Back to playing baseball and to flipping cards. But I felt like I was walking under water. I was separated from everything and everyone. It felt like it was a mistake that I was alive. I watched a lot of TV. No one stopped me. I saw a show in which a man was poisoned. He drank something, grabbed his throat, gasped for air, and fell down dead. It looked painful. And it occurred to me that my parents would do that to me. Mom said that I should be dead.

I started to refuse to eat any food that they gave me. I trusted Grandma, and would eat what she brought me. But mostly she didn't bring me anything. Days went by and I didn't eat or drink anything. I stayed in my room. I began to get weak.

The other Grandma came to our house. She said that she could get me to eat. She came up to my room with a bowl of soup, tried to hold my mouth open, and to pour it down my throat. I had to protect myself. There was evil emanating from her eyes. I spilled the soup on her dress and she left screaming. Eventually, I was taken to the hospital. I had double pneumonia. I was on an IV. I didn't care about anything. I was overwhelmed with the realization that I didn't deserve to live. There was no reason to fight back.

I believe that an angel began coming to my room. The angel had a glowing smile. She told me that I was a beautiful, intelligent boy. She told me that I did deserve to live. She told me that I should be outside with my friends playing baseball.

She told me that I ought to be happy. She told me that Sheryl knows that I love her. My parents came in one day with a bowl of vanilla ice cream. They handed it to me. I didn't know what to do. The angel looked at me, smiled and nodded her head. I put a spoonful in my mouth. Dad opened and closed his mouth along with me as I was eating. Mom cried. Did they really want me to live? Or, did they just not want someone else to die?

Eleven

IN SEPTEMBER, 1959, I STARTED third grade. I went back to school missing something. I didn't exactly know what it was or how to get it back, but definitely I was different. I know that I was missing Sheryl. She would have been in first grade and her class would have been in the same wing as mine. Keith was only two years old, so I was the only Goldstein attending Shore Road. Vinny had a younger brother, Ralphie, who I very creatively referred to as, Little Vinny. He was Sheryl's age and in first grade. Most of my friends had siblings at school. Even Albert had a brother and a sister in school, and Paul had a brother named Seth.

Sometimes we'd be picking on each other, or there would be an argument, and someone would say, "Leave him alone. His sister just died."

Even if I wasn't thinking about it, someone else was. It felt like I stood out, not because I was number two in my class, or not because Mr. Deluca said that I was fast, but just because I was alive and Sheryl wasn't. I felt guilt along with my grief, and realized that I was feeling anger. I never smiled.

There was so much churning inside of me, and it seemed that I could run even faster. We started to play flag football in gym. When I had the ball, I discovered that I could quickly fake one way, go the other way, and run down the field without anyone touching me. I felt unstoppable. I wanted to play all the time. We had games at recess and after school, and everyone wanted me on their team. They wanted me, the boy who was fast, not the boy whose sister died. I felt like two different people.

Jeffrey Goldstein

In gym class, while we were all standing at attention, Mr. Deluca did his usual rant, criticizing boys for being fat and lazy. My mind was drifting away until I heard him again put the spotlight on me. He was talking about my speed in football. He also mentioned other boys who had great throwing, catching, running or blocking skills.

"I am going to enter a team in an intramural flag football league," he said. "We will play twice a week after school. Those of you who have done the best in class will be chosen for the team. Your great efforts have earned you this honor. The rest of you need to get off your lazy butts and work harder. The list will be posted on my office door tomorrow at recess."

I smiled for the first time in months. He mentioned my name, everyone picks me for their team, so obviously I'll be chosen. I'll get to play football twice a week. Somebody important, Mr. Deluca wants me. I pictured myself running past other kids and scoring touchdowns. I let myself feel the exhilaration of running, competing, and winning. I wanted to tell Mom or Dad, but even though they were there physically, they were really not there.

The next day, we could not wait to see the list. When the recess bell rang, those of us who thought we were chosen, ran out of class to Mr. Deluca's office. We did not even try to hide the smiles on our faces.

"There's the list," we shouted. It was in alphabetical order. Kids saw their names, screamed, and slapped each other's hands.

"Wait, where is Goldstein's name? Maybe he put it somewhere else. I can't believe it's not there. Wow, too bad, Goldstein."

I stood there while the others happily ran away. My heart had been ripped out and thrown against the wall again. I looked into his office. He was sitting there. I stared at him through the window until he beckoned me in. I glared at him, unable to talk, trying to hold back my tears.

"Goldstein," he said, "Football is a dangerous sport. Your parents have already lost one child. I don't want to put you in a position where you might get hurt. It would be too much for your family."

"But I run faster than everybody else. No one ever touches me. I won't get hurt." I wanted to say these things, but nothing came out. I looked at the floor. I was numb, empty, dejected. I didn't move until the bell rang and he told me to get to class. Once again, it was like my world was collapsing around me. Mr. Deluca was telling me that I should be dead. As I walked away, I imagined ripping his head off of his shoulders.

Twelve

SHERYL NO LONGER WAS physically at my house, but I felt her presence. Grandpa was gone, and we no longer had a reason to visit Brooklyn. Grandma moved in, slept in Sheryl's room and we now had borscht in the refrigerator. Mom and Dad were always fighting and I tried to avoid them. They put another bed in my room for Keith. I enjoyed having him there. I could still read at night because he went to sleep with the light on. He couldn't say my name, so he called me "Fruffrey".

We found out that Dad had lost his job, even though he was ostensibly leaving for work every morning. He had borrowed money from almost every friend, neighbor and relative that he knew. Bill collectors and other people began coming to the house demanding to see him. The family began paying the bills and living expenses from Grandma's savings. I tried to be at home as little as possible.

Sometimes, Vinny would invite me over for dinner. I called his father, Mr. "Vinny". No one on in his family talked very much, as opposed to mine, where everyone was always arguing. Mr. Vinny seemed to always have a martini in one hand, and a cigarette in the other. He only had gray hair around the side of his head, and the top was totally bald and shiny. He owned some sort of factory in Queens.

Mrs. Vinny was plump and always seemed to be munching on chocolates. She always was wearing an apron and either dusting the furniture or cooking in the kitchen. Their kitchen was next to the living room that we were forbidden to enter.

Mr. Vinny usually got home late from work, smelling of

cigarettes and alcohol, and we would be sitting at the table silently eating when he walked in. He would always look at us and say the same thing, "What a motley crew." No one ever responded. When we couldn't play ball outside, we played ping pong in Vinny's basement.

Most of the other neighbors didn't want anything to do with us and I was told that it was because Dad owed them money. The one exception was the Dorfman family, who lived three houses down the block to the left. Michael Dorfman was a year younger than I was, and Dean Dorfman was three years younger. The boys were not very bright, and as far as I could figure out, they did nothing but watch TV. They never would play ball or any other games with us.

Mr. Dorfman, Murray, was about 6 feet 4 inches tall, very thin and wiry, and he was a truck driver who worked as a handyman on the side. After Sheryl died, he would bring us melons from his truck and fix anything in the house that needed to be repaired. He helped me re-string my baseball mitt and he waxed our floors.

The first summer that we lived there, the Dorfmans erected an above ground pool in their back yard and had a block party. People were very loud and I could hear all the laughing and talking, and the music from their yard. Apparently, Dad and Mr. Dorfman got into a fist fight, and they fell on the pool and collapsed it. I remember Dad coming home all wet with a bloody face. It was obvious that the Dorfmans hated Dad. It seemed like everybody did, but they liked Mom and were nice to me.

Mrs. Dorfman, Shirley, was about 5 feet 2 inches and extremely fat. She had diabetes and was missing some teeth and some toes, but wore open toed shoes, anyway. Everyone made fun of how they looked as a couple. Shirley was very friendly in a motherly way. If she saw me outside, she came over and asked me how I was. I never said anything other than, okay.

At the end of the summer after Sheryl died, and after I was home from the hospital, I had developed some sort of facial rash. The doctor gave me a yellow cream to put on it. I had just put some on and was walking out of my house when Shirley came by. She looked at my face and said that I still had some of my breakfast on it. Before I could say anything, she wiped it off with her finger and stuck it in her mouth. "Oh, tastes like you had eggs for breakfast," she said.

Shirley often invited me to dinner when I didn't want to be at home. The dinner talk was very friendly, and there was plenty of good food, but after dinner everyone plopped themselves down in front of the TV. They all had a specific spot on a big couch where they always sat. I sat on the rug. I wanted to go out and play ball, but I felt guilty about leaving right after eating, so I'd watch with them for a while. No one talked or made a sound while the TV was on, and they would often fall asleep. But, I was glad not to be at home.

In September, 1959, we were told that Mom was pregnant.

Jeffrey, and Keith (both 2nd from the right), and cousin Jackie (far right), at birthday party, 1959

Jeff and Keith at beach

Thirteen

MRS. HOBBY WAS MY THIRD grade teacher. She was the oldest teacher in the school. Her hands shook and her voice quivered when she spoke. We all liked her, but I felt compelled to challenge some of her pronouncements. During a spelling lesson at the beginning of the year, Mrs. Hobby told us that it is impossible for a word to have four consonants in a row. I raised my hand. "That's not true," I informed her. "My name, Goldstein, has four consonants in a row".

She smiled. She always smiled when she spoke to us, and informed me that Goldstein was a name, not a word.

I thought quickly and said, "What about subscription, that has four consonants?"

She smiled and said, "Dear, dear. I guess there are always exceptions to any rule. Thank you Jeffrey for pointing that out." My insides were always churning and it infuriated me that she was always calm. But, there was no way to get her angry.

Another time, Mrs. Hobby told us during an arithmetic lesson, that when you say a number, never use the word, "and". For example, the number 101 is pronounced one hundred one, not one hundred and one.

I defiantly raised my hand and said, "That's not always true. When you are talking about money, you would say, one dollar and one cent, not one dollar one cent. In fact, when there is a decimal or a fraction involved, you also say the word 'and'. For example, 1.01 would be 1 and 1 one hundredth"

"Jeffrey, you are so smart. Thank you for enlightening us." I could not get her flustered.

Caught in the Undertow

In third grade, we began to learn about music. First, we all learned to play a little musical instrument called a recorder. After listening to songs for so long, it felt amazing having the opportunity to play them. Then, after a few weeks, Mr. Herman, the orchestra leader, and Mr. Brown, the band director, demonstrated all the different types of musical instruments. We listened to brass, woodwind, string and percussion. They explained the difference between them, and told us which ones we could play in the band or in the orchestra. Shore Road School combined with Winthrop Avenue School to form both a band and an orchestra.

I couldn't believe it. I was mesmerized by the sound of the instruments. I couldn't wait to make music. This was the most excited that I had been since getting my new baseball mitt. I felt chills when Mr. Herman played the violin. The sound made me feel connected to Grandma and to Poland. The sound was so haunting and enticing. There was no doubt that I would choose the violin.

The next week, we divided into groups based on the instruments we had chosen. There were kids there from Winthrop Ave. The string instrument group was a small one and there were mostly girls. I found myself standing next to a boy I had never seen before and he asked me if I was waiting for Mr. Herman, also. I said yes and he said, "Mr. Herman is a German." This was the first conversation that I had with the person who was about to become my best friend. This was the person who helped me survive my childhood.

Fourteen

MY FRIEND BOB—Robert Allan Petrocelli—lived in a small white house on Farmers Avenue. It was located on the other side of Merrick Road, with all the Gentiles and old houses. Bob was an only child. His parents tormented him, but much differently than mine did.

His Irish mother, Terry Petrocelli, was incredibly controlling. She monitored everything that he ate, and he was forbidden to eat candy or chocolate. He could only drink Saratoga Springs water, which came in glass bottles. My parents never had any idea where I was. Bob's Mom had to know where he was at all times. Bob's Mom had to know everything about me to see what type of influence I would be. She even checked his bowel movements, as Grandma did with mine. But Grandma did this when I was a lot younger.

Bob's Italian father, Johnny Petrocelli, was the foreman in a factory. He was totally dominated by Terry. He never learned to drive, and Terry drove him to and from work each day. Johnny had barber skills, and would cut Bob's hair, and sometimes mine. Terry and Johnny never associated much with their relatives, much the way that my parents didn't with theirs.

Bob and I connected because we both read, and we talked to each other. We talked about things that other kids just didn't talk about. We talked about things that I had only talked about with Sheryl. And we talked about a great deal more. We came from totally different backgrounds. We were both friends with kids that the other person didn't like. We looked very different from each other. We were raised differently. We went to different schools. But we understood the world in a way that others couldn't. We transcended our surroundings and realized that we didn't belong in our families. We wanted to find a place to belong somewhere else.

Mrs. Hobby posted a list of the class rankings every five weeks. I was still number two, but not behind Albert. Albert was now in a different class. Number 1 was someone who had never been in my class before. His name was, Bobbie Blake. Bobbie was also a great athlete. When we played flag football in gym, and he guarded me, he stuck to me like glue. I had to work as hard as I could to get open for even a second. And I would guard him as closely. It was an exciting challenge playing against Bobbie. He was taller, and that gave him a slight advantage. We liked and respected each other, both academically and athletically, but were not friends. Bobbie was part of the most popular group of boys in the school. I believed that I was as good an athlete as any of them, but they had one thing that I didn't. Self confidence.

One day, near the end of school, Mrs. Hobby gave the class a difficult riddle to think about. She said that if anyone could figure it out, we would not have homework that night. Everyone turned to look at Bobbie and me. I came up with the answer first. The riddle was, "What comes once in a minute, twice in a moment, but never in a thousand years?"

I knew the answer. It was the letter, "m". Bobbie turned and smiled at me. He gave me a look of approval. I realized that I was not getting that look anymore from my parents. I was not getting the look that a younger sister gives to her older brother, either. Everybody else also gave me that look and patted me on the back on the way out of class. I let myself smile.

I liked going to school. I felt safe and important there. Mrs. Hobby was always kind and complimentary, even when I was obnoxious. I did not feel safe at home. I was being verbally abused, and when I crossed paths with Dad, physically abused. Grandma, when she wasn't crying, was always nice to me. The first time that I saw her really angry was when we found out that Mom was pregnant.

"How could you have another baby with that man?" Grandma screamed. The story was that Mom and Dad only slept together once, a month after Sheryl died. Mom desperately wanted another girl. And she conceived after just one try. Meanwhile, the bill collectors kept coming to the house, Mom and Dad were always fighting, and I tried to stay out of the way.

Mom and Grandma believed in curses and superstitions. *Einhoreh*, the evil eye, was very real to them. As proof, Mom told us about our mailman. The mailman's daughter was diagnosed with leukemia. A few days later, Dad, Keith, Sheryl, Grandma, Grandpa, and I were sitting in the living room. Mom was at the top of the stairs and looked down at all of us. She was *Kvelen*, glowing with pride.

"Thank God for my healthy family!" she said. A few months later, Sheryl was diagnosed with leukemia. A few months after that, both Sheryl and Grandpa were dead. To them, there was cause and effect. I tried hard not believe in their logic, but they kept hitting me over the head with the same message. Do not feel too happy because then bad things will happen. They were all angry at God. Despite this anger, I was expected to start going to Hebrew School in third grade, and to prepare for my Bar Mitzvah.

At the end of our housing development, towards the ocean, there were marshlands, swamps, and tall weeds, some taller than we were. Vinny and I, along with a group of neighborhood kids, had built a hidden secret clubhouse out of the weeds and other discarded items. There were piles of wood, shingles and pipes left over from the housing construction, so we had as much building material as we needed for construction. We borrowed hammers, nails and other tools from various fathers. Different groups of us worked on this a little at a time all summer, and finished it in the fall. To get to our clubhouse, you had to put boards over streams of water. We would pull the boards back after we walked over them so that no one else could get to our private dwelling. Everyone had to take an oath to uphold the secrecy of the location. We had the most fun just getting there and coming back. We felt special belonging to this exclusive group. No one ever told Eck about it because we didn't want to be alone with him in a desolate area.

Paul tried to follow us one day as we began our surreptitious trek to our secret hideaway. Someone saw him, we yelled at him to go away, but he kept coming. Feeling threatened that the location would be discovered, and that the sacredness would be violated, we huddled up and discussed the situation. I don't remember whose idea it was, but we came up with a plan. We told Paul that he could come with us, if he put on a blindfold. We made one out of a rag that was on the ground, he held on to someone's shirt, and we took him with us. We'd stop every few minutes and spin him around a few times, as Vinny had seen them do on TV. This was to ensure that he didn't know where he was. We walked for about twenty minutes, took him to a totally different part of the marshlands, and sat him down. We told him that if he stayed still, we would be back for him in a minute. We all ran away, back to Vinny's house, and left Paul there. He never followed us again.

Dad would get jobs, lose them and pretend that he was working, and get other jobs. He always went to the train station and took a train somewhere. In November he brought home some new stylish boys clothes that he wanted me to wear for Thanksgiving. He took me up to my room and ordered me to try them on. I hated the way they looked and felt. The clothes felt stiff and uncomfortable, but I didn't say anything. I put a polo shirt on over my head, and he buttoned the top button. I felt like I was choking. I quickly tried to pull it back over my head. The shirt got stuck and the button popped.

Dad went crazy. He told me to pick up the button. When I bent over to find it, he kicked me as hard as he could in the butt. Then he threw me across the room, and my head hit the side of a dresser. I was bleeding all over the clothes. He lifted me up by the neck and started to choke me. Rage flew out of his eyes as I struggled to take a breath. I wanted to fight back but my arms hung limply and I became disabled. He finally calmed down, tried to stop the bleeding, and ended taking me to the emergency room of Meadowbrook Hospital. That was the place where Sheryl and Grandpa died, and where I had been with double pneumonia. I needed stitches for my head.

I told the doctor that my butt hurt. He looked at it and said, "That's quite a bruise you've got."

Dad came in and joked, "He's always getting hurt playing ball. When I was a boy, I always had cuts and bruises from playing, too."

The doctor believed him.

Fifteen

IN FEBRUARY, 1960, TEN MONTHS after Sheryl died, Mom went into labor. She wanted to have the baby in Brooklyn, so we all drove to Grandma's sister Yetta's apartment, and Mom went into the hospital. Grandma, Grandpa and Mom had lived in the same apartment with Aunt Yetta for a while in the 1930's after Grandpa lost everything in the Depression. This is when Mom became close to her cousin Milton, Yetta's son. Yetta's husband, Sam, was an inveterate drinker and gambler, and Sam died soon after they had a second son, Richard. My Aunt Yetta was very short, had light hair, and always hugged me and tried to get me to eat something. I was very comfortable around her, and felt safe, unlike the uneasiness I experienced around Dad's relatives. Grandma and Mom, when they talked about Yetta, called her a little *vantz,* or bedbug. I had become very familiar with all the Yiddish insults and derogatory words that were mostly directed at relatives.

Richard was fifteen years younger than Milton, and he was still living in his mother's apartment. He was in his 20's and they called him a bachelor. Keith and I were taken to the apartment, while Mom, Dad, and Grandma went to the hospital. Richard greeted me and shook my hand. I was invited to see his room. There were posters of musicians hanging on his wall and I saw a guitar sitting on a chair.

"Do you play that?" I asked.

"Yup," he replied. "I love rock and roll."

"What's that?"

"It's music with a beat. Like Elvis." Richard picked up the

guitar and I watched as he played. I bobbed my head up and down to the rhythms of the songs.

"I'm learning to play the violin," I said.

"Then you should be able to play this." Richard handed me the guitar and showed me how to strum and play some simple chords. My hands weren't big enough to cover the whole fret but I managed to make some pleasant sounds.

"Why don't we ever see each other?" I asked.

"My mom and your grandma don't get along. Maybe they'll get over it someday," he replied.

"Can I play your guitar again later?" I asked.

"Sure, anytime. So, do you want to have a new brother or new little sister?" he asked.

"Probably everyone would be happier with a girl. I really miss Sheryl." That was the first time that I had said that out loud. I fought back the tears. Richard held my hand and gave me a weak smile.

That night, I was told to sleep on the hard couch in their living room. Aunt Yetta's furniture was very old and the couch had white doilies over the arms and the back. I couldn't get comfortable. I stayed awake staring at the plaster designs on the ceiling. I thought about Sheryl and felt empty. My chest burned and there was no way to put out the fire. I was exhausted. Where did I fit into my family? Where did I fit into the world? I looked at my watch and it was three in the morning. I had never been up that late before, and wondered if I would ever fall asleep.

At 5:30, Dad came in. His face was blank as he told me that I had a new baby sister. Keith stayed asleep on a cot near the couch. I cried. It was February 6, 1960, and my sister Michele Stacy came into the world. The "M" in Michele comes from Max, Grandpa's name, and the "S" in Stacy comes from Sheryl. Mom now had her daughter. I had a new sister. I dared to feel some hope for the family.

Sixteen

MICHELE SLEPT IN A CRIB in Mom and Dad's room. Dad was working again, and, except for the sound of a baby crying, our house was a lot calmer. In the spring, we began playing stickball at Shore Road School. We drew a box on the back wall of the school. The box represented the strike zone. The batter would stand in front of the box, and if the pitcher could hit the box without the batter hitting the rubber ball, it was a strike. If it went outside of the box, it was a ball. We each had our own special stick that we used as our bat. Mine was an old broom handle. Playing the game improved our hitting reflexes. This was important to me because little league tryouts were coming up, and I was better at fielding than I was at hitting.

Tryouts were again at the baseball fields near Winthrop Ave. School. I felt confident that I had done well, and waited to find out which team I was on. We waited for the coach who picked us to call. Neither Vinny nor Bob wanted to be in Little League, even though they both played stickball and other baseball games with me. Finally, a few days later, the phone rang, and Mr. O'Malley wanted to talk to me. I was chosen to play in the Minor Leagues on a team called the Wildcats. I was chosen! I did well hitting and fielding at our practices, and Mr. O'Malley told me that I could play center field. The same position as Mickey Mantle! I was bursting with pride when I received the uniform. I was number 5, the same number as Joe Dimaggio.

When the games started, an older kid named Tom played

center field for the first few innings, and I played for the rest of the game. I used my speed to track down any fly ball hit near me. When a ball was hit into the outfield, Mr. O'Malley would shout, "Goldstein, get on your horse and ride!"

After a while, all the kids would shout to me, "Goldstein, get on your horse and ride!" I also batted leadoff, and if I hit a ground ball, I could almost always beat the throw to first. I also drew a lot of walks, so I was on base most of the time, even though I rarely hit the ball to the outfield.

Halfway into the season, Dad came to a game. He drove me there, and I felt proud that he was going to see me play. I put too much pressure on myself, and I struck out twice, and dropped a popup. Mr. O'Malley patted me on the back and said, "Don't worry kid, you'll get 'em next time."

In the car on the way home, Dad exploded. "You are totally useless! I am so embarrassed!" He loudly continued to berate me, and slapped me on the face with the back of his hand. I turned my head away, looked out the window, and smiled, in an attempt not to cry. The more I felt like crying, the harder I smiled. He would not ruin my love of baseball. I wondered if he realized how much I hated him at that moment.

July 1 was my 9th birthday. I was hoping for a new bike. My old bike was small and beat up, but I doubted that I would get one. That evening, as we were playing in Navy Court, Dad, in his suit, rode down the street on a big, new black bike. It was a three speed English Racer with hand breaks. It was a premier bike, the Cadillac of bicycles. He bought it at a bike shop in Wantagh, the next stop on the railroad. He then rode it back, about five miles, to our house.

Dad got off the bike and said, "Happy birthday!" He got a wrench from the house, and lowered the seat as far as it would go. I got on and could barely reach the petals, but I still was able to control it. He had now given me the two best presents in my life, my baseball mitt and a new bike. I rode it away to show my friends. That day, I didn't hate him.

Caught in the Undertow

Riding my new bike was exhilarating. I applied the three speeds to effortlessly go as fast as I wanted. The hand brakes, front and rear, enabled me to stop on a dime. I could go to Bob's house in a few minutes, and would glide around the neighborhood feeling like I was flying. I had the ability to cross Merrick Road and soar through foreign neighborhoods. Sometimes, I would spend time peddling up and down each street so that anyone outside could see me on my luxurious machine.

A week later I rode to Robin Hoods, purchased two deep baskets that fastened over the rear wheels, and my bike became a pickup truck. I had the ability to put my mitt, a baseball, my bat, a sweatshirt, lunch, and a thermos in the baskets, with room to spare. My friends and I would leave for Bart's candy store, but I'd pull away and shout, "I'll meet you when you get there," because my bike was so much faster.

Bart's became a place to hang out when we weren't playing ball. We sat at the soda fountain counter and drank egg creams, vanilla coke, cherry coke, thick milk shakes, or root beer. We read comic books as we drank. And, of course, we bought baseball cards. There was still tremendous excitement and anticipation as we each ripped open our new packs.

Across the road from Bart's, there was a bridge that went over a stream with a strong current. Each of us would grab a leaf or a piece of grass, drop it in the stream at the same time, and have a race. The grass or leaf that was carried to the next bridge first, won. Sometimes we bet baseball cards on the race. It was especially fun to sit by the stream when we had a hot, lazy summer day. When you are 9 years old, and it is summer time, there is nothing to do but have fun, and have adventures.

A requisite activity for summer fun was stickball. We played with as few as two players, Vinny and I, or as many as ten or eleven. A few weeks after my birthday, eight of us rode our bikes to the school for a game. I put some other kid's gloves and sticks in my baskets to free up their hands while they rode their smaller bikes.

We were playing intensely, and the game had been going on for over an hour when we heard a group of boys coming towards us. It was Randy Strong and his gang. Randy never was alone, but always had a group of kids with him and they always were looking to disrupt other kid's activities. They started to taunt us, and we told them to get lost. They tried to engage us in what we called, "rank outs". A kid insulted you, and then you insulted him. This would continue until one of the kids failed to come up with a good retort. At that point, the spectators would all shout, "Rank out!" as an insult to the loser. I was particularly good at this having used many of the insults that I heard from the comedians in the Catskills.

I was up at bat at the time, and did not want to stop the game. Everyone again shouted, "Get lost, can't you see that we are playing a game!"

What happened next became folk-lore around south Bellmore. Everyone who was there remembers it differently. Randy and his goons took out water guns and ran at us while shooting them and squirting us. The way I remember it, Vinny had already pitched the ball, and I was in the process of swinging my stick when Randy ran in front of me. He was hit by my swinging stick in his elbow and fell down screaming. He had a fractured elbow.

Some kids say that I hit him on purpose. Some say that I was defending myself. Other kids, including Vinny, corroborate my version that it was an accident. "Goldstein broke Strong's arm with his stickball bat" became the topic de jour.

A few days later, Randy, and some other adults, came to my house. Randy was in a cast and yelled that he wasn't going to be able to go swimming all summer because of me. One of the adults was from their insurance company, and he asked me a bunch of questions about what had happened. They interviewed most of the kids who were there, and I never found out how it was resolved. I was left with another question without an answer.

Jeff and Keith

Seventeen

IN SEPTEMBER, 1960, I ENTERED 4th grade at Shore Road Elementary School. My teacher was new to the school. She was a very tall, big boned woman named Miss Lindbloom. I immediately noticed that she had four consecutive consonants in her name, and wanted to tell Mrs. Hobby. I was surprised to find out that Mrs. Hobby had retired. I had trouble imagining Mrs. Hobby not being a teacher. I pictured her at a grocery store telling the cashier, "Dear, dear, you did such a good job. Thank you for bagging my food!" I looked around the class, and noticed that both Albert Frankenstein and Bobbie Blake were in my class. David Beagler, who had been number one in his classes, was also there, as well as Paul Baldwin. I eagerly anticipated some intense academic competition.

At school I felt a reprieve from the horrible feelings that overwhelmed me at home. There were no adults to hit me or to yell at me. I actually received positive recognition and I thrived in Mrs. Lindbloom's class. She challenged us academically, and I loved the discussions and debates. Mrs. Lindbloom especially liked social studies, which Mrs. Hobby had called citizenship education. This became my favorite subject.

I began reading about history on my own at home. We still had Mom's childhood set of the *Encyclopedia Britannica* from the 1930's. It referred to World War One as, "The Great World War" because World War Two hadn't happened yet when it was printed. I spent many hours reading through moldy smelling volumes. That fall, Mom began buying the *World Book Encyclopedia,* a more modern reference book. She bought it one volume at a time, at Waldbaums, a grocery store which touted itself as a "supermarket". We eventually had the whole set for 1960, and the yearly supplement. The two sets were put on a book shelf downstairs in the utility room, which contained the oil burner that heated our house. In that room I was also able to feel Mom's warmth when she took the time to answer my questions about her historical recollections.

The best part of class was when we studied history in the making by examining current events. We all had a subscription to a weekly news magazine for kids. Every Friday we would read it together and debate the different controversies. The biggest issue that fall was the presidential election. I was enamored with John F. Kennedy. Most kids were. He seemed to be glowing with hope and energy. Richard M. Nixon, from my nine year old perspective, seemed mean and sinister.

Martin Luther King Jr. and the civil rights battles were just beginning to enter into our consciousness. There were no black families in Bellmore, but I vividly remembered the ones in Brooklyn, and my friend, Willie. Kennedy seemed to be the champion of equal rights. Dad was a World War ll veteran and a staunch Republican. He actually let me watch some of the presidential debates on TV, and then calmly discussed them with me. I made a mental note, we could talk about the Yankees and politics without Dad erupting.

We were also being inculcated as to the malevolence of communism. Fidel Castro was our enemy and he had nuclear missiles pointed at us in Cuba, just ninety miles south of our country. Nikita Khrushchev was the evil dictator of the USSR, and Mao was the wicked leader of China. They often put those names together, Castro, Khrushchev, and Mao. They were the modern day Hitlers. They were the reason that we had to have air raid drills and duck and cover next to the wall in the corridor. They were the reason that the world might end. They were the reason that my sense of security at school was sometimes violated.

My good feelings at school were also threatened when Mom, who had been an elementary school teacher before she was married, began to sub at my school. We needed the money. Dad apparently still wasn't working and we continued to live on Grandma's social security. I prayed that Mom wouldn't fill in for one of my teachers.

At the end of September Mom subbed for another fourth grade teacher. At the end of the day, she tried to talk to me as I left the school building, but I ignored her. Randy Strong confronted me outside the gym. "You ruined my whole summer, and now I'm going to beat the shit out of you!" I put up my fists to defend myself. Randy threw a punch, and I ducked. I then threw a right hook that hit him square on the side of his jaw. He crumpled to the ground, with me standing over him, and my fist still waving in the air.

An older kid ran over, pulled me away, and yelled, "Haven't you already done enough to him?" I was incredulous that I had knocked him out with just one punch. I felt a deep, painful guilt. I had done to him what Dad was doing to me. My throat muscles tightened as I thought of Sheryl. I turned red as I became aware of Mom's presence nearby.

Aunt Esther and Uncle Max

Eighteen

In 4th GRADE, I BOUGHT my first transistor radio. I had been told that my cousin Milton, who was some type of engineer, was a member of the team that developed a way to make transistor radios. They seemed like an incredible innovation. It was small enough to fit in my pocket, and it came with a single earphone so that I could listen privately. I could pick up over a dozen stations, mainly emanating from NYC. I tuned into Yankee games, popular music, and the news. In October, we had tried to listen to the World Series secretly at school. The games were all during the day. Mrs. Lindbloom discovered what we were doing, took away our radios, stored them on her desk, and told us not to bring them back. I continued to take my radio with me wherever I went, except, to school. Sometimes I felt saddened when I listened because I couldn't spend more time with Milton and my cousin Jackie.

In November, 1960, I heard on my radio that JFK was elected to be our 35th president. Grandma had told me about FDR and how adored he was when he was the president. Now we had a president that I could admire. JFK, just like FDR, was also referred to by his three initials. I felt a bond with Grandma. In January, I listened to Kennedy's inaugural address and felt chills. His speech was printed in the newspaper the next day, and I memorized parts of it. So many phrases in it resonated with me. "Let us never negotiate out of fear, but never let us fear to negotiate." I knew that I didn't understand all of it, but it sounded like music. Dad had voted for Nixon and was very unhappy, but Grandma was thrilled. Mom didn't seem to have an opinion.

Caught in the Undertow

January, 1961, we were told, was the beginning of an historic year. I tried to imagine what the encyclopedias of the future would say. JFK took office as the youngest president to ever be elected, the first Catholic president, and the winner of one of the closest elections ever. It was also historic because of the number, 1961. The number looked the same upside down and right side up. The first *Mad* Magazine of the year had a big 1961 on the cover with the caption," It's Going to be an Upside Down Year." We tried to figure out the last time that this happened, and came up with the year, 1881. We thought that the next time would be 6009.

At school, we continued to have fascinating discussions about the news and world events. During the course of the year, Mrs. Lindbloom posted our class rankings, just like our other teachers had. Albert was always number one, Bobbie Blake and I kept trading places for numbers two and three, David Beagler was always number four, and Paul Baldwin had fallen to number five. The competition was fun, even though we couldn't figure out the basis of the rankings. Bobbie, David and I discussed the topic and realized that we all consistently received A's on all of our work. We all were in the highest reading, math and science groups. We all had great class participation. We began to believe that it was rigged so that Albert would be number one. He had a mystique about him and was so weird that everyone assumed it was because he was a genius. I loved to read, but Albert read while we all played games during recess. He read science books and probably never heard of the Hardy Boys. He didn't have any baseball cards. Mr. Deluca always left him alone in gym. I could still beat him most of the time at chess. But everyone expected Albert to be number one, and so he was.

I had many friends at school, but was unhappy at home and yearned for an extended family. We saw no relatives, except for during Passover, when we drove to Far Rockaway, Queens for a Seder at Aunt Esther and Uncle Max's apartment. Aunt Esther was Grandma's oldest sister. Aunt Esther and Uncle

Max were Orthodox Jews. Uncle Max always wore a yarmulke, and went to Temple regularly. They both were kosher, and always asked me about Hebrew School. They never had any children, and Grandma said that it was too bad because Aunt Esther had big hips and could have had a lot of babies. When I asked Grandma why they never had children, she said it was because Uncle Max was too nervous and couldn't do it. Thanks to Willie's brothers, I knew what "it" was. They had very old furniture, no radio, and a small TV. They only had books written in Hebrew or Yiddish, a daily newspaper that was written in Yiddish, and spoke only Yiddish to the other adults. Grandma told me that they had never been anywhere since they came here from Poland.

Aunt Esther always said, "Why go anywhere, you just have to come home again."

I never said anything at their apartment, except, "Good," when they asked me how Hebrew school was. I often wondered why I had to go to Hebrew school when religion seemed so unimportant to Mom and Dad. Mom often talked about being angry at God for taking Sheryl away. On the way home I listened to my transistor radio in the car and thought of Milton.

Night time was the worst part of the day. I still thought about Sheryl. When strong winds blew, and tree branches or shutters rapped against the house, I imagined that it was Sheryl wanting me to meet her in the hall. Sometimes I was overwhelmed with fear and terror. I believed that Sheryl was coming to trade places with me. I was overwhelmed with the feeling that I was the one who was supposed to be dead. My memories of her began to fade away and mostly, I felt a profound emptiness.

In the spring, my spirits were lifted when I tried out for Little League again. As a 4th grader, I was eligible for the Majors, but I was told that hardly any 4th graders make it. I ended up being called by Mr. O'Malley, and being told that I was on the Wildcats again, but that I did very well at tryouts and would play most of the game in centerfield. Mr. O'Malley talked to me after the first practice and said that players are often brought up to the Majors if someone gets hurt during the season. He said that there was a good chance that I might get called up. When our games started, I didn't give Dad the schedule.

About two weeks into the season, I got a phone call from Mr. Hill. He was the coach of the Bankers, the best team in the Majors. One of their players broke his collarbone and he was out for the season. I was invited to the next practice. I was ecstatic. The Bankers won the championship almost every year. Mr. Hill had been coaching for years, one of his sons was the assistant coach, and his grandson was on the team. Mr. Hill was considered the best coach around. It was like being drafted by the Yankees. I got on my bike, and told everyone I could find.

At the first practice, it was obvious how organized they were. There were different coaches for hitting, for throwing, for pitching, and for fielding. The players rotated through the different stations, and all the coaches were encouraging and enthusiastic. They all welcomed me to the team, and introduced me to the other players, most of whom were 6th graders. No one yelled at you if you made a mistake, but instead helped you do better the next time. Even the kids were nice to each other. Mr. Hill always had a different pep talk to deliver to us at the end of practice. Sometimes, some us would stay after practice and discuss professional baseball and talk about baseball cards with Mr. Hill. He was always friendly. I sometimes wished that he was my father.

My season in the Majors started. Mr. Hill explained to me that because it was my first year, I would only play about two innings a game. Two innings, however, was more than enough time to show everyone how good I was, he explained. Mr. Hill would always make sure that I got at least one at bat.

After my first game, Mr. Hill told me everything that I did well. I always knew where to stand in the field, I always was alert, and I had real good cuts at the ball, even though I struck out. He built up my confidence, even though playing with older and bigger kids was very intimidating. Eventually, I got my first base hit, and the whole team stood up and cheered. We played more games than we did in the Minors, and I started to get more playing time.

Dad found out that I was on the Bankers, and came to a game. I choked again, and did terribly. Dad came up to Mr. Hill after the game, introduced himself, and said that he was sorry that I did so poorly.

Mr. Hill said that I was an excellent player, and just had a bad day. We went to the car, and I told Dad that I was going to walk home on my own. I left before he could say anything. It was a twenty minute walk. I avoided him when I got home, and went straight to my room.

The next day at practice, Mr. Hill asked me why I didn't go home with my father. I said that I felt like walking. Mr. Hill said that if there was anything wrong, I could tell him. I never did. I never told anyone, not even Bob. Part of me felt as if I deserved to be beaten for being alive instead of Sheryl.

Nineteen

GRANDMA HAD MOVED INTO OUR house after Sheryl and Grandpa died, and I spent a tremendous amount of quality time with her. When I was in fourth grade, Grandma began to take me on trips into Manhattan during Christmas and Easter vacations. She'd get dressed up, put on her big white earrings, a hat, and a skirt, and I would put on a dress shirt, dress pants, and Buster Brown shoes. We'd go to the Bellmore train station, and take the southern line of the Long Island Railroad into The City. I always sat by the window and watched as we stopped at each village along the way; Merrick, Freeport, Baldwin, Rockville Center, Lynbrook, Valley Stream, and then Jamaica, Queens, the hub station. I'd look at all the stores, houses and trees that flew by us and wonder about what it was like to live somewhere else. I'd stare at the people getting on or off the train and try to imagine what their lives were like. Sometimes, we'd switch trains in Jamaica, and sometimes, we'd stay on our train as the other passengers switched. The train then travelled through a tunnel that went under the river, it got very dark, our ears popped, and we'd end up in Penn Station in Manhattan.

The train ride was always exciting, and Grandma was always uninhibited on the trip. It was like a weight was lifted from her shoulders when we left the house. We both felt free. She answered any question that I had the temerity to ask. It was on the train that Grandma told me about Aunt Esther's big hips and Uncle Max's nervousness. I asked Grandma to tell me why Mom was her only child, and she had the candor to inform me that Grandpa, "finished too quickly" and she couldn't get pregnant again. Grandma told me about the different feuds that had occurred in the family, and about how she had warned Mom that Dad was no good and not to marry him. She'd tell me stories about Poland, her childhood, and explained obscene Yiddish expressions that I had heard but didn't know how to translate. We felt very comfortable with each other.

Penn Station was huge and filled with dozens of trains on dozens of tracks going to dozens of destinations. We'd walk by store after store selling everything from magazines to jewelry to clothes. There'd be men kneeling down and shining business men's shoes. The air vibrated with sounds of clarinets, guitars, and all the instruments played by the street musicians. Sitting against the dirty walls were homeless people who smelled like urine.

Outside of the station we were thrust into the raucous city. The sound of honking horns from the swarms of vehicles filled our ears, the pungent aromas from the street vendor's food filled our noses, and the heavy air hit us in the face. I'd look up and take in the sight of the tall buildings, and I'd gaze at the hordes of rushing people scurrying across the sidewalks. Grandma and I always stopped for lunch at the Automat. I'd enjoy having a hamburger and vanilla shake.

During Christmas vacation, Grandma took me to Radio City Music Hall. We'd enjoy a show by the Rockettes, and then see a movie. The first year that we went we saw the movie, *Exodus*.

During Easter vacation, Grandma took me to a Broadway musical. The first year we saw *Bye Bye Birdie*, and later we saw *Camelot, Oliver,* and *Fiddler on the Roof*. I sat enthralled with my mouth open. I was captivated by the beauty of the story, the depth of the characters, the operatic voices, and the majesty of the music. If we could see the orchestra from our seats, I would watch the virtuosity of the violinists and other musicians. I was moved emotionally, and sometimes had tears in my eyes. I looked away if Grandma turned her head towards me. After each musical, I begged Grandma to stop at a record store so that we could buy the record album from the play, and within a week, I had all the songs memorized.

The Broadway musicals inspired me to practice playing my violin even more diligently. I was taking lessons during the school year, and once a week during the summer. Mrs. Kunicki, a young new teacher, gave the lessons. Bob and I were able to go to lessons together. Bob had a portable electric organ at his house, and sometimes Bob's mom would accompany us. Bob always played more skillfully than I did, but he always said that he was only playing the violin until he could learn to play the guitar.

In the spring of each year, the Shore Road Elementary School orchestra gave a concert. Mom and Grandma never showed any interest in my sporting events,ced but they came to all of my concerts and recitals. Music was the one thing we all loved. We played classical music pieces and songs from musicals such as *Carousal*. Bob and I were first violins in the orchestra. It seemed to take an incredible amount of time and effort for all of us to get the sound right. There was always someone who played out of tune or who played the wrong notes. When we finally gelled, I felt the same feeling of awe that I did listening to the Broadway orchestras. I felt proud being a part of something that sounded so amazing. I loved the sound of the applause when we were done. On the way home, Mom and Grandma would always tell me how beautiful the concert was, and that the way I played brought them *naches*, or great happiness. They felt *farklempt*, or brought to tears. The music connected us.

If Dad came, he made a point of criticizing the way I was dressed.

Twenty

I BECAME A FIFTH GRADER in September, 1961. My teacher was Mr. Boblewski. He had a tremendous round head which looked like a big bubble to me, and I called him, Mr. Bubble Brain. He also had a terrible temper, and would often throw chalk, erasers, pens, books or whatever he was holding at someone. He had enough control that the object would soar above our heads, but once he threw a big metal stapler, and most of us stopped fooling around after that. I didn't have to spend much time with Mr. Bubble Brain because we began to be departmentalized in fifth grade and went to different rooms and teachers for our different subjects. He was my science teacher. In fifth grade, they also stopped posting the student rankings.

About a month into the year, the situation that I had dreaded actually happened. Mom, who was still subbing, subbed for my reading teacher. The other kids, naturally, all teased me on the way to class, and as soon as I entered the room, my face turned as red as Grandma's borscht. I refused to make eye contact with her, but I could see other kids smirking at me. Mom handled it well, she acted as if I wasn't there.

On the way out of class, Bobbie Blake yelled at me, "I bet you got a perfect score on all of your work today."

I responded, "Perfect *is* the correct word to use to describe me."

Bobbie replied, "Yeah, a perfect mess."

"It takes one to know one," was my brilliant retort.

Everyone waited for our conversation to escalate into a rank out session, but the bell rang and it was time for our next class.

The fact that I had the skill to quickly hurl insults earned me the respect of the other kids and I was always searching for the approval that I wasn't receiving at home.

Most of the time at home I was angry and avoided everyone. Sometimes, I became aware of my siblings, and wanted to take care of them. Dad didn't seem to pay any attention to any of us, except for when he would explode at me. Keith was now four years old, and I felt very paternalistic towards him. I played catch with him, and taught him to play chess while we listened to my records in our bedroom. Keith chose to occupy his alone time differently from me. He had many sets of little plastic toy soldiers and he spent hours moving them around in imaginary battles. Keith also showed a great deal of artistic talent at a young age.

Michele was only a year old and I didn't interact much with her. I read children's books to her now and then, and she had dolls that she played with. I really didn't know how to connect with her. Mom and Grandma were always doting on her. I wanted some positive attention from Mom also, but at the same time, I was happy that she wasn't yelling at me.

Mom was subbing almost every day, and Grandma did most of the cooking. Dinner time was one of the only occasions where the whole family was together. We ate many Jewish foods; kishke, gefilte fish, kasha varnishkes, blintzes, knishes, chopped liver and onions, salmon croquettes, and matzah ball soup. Sometimes we had spaghetti covered with ketchup as a side dish. I loved lamb chops, which we only had infrequently due to the price, and also enjoyed tongue. About once a week, Grandma brought home a big beef tongue and cooked it for dinner. I was then able to have sliced tongue sandwiches on rye bread for lunch. I always brought my lunch to school. I ate a sandwich, (tongue, pastrami, or roast beef), an apple or orange, and a few chocolate coconut cookies. I drank a small carton of milk which I purchased with my milk card. It cost ten cents for a weekly milk card. It was not kosher to have milk and meat together, and we didn't at home.

Every few weeks we ate dinner at a restaurant, usually The

Charcoal Chef, on Sunrise Highway in Merrick. We ate only kosher meat at home, but we were allowed to stray from that when we dined out. Grandma still would not eat *traif* or non kosher meat, and she would always order fish. She had never eaten pork or bacon, or any type of shellfish. I always ordered a menu item called, Chicken in a Basket, at The Charcoal Chef. I would receive fried chicken on top of French fries in a plastic basket.

On days that we had violin lessons after school, I saved a few chocolate coconut cookies to eat after we were done. Bob's mother was always very strict about what Bob was allowed to eat, and he was prohibited from eating any chocolate. She said that Bob was extremely allergic, which he denied. One day, he asked for one of my cookies, and ate it. When Bob's mother found out, she called my house and yelled at me over the phone. She said that Bob could have died. That was the first of several times that Bob was banned from seeing me. Bob and I thought that we were the only kids with such awful parents and we spent a great deal of time discussing the fact that we didn't want to be a part of our families.

Grandma seemed to be the only real Jewish person in our house. The fact that my religious training was so important to her made it more palatable to me. In fifth grade, I was in my third year of Hebrew school. I went to The Merrick Jewish Center on Tuesday and Thursday nights, and on Sunday mornings. We were also required to attend a few Saturday morning Sabbath services, and to attend services on the High Holy Days and other holidays.

During the week, we learned Hebrew, and we studied Jewish history on Sunday. I enjoyed learning history, and hated the Hebrew part. We learned to read Hebrew, to speak it, but not much about what the words meant. No one wanted to be there, and most of the kids fooled around the whole time. I was proud of being Jewish, and felt connected to the culture and historical aspects, but did not relate to the Hebrew part. I actually felt sorry for the teachers. They were shown no respect and they seemed sincere about trying to teach us.

I never wanted to go to services on Saturday, but I felt a part of something bigger when I did go. The group singing, chanting and responsive reading, gave me the same feeling of awe as when I played in the orchestra. I felt part of a consciousness that included my ancestors and all the Jewish history that came before me, and I felt Sheryl's presence. I also became aware of how out of alignment Dad was with everything going on at the services.

We car pooled to Temple, with different parents taking turns driving us kids. I became friends with Cliff West. We told jokes on the way there and back, and Mr. West was the only parent who would laugh. One Sunday, Cliff and I came up with a secret plan. We went into class, stayed for attendance, and then snuck out. We walked across Merrick Road to the Gables movie theater, and watched the movie, *Barabbas*. We thought that this was ironic because *Barabbas* took place around the time of Christ's crucifixion. We were learning history, we said, and it was exciting seeing the gladiators and watching events that took place two thousand years ago. We chose *Barabbas* because it was scheduled to end about ten minutes before our class was over.

After the movie, we went back to the temple, and went home in the car pool. Cliff and I had a loud conversation in the car. "Did you ever hear of the movie *Barabbas?*" I asked.

"No, what's it about?" asked Cliff.

"It's a historical movie that takes place in Roman times," I said.

"Wow, we could probably learn a lot that would help us in Sunday school if we saw it," replied Cliff.

"Yeah, I hear that Anthony Quinn is in it. I wish that I could see it," I sighed.

"Me, too," says Cliff.

The other kids in the car giggled, but none of the parents ever found out. It became a running joke to bring up the name of that movie each Sunday in the car pool. We were being forced to go to Hebrew school and it felt empowering to put something over on them.

Twenty-One

THAT SPRING, THE TOWN OF Hempstead, which was comprised of several villages including Bellmore, opened up a series of public parks. Around the corner from Navy Place, and down the next block, was the entrance to Newbridge Road Park. The Park was like heaven to us. It took us only four or five minutes to make the walk, and less than two minutes to run there. It was located where the tall weeds and marshes were that once hid our secret clubhouse. The wetlands were now filled in with a modern park that contained six separate baseball fields, four tennis courts, three full basketball courts, handball courts, an indoor ice skating arena, three separate playgrounds, and a big swimming pool. A big running track surrounded everything, and the south end of the park contained a dusty trail and mounds of dirt and was used as a bicycle racing area. South of that was the Atlantic Ocean. We played stickball and flipped baseball cards on the handball courts, played baseball and football on the well groomed fields, raced our bikes on the dirt track, and began learning to play basketball. There was no reason to ever go home.

Sunday was the best day to go to the park. The older kids organized a "continuous baseball game" that started at 9am and lasted until dark. Players would come and go, and the teams would rearrange to fit the people there. If you came, and you could play, you were put on a team. The game was always on the furthest field from the entrance, supposedly the best field, and the players could see you approaching way before you arrived.

When the older kids saw me coming, they'd shout, "Hey, it's Goldstein. Goldstein, get on your horse and ride!"

I'd jog a little faster and they'd scream, "Your horse is a little pokey today. Better feed it some more oats."

I'd run full out and hear them tell the kids who didn't know me, "He's fast. You should put him in centerfield. And he always gets on base."

No matter how fast I got there, they'd say, "Goldstein, what took you so long. We just played nine innings waiting for you to get here," and they'd laugh and muss up my hair.

I felt like I belonged, like I was welcome, like I was important. My insides glowed and felt warm. Not the profound emptiness I felt at home. The sun energized my body, the salty air refreshed my lungs, the calming sound of the ocean and the sea breezes pushed away my pain. My mitt caressed my hand, my baseball cap was a crown on my head, and I could run uninhibitedly. This *was* heaven.

Often, school also became heaven. In May, the whole 5th grade took a one day field trip to Washington D.C. This was the home of the president we so idolized, John F. Kennedy. President Kennedy! JFK! Jack and Jackie! Even as 5th graders we were totally in awe of him. JFK was larger than life. He started the Peace Corps. He fought for equality and civil rights. He stood up to Russia and the communists. And we were going to take a tour of the White House.

"Do you think that we'll get to meet him?"

"Nah, he won't come out to see a bunch of kids."

"Yeah, I wouldn't want to meet us either."

We all went to the Bellmore train station while it was still dark, earlier than I had ever been up before, and travelled on a 5am train into Penn Station in the City. There we boarded a train with luxurious accommodations that was bound for Washington D.C. The train cars had big cushioned seats that reclined, bathrooms, a food car, and tray tables that folded down from the seat in front. There were big tinted windows, and shades that you could pull down to cover them. Unlike the Long Island Railroad, the train moved fast and quietly, and was going non-stop all the way to D.C. I spent time either walking around and talking to different people, or sitting quietly and staring at the ever changing view. Most of the time, we were all too excited to sit still. We might see JFK later!

In Washington, we went on a walking tour. I gazed in amazement at the National Mall, the Washington Monument, the Lincoln Memorial, the Jefferson Memorial, and then the many buildings of the Smithsonian. My group went into the Air and Space Museum and we saw the Wright Brothers wood and fabric biplane, which we learned was called, *The Flyer*. We were next to famous landmarks that we had only seen in pictures in our books or encyclopedias.

Then, after lunch, we went on our tour of the White House. There were different tour guides for our various small groups. We all ended up in the same big room, and then it happened. It *really happened*. JFK. Our 35th president. With a smile and a dark suit he walked into the room. We all stopped breathing and stared. Our jaws dropped and our eyes grew huge. He was standing in the same room!

"I heard that there was a group of students here and I want to welcome you all to the White House. I hope that you are enjoying your trip, and that you are learning a great deal," he said with his presidential New England accent. "Keep studying hard and maybe one of you will grow up to be President of the United States."

"Yeah, if you have a rich daddy, too," I heard Mr. Bubble Brain mumble.

I had another reason to dislike Bubble Brain, but no one could diminish the enormity of this moment. I breathed the same air as JFK! This was by far the greatest moment of my life.

We all were exhausted by the time we boarded for the trip back home. We ate dinner on the train, and several kids fell asleep. Many of us were too excited to sit still, and we walked around bothering the chaperones and kids who wanted to sleep. At around 1am, my eyelids were very heavy, but I refused to sit still.

"You look funny when you are tired," said Debbie, a girl that I liked.

"You look funny all the time," I replied.

Twenty-Two

JONES BEACH WAS ABOUT FIVE miles away from Bellmore, and it was the big summer destination for families and kids. When we were younger, a school bus took us to an inlet called Zach's Bay, where we took swimming lessons. Zach's Bay had no waves, and everyone called it the "Polio Pit." Zach's Bay was located at field 5. Jones Beach contained several different fields that were located at various parts of the ocean. The summer after 5th grade, we began taking the public bus by ourselves to the beach. We would walk about ten minutes to Merrick Road, pay twenty-five cents for the bus, and arrive at field 4. Field 4 contained the famous Jones Beach Tower, a long boardwalk, and a big sandy beach on the ocean.

We had become strong swimmers and spent many hours body surfing in the ocean. We'd normally swim all morning, and then went to the boardwalk food stands for lunch. For a nominal amount of money, we purchased big, juicy cheeseburgers fresh off of the grill, orangeade, and a "Mello Roll" for dessert. A Mello Roll was a cylindrically shaped roll of ice cream that came wrapped in paper, which you unwrapped and dropped sideways into an ice cream cone with a flat cylindrically shaped top. They came in vanilla, chocolate, and strawberry. A popular rank out was, "Up your hole with a Mello Roll." Many rank outs consisted of invitations to shove large objects into small orifices of the other person's body. If the rank out rhymed, it was more effective. "Up your ass with some Mobil gas," and "Up your nose with a rubber hose," were also popular.

Caught in the Undertow

We usually had enough money to go to the beach two or three times a week. One Sunday in July, we walked down the beach to a closed area with no people or life guard. It was forbidden to swim in roped off areas like that, but Eck had talked us into it. "We'll have the ocean all to ourselves," he said.

We had been body surfing for a while, and I decided to swim out deeper than I had gone before. When our family went to the beach, Dad, who learned to be an incredible swimmer in the Navy, would dive into the ocean, and swim out of sight. The lifeguards stood and blew their whistles at him, but he kept swimming further and further away. He would finally come back an hour later.

I thought that I could do this too, and swam straight out away from the shore. When I tried to swim back in, I got caught in a strong riptide, which we called an, "undertow." The harder I struggled, the further away from shore I ended up. I was breathless and getting panicky. There were no other people near me. It took all my energy to stay afloat, and my situation seemed hopeless. I didn't feel calm and peaceful like I did when I fell off the boat in the Catskills. I feared for my life, and began to breathe in water.

I flailed around for what seemed like an eternity, and ended up even further from the shore. I decided to conserve my energy, and calmly floated on my back. I then remembered that we were told in our swimming lessons, that if we were caught in an undertow, we should swim parallel to the shore and find the area where the undertow ended. I used the side stroke, which I could do with less effort, found that area, and eventually made it to shore. I collapsed on the sand, rested, and walked back to where the other kids were sitting on the beach.

"What happened to you? We thought that you drowned!"

"I was just having too much fun to come in," I said. "Let's go eat."

I replenished my energy with my standard lunch, a cheeseburger, orangeade and vanilla Mello Roll. The board walk also had shuffle board and paddle tennis courts. Paddle tennis was played on a small tennis court and the players used a wooden racket and a black paddle ball. Eck, who had never been beaten, challenged me to a match. He was definitely better than I was, but I kept hitting the ball to opposite sides of the court, kept running around, and wore him out, even though I was exhausted. I beat him for the first time, and his reaction was, "Up your hole with a Mello Roll!"

"As long as it's vanilla," I replied. I could easily beat Eck in a rank out contest, but I didn't want to provoke him. I knew that he was as volatile as Dad. So I gave a nonthreatening response.

We spent the rest of the afternoon swimming, this time in an area with a lifeguard. Everyone had figured out what had happened to me, and even Eck wanted to play it safe. At the end of the day, we washed the sand off our feet at the water faucets by the boardwalk, took the bus, and walked back to our houses.

I was eating dinner, when another group of kids came to my house and asked me to play football with them at the park. I welcomed any excuse to get out of the house, and went with them. We played for a few hours, and I ran as hard as I could. After all, I had a reputation to live up to. When darkness came, I hurried home.

At home I realized that every time I tried to take a breath, I coughed. I sat down outside my house and felt like I was suffocating. The more I tried to breath, the more I coughed. The only other time I felt this way was when I was in the hospital with pneumonia. Dad heard me, and came out of the house. I was reluctant to tell him what was going on. He usually got angry at me when I was sick. Between coughs, I sheepishly told him everything I had done all day. He said that I probably had too much blood in my lungs, from too much exertion, and that I should relax and go to bed. He put his arm around my shoulders and walked me upstairs. I fell asleep as soon as I got into bed. For the first time in a long time, Dad acted like a father.

Our other big summer activity was following the New York Yankees. Every game was on TV and the radio, and Phil Rizzuto, Mel Allen, and Red Barber were three of the announcers. Each had their own distinctive style. "Holy cow!" was Rizzuto's catchphrase, and Mel Allen would enthusiastically scream, "That ball is going, going, gone!" when a Yankee hit a home run. When a player was doing well, Red Barber, who had been a Brooklyn Dodger announcer, would say, "He is sitting in the catbird seat!" We mostly watched games at Vinny's house, and we listened to them on our transistor radios when we played ball outside.

We all knew who all of the Yankees were, and we knew their starting batting order by heart. Shortstop Tony Kubek, was leadoff, followed by Bobby Richardson, Tom Tresh, Mickey Mantle, Roger Maris, Joe Pepitone, Elston Howard, Clete Boyer, and the pitcher. These were the names of gods. We argued endlessly about who was better, and who was most valuable to the team. We prized their baseball cards.

Every summer we would get especially excited about the Old Timers Day game at Yankee Stadium. Retired players such as Joe Dimaggio and Don Larsen would play former Yankee opponents in an exhibition game. In July, a few days after my birthday, it was time for the 1961 version. I walked over to Vinny's house, and down the side yard past Hunter. Hunter stood up and banged against the wall of his pen, exposing his big genitals and threatening me with his loud bark. I noticed that Hunter was getting grey hairs, and thought that he wasn't as intimidating anymore. The smell of the piles of his dog poop was as rancid as ever, so I ran around to the back door. No one was home. It was Old Timer's Day! Where is Vinny? I tried a few other houses, and had the same bad luck.

I dejectedly went home to watch the game alone in our den. I was immersed in the sounds and sights of the game on TV, when Dad suddenly burst into the room.

"Get outside and play!" he shouted.

I was oblivious to everything but the game, and replied, not even aware of whom I was talking to, "I'm watching the Old Timers game."

"When I tell you to leave, you leave!"

Then, he went into his violent routine. He lifted me up,

threw me against the metal door to the garage, and I collapsed onto the floor. He lifted me up by my neck, held me against the door, and screamed at me with his putrid breath filling my nostrils. He had his hands wrapped around my throat and choked me so hard that I couldn't catch my breath. I thought that he was going to strangle me to death. I became limp. Hopelessly powerless. As soon as he let go, I ran out of the house. I did not want anyone to see the battered, guilty person that I was. I sat in the back yard. My internal agony drowned out my body's aching muscles.

After a while, I wiped off my face and went down the block to the Dorfman's house, where I was always welcome. I got to watch the game, and even was invited for dinner. I watched TV with them after dinner, they seemed to always be watching TV, and was sent home when it turned dark. Afraid to go back into my house, I curled up on the ground in the back yard. I woke up a few hours later, covered with mosquito bites, and thirsty.

"No one even cares that I am not inside," I thought. "Should I just lie out here until I die? Did the wrong child live? Do I have the right to go back into my house?" I curled up on the back lawn and listened to the crickets and a dog barking in the distance. I was a worthless, old piece of newspaper waiting to blow away in the wind.

Twenty-Three

I BEGAN MY LAST YEAR AT Shore Road Elementary in September, 1962. I was a 6th grader in Mr. Tydeman's class. He was my teacher for homeroom and for social studies. Mr. Tydeman was a very friendly, personable man in his 20's, and he let us joke around with him. In social studies class, he assigned us group projects that required us to do a great deal of research and to be creative. He gave long lectures on world history and expected us to keep notebooks. I was fascinated by the Romans and their concept of a sound mind in a sound body, "mens sana in corpora sano." He taught us Latin phrases when we learned about Roman history. The concept of a healthy mind and a healthy body inspired me and I began reading about nutrition and exercise. I made up lists of healthy foods for Mom to buy, started doing calisthenics each morning, and also began reading poetry and nonfiction in addition to novels. There were so many things happening that were out of my control and I felt empowered by living a healthy lifestyle.

Mr. Tydeman paced back and forth in front of the room when he was lecturing. Someone asked him why he did this and he replied that it helped him think. When we got our first report card, his name was listed as A.C. Tydeman. The next day when he was lecturing, I shouted out, "I know what your initials A.C. stand for. They stand for, Alternating Current." Everyone laughed, including Mr. Tydeman. The fact that he laughed instead of getting angry made us like him even more.

Mr. Tydeman also lectured us about how we should help

and support our classmates. He paired the good students up with students who were struggling as part of his peer tutoring project. I was assigned Robert Hall. I had never talked with him before, even though I had known who he was since first grade. Robert had long, greasy blond hair, was tall and very skinny, and was extremely shy. I didn't remember ever seeing him talk to anyone. I helped him with his assignments during homeroom, and felt very nurturing towards him. He seemed so sad and lost.

A few weeks into the year, I agreed to go over to his house to help him with his homework. He lived in an old, run down wooden house that desperately needed to be painted. The house was buried in the tall weeds on the other side of Newbridge Park in an area that I didn't even know had existed. There was a goat, several cats, and some big, dirty, friendly dogs in his yard. His mom was very old and sad looking, and she offered me some milk and homemade cookies. I thought about all the times that I played in the park without ever knowing about the house and family living on the other side of the fence.

I went to Robert's house every other week or so to help him. He had no knowledge of sports, or music or anything that my friends and I talked about. We mostly talked about school work. I had fun making up rhymes to help him remember facts, and felt very proud when he did well on a test. Even though I had endured many painful things in my life, I felt fortunate not to be living in an old run down house that was hidden in the weeds.

Mr. Fitch, a fifth grade teacher, began giving dance lessons to us sixth graders at the end of September. We met in the gym on Fridays after school. He played current rock n roll records, and taught us the dances that teenagers were doing on TV shows like *American Bandstand*. This was the first time that most of us boys had ever had close physical contact with a girl. We were paired off randomly, and as the saying goes, I was "stiff as a pair of new jeans." Learning to do something totally new, and holding hands with a girl at the same time, was about as stressful as a situation could be.

Nancy Duran was the most beautiful girl in the grade. Everybody talked about her, and all the boys wanted to be her partner. But I knew that if she were my partner, I would be unable to move. At the same time, no one wanted to be with Wendy Scarscelli. She had cooties and always smelled like she wet her pants. We called her, "Wendy Scar smelly." If she was your partner, you had to stand as far away as possible. Every few songs we had to change partners. This was a good thing if you were stuck with Wendy and a bad thing if you had to leave someone nice to get stuck with Wendy.

Later in the year, the school had 6th grade dances on weekends every month or so. A big group of us boys met up and walked to the school together. We all bragged about how we were going to make out with a girl, but we secretly knew that none of us would have the courage to do that, or even know how. At these dances you had to ask a girl to dance, so most of the time we just watched the more daring kids dance. I was friends with Debbie Goldblum. She always was in my classes and was very easy to talk to. She knew about baseball. I asked her to dance a few times and glowed with pride when my friends, who were afraid to dance, saw me dancing. I bragged about how I was going to make out with her.

We were very curious about sex and talked about it often. I had shared the knowledge I was given years ago by Willie's brothers, and what I had read in encyclopedias. I was the resident expert on menstruation. I once had even stolen a tampon from a box in Mom's room and shown it to the gang. We were all fascinated by it. Our friend Alan, had stolen a condom from his father's dresser and brought it to our informal show and tell. The most difficult thing to believe was that his parents were apparently having sex.

Many of our conversations took place in Vinny's basement. He had a ping pong table and we could play and talk at the same time. One day, the ball rolled around the basement floor, and someone discovered a small trap door in the far wall. We opened it up, and found a set of 8 millimeter reel to reel movies. We talked Vinny into taking out his family's film projector. We set up a screen and began the movies. It started out as an old black and white movie. The clothes looked like the 1940's, but soon no one was wearing any clothes, except for some of the men who were still wearing socks. It was a stag movie. Naked men and naked women engaged in activities that we had talked about but never seen. Naked men and naked women engaged in activities that we had never talked about. We didn't even have words for many of the things that we witnessed. Sex education was thrust upon us. No one could talk or take his eyes off the screen. We were mesmerized. Dumbstruck. Afraid to look at anyone else. But, I would never look at Mr. Vinny the same way.

"So that's what it looks like," someone finally spoke. I left feeling even more afraid of girls than I was before.

Twenty-Four

IN SCHOOL WE SPENT A great deal of time discussing current events, and we boys were especially worried about our futures. No matter how good our lives were now, the Draft was hanging over our heads, like The Sword of Damocles, ready to impale each of us when we turned 18. Even though that seemed to be very far away, Mr. Deluca reminded us every time we had gym that the Army was waiting. We still were forced to stand at attention, perform left face, right face, and to march in columns. Deluca continued to berate the kids who were out of shape, and warned that the Russians were going to take over unless we were strong enough to stop them. We were scared of the Russians, and we were scared of nuclear war. The level of our fear went off the charts in October of 1962.

No one could escape the news of the Cuban Missile Crisis. US spy planes discovered that the Soviet Union had placed nuclear missiles in Cuba. 90 miles from the US! The news was relentless.

"The Soviet Union has nuclear missiles pointed at us, 90 miles from our border!"

"We are on the verge of Nuclear War!"

"An attack by Cuba will be considered an attack by the Soviet Union."

"The United States is preparing for Nuclear War!"

"President Kennedy's response is to execute a naval blockade of Cuba."

"A naval blockade is considered an act of war."

"The Soviet Union vows to protect Cuba."

President Kennedy was on TV every day and the news was always bleak. At night, I could see his face and hear him talk as I stared at the ceiling and tried to fall asleep.

Adding to our fear was the fact that we stepped up the amount of air raid drills in school. It had reached the point where no one took these drills seriously, but in October, 1962, no one was smiling as we did "duck and cover." We were forced to watch the "Duck and Cover" movie, again.

"There was a turtle by the name of Bert. Bert the turtle was very alert. When danger threatened him, he never got hurt. He knew just what to do. He would Duck! And Cover! He would Duck! And Cover!"

We learned about, "MAD," "Mutual Assured Destruction." If the Soviet Union and the US launched their nuclear missiles, the whole world would be destroyed. We had known about this for years, and now it seemed to be becoming a reality. We read books like, *On the Beach,* and *Fail-Safe,* saw apocalyptic movies and TV shows, and learned facts in school that brought to life the realities of nuclear war.

The crisis finally ended. Our fears didn't.

After the crisis had died down, I went to Robin Hoods and bought a reel to reel tape recorder with money I had saved from my birthday. I wanted one for a while, and the price had finally come down. Bob and I had been listening to music on the radio, and now I had a way to record the songs that I liked. We also purchased 45 rpm records at Robin Hood's for twenty-five cents apiece. Music became a way that I could connect with Mom. She and Grandma always came to my school concerts, they listened to the songs I recorded, and they listened to my explanation of the lyrics. They were both very generous with their money, when they had some, and they helped me pay for new records and blank tapes.

My new tape recorder had a suction cup type microphone that attached to telephone receivers and enabled you to record conversations. We had just started participating in the childhood ritual of making prank phone calls, and now we could record them and enjoy the exchanges over and over again. Both of Vinny's parents worked until about 5pm on weekdays, and that gave us about a two hour window of opportunity to use the Vinny phones. There were two extensions, one in the den, and one in their parent's bedroom, so we could all listen at once. I was usually the person who did the talking.

I started out making the obligatory common ones, such as, "Is your refrigerator running? Then you better go catch it." "Do you have Prince Albert in a can? Then you better let him out." Then I started asking people to please explain to me where babies came from. I would also talk in a deep voice and pretend that I was calling from a radio station. I'd play part of a song and tell the person that they would win a brand new car if they could give the title and artist for the song. The goal was to keep the recipient on the line for as long as you could. I was good at this, and gradually kept getting more creative.

Everyone wanted to prank Paul Baldwin, and I finally came up with a plan. Both of Paul's parents worked, and he had to go straight home after school. We learned that his evil mother called him every day at 3:30, and if he didn't answer, he was in deep trouble. As part of my plan, I sent Vinny and Eck to Paul's house and they stood in the backyard in a spot where they could hear the phone ring. I waited until about 3:25, and called Paul's house. I talked in a deep voice and told Paul, "I am a repairman from the Telephone Company. We are working on your phone lines. If your phone rings during the next 30 minutes, do not answer it. If you do, the repair man will be electrocuted and killed. I repeat, do not answer your telephone or a man will die! No matter how many times it rings, Do Not Answer!"

I hung up and immediately called again. Paul's phone was ringing, and I knew that he could not resist answering. I heard it ring five times, ten times, twenty times, and after about fifty times, Paul picked up and said a meek, "Hello." As soon as Vinny and Eck heard the phone stop ringing, they screamed as loud as they could, and banged on the back wall of the house. They came back to Vinny's house laughing and celebratory and said that I was a genius. I was proud, but felt guilty. What if Paul really thinks that he did kill someone? I wrote an anonymous note saying that the phone call was a joke, stuck it in his front door, rang the bell and ran back to Vinny's.

Besides the prank phone calls, another childhood ritual was to sing the many silly and ridiculous songs that spread through our school. Sometimes we would call random people and sing to them until they hung up. Once in a while, we would get someone who would sing along with us.

Mine eyes have seen the glory of the coming of the Lord, He is driving down the highway in his 1960 Ford, He has one hand on the throttle and another on a bottle, Of Pabst Blue Ribbon Beer, Glory, Glory Hallelujah, The teacher hit me with a ruler, The ruler turned red, and the teacher dropped dead, But her shoes kept marching on.

Because of the threat of nuclear war, there were silly songs about death.

Do you ever see a hearse go by, And think that you will be next to die, They wrap you up in a big white sheet, From your head then all the way down to your feet, They put you in a big black box, And cover you up with dirt and rocks, It all goes well for about a week, Then your coffin it begins to leak, The worms crawl in and the worms crawl out, They eat your guts and they spit them out.

Joy to the world, Khrushchev is dead, We barbequed his head, And what about his body, We flushed it down the potty, And round and round it goes, And round and round it goes, And round and round and round it goes.

We'd change the words and make up songs about teachers or other kids. A popular one was, "Vinny and Sally sitting in a tree, K-I-S-S-I-N-G, First comes love, Then comes marriage, Then comes Vinny with a baby carriage."

I began making attempts to write my own songs, but none of them were good enough to share with others yet.

Bob and I kept taking our violin lessons and practicing at his house. The music that we were assigned became more and more challenging, and very difficult for us to master. We couldn't focus for long periods of time and took breaks from the music by having baseball catches in front of his house. Bob enjoyed baseball, but not as much as I did, and we spent a great deal of time talking while tossing the ball. Bob lived in the much older, blue collar section of Bellmore, and the houses were smaller. There were more trees, and there were bigger trees. The streets were wider, there were dogs and cats roaming the streets instead of being fenced into yards, the cars were older, and there was a weird assortment of kids.

Alan Bell lived around the corner, and he and Bob had an affinity towards each other. Al was a year older, had very thin blonde hair, and was extremely intelligent. Al was totally non athletic and apathetic about sports, but he enjoyed showing us how developed his calf muscles were. He spent almost all his time reading and wanted to be a professional writer. Al sometimes played catch with us, but when he caught the ball, he invariably held it for five minutes and talked before he threw it back. Al was reading and thinking about philosophical concepts that were years ahead of what Bob and I were thinking about. Al was not able to connect to the other kids, and Bob was his closest friend. Al fascinated me, and scared me. I was trying to get away from my thoughts and feelings, and he was trying to get closer to his.

Bob and I were informed later in the year that we were the two violinists from our district who were chosen for the All Nassau County Elementary School Orchestra. There would be two rehearsals with the musicians from the other elementary schools, and then a big concert at Hofstra University. Mrs. Kunicki said that she would help us prepare during our lessons, and then gave us the most ridiculously difficult music to practice that I had ever seen. There were two pieces that I could not relate to, but I wanted to be part of the All County Orchestra and was determined to master them. I never quite did, and I was told that I would be a second violinist. Bob was chosen as a first violinist.

Stanley Applebaum, a famous orchestra leader, composer and arranger, was announced as our conductor. He had written a series of music books that we used for our lessons. The same picture of his face adorned all of the covers. We were all very excited about meeting him at the first county wide rehearsal. Bob's Mom drove the two of us to Hofstra for the first weekend, and we were directed to a big band room containing dozens of kids. We all wore name tags that included the name of the school that we were from. I felt very uncomfortable about the fact that there were very few boys in the room, and that no one looked like a kid that I would want to be friends with. I imagined what Dad would think of these kids. He already had been very critical of Bob, but I still enjoyed making music.

Mr. Stanley Applebaum came out and we all found our seats. He congratulated us for being the best elementary school musicians in our county, and we began our rehearsal. He had a very easy going, positive, but authoritative way of conducting us, and I was amazed at how professional we sounded. The pieces we were playing finally made sense to me. I was also struck by Mr. Applebaum's stature. I had pictured a big man, and he was very short and slight.

After the rehearsal, Bob and I were walking down a hall. We talked about how good the orchestra sounded, what a nice guy Stanley Applebaum was, and I mentioned that I was very surprised at what he looked like.

"I can't believe how short he is," I said. "I think that he's my height and I'm 11 years old."

Bob was putting his finger over his lips and telling me to "shush," but I didn't notice. I finally realized that Stanley Applebaum was right behind us and heard what I said. He smiled as he walked past us.

Twenty-Five

THE SPRING OF 1963 BEGAN the countdown to the end of our final year at Shore Road Elementary School. We were looking forward to moving up to Junior High School. We all received little memory books, filled with different colored blank pages, and asked the other kids to sign them. On the first page of mine I wrote, "Ha, Ha, what a laugh, to sign my own autograph." Then I signed the fancy signature that I had developed. Other kids wrote silly little rhymes like, "God made the bees, the bees make the honey, we do the work, and the teachers make the money," and signed their names. Everyone tried to come up with a different rhyme to write.

Robert Hall, as he normally did, was sitting by himself. I went up to him, and offered to sign his book. I noticed that no one else had written in it, and I wrote my usual, "Roses are red, violets are blue, some poems rhyme, this one doesn't." I also added, "I have enjoyed getting to know you this year." I gave him my book, and expected that he would write something nice, since I had spent so much time with him. He wrote, "I have nothing to say, so I will just sign my name."

This was also my final year of Little League. I was graduating from the Bankers and from Mr. Hill. Mr. Hill had always told us, "Baseball is like life. It is a series of habits. If you develop good habits, you will be successful at baseball, and successful at life." I had learned so much from him in terms of baseball. I learned to run to a fly ball with my glove down and to wait until I got to the ball before I lifted up my glove. I learned to wait for my pitch. I learned to be aware of everything that was happening on the field. I learned to play with determination, a positive attitude, and to never give up. I learned that I was always part of a team.

I also learned about what it was like to be a human being. Mr. Hill was a role model. He was always supportive, and always treated everyone with respect. If you struck out, you got past it, encouraged your team mates, and went up to the plate the next time with confidence. Most of all, you should enjoy playing the game. I realized that Mr. Hill was the kind of person that I wanted to be.

At the end of the season, Mr. Hill came up to me and shook my hand. He kept holding it as he looked me in the eyes and said, "You are going to have a great future. I know that you are going to make a difference!"

With Mr. Hill holding my hand, I knew that he was right.

In June, I graduated from Shore Road, and left with my name, and Sheryl's, in the cornerstone. The summer after 6th grade was when I first started to go to Yankee Stadium. Dad managed to get several sets of tickets, but never went with me. Each time I went with a different friend on the Long Island Railroad. The trip took over an hour, as we had to switch trains once or twice to get to The Bronx. We always went to day games so that we wouldn't be alone on the train at night.

The first time I went, I took Skinny Vinny. I looked at him slumped in his seat, and was amazed at how skinny and small he looked. His front tooth had been knocked out when he was younger, and it was replaced with a false one. He had the habit of moving it up and down with his tongue when he talked. He rarely talked, however, and spent most of the trip staring out the window. He didn't even talk at Yankee Stadium. I decided that I wouldn't ask him to go with me again.

The next time I went, I took Alan Lawson, a friend and fellow violinist from orchestra. He invariably turned any conversation to the topic of sex. At that point, we had become aware of the fact that we were going to be the class of '69 when we graduated from high school. I didn't understand the significance of this fact, so Alan launched into a long explanation as to the sexual meaning of the term, "69." He was fun to be with, and shared my excitement with being at a Yankee game.

The friend that I most wanted to go with was Bob. His overprotective mother wouldn't allow him to take the train. However, she said that he could go if she drove us. We went into the Bronx in her little green Rambler, and she lectured us about what we could do and what we couldn't do at the game. It was more fun sitting next to Vinny. When we got to the stadium, she informed us that she was going to keep driving around, listen to the game on the radio, and meet us outside Gate 4 when the game was over.

Bob was also a Yankee fan, and we knew who every player was. It was an exciting game, and we both got hoarse from cheering so loud. It was a very hot and sunny day, and we were sweating as we sat on the hard wooden seats. We ate hot dogs and cracker jacks and foods that Bob wasn't allowed to eat. We didn't share any of this with Bob's mother after she picked us up.

The next day, Mrs. Petrocelli called my house. She was livid. She said that Bob had developed a boil on his butt from sitting on the dirty wooden seats at Yankee Stadium. She should never have allowed him to go with me. We were too young to go, and I was a bad influence on Bob. He was not allowed to see me anymore.

Bob would just laugh and shrug his shoulders, and wait for the storm to pass. He knew that his parents were messed up and that he was powerless to do anything about it.

"I hate living with them," he said. "Being at home is hell!"

"Do you ever feel that you belong in a different family?" I asked.

"All the time. I can't believe that I'm related to them."

"Me too. Sometimes I feel like an alien from another planet when I'm home."

"Do you ever think about other planets, and the universe, and infinity? How can that make any sense? How is it possible for the universe to go on and on forever without an end?"

"Sometimes I think about that as I'm trying to sleep. The more I think about, the more confused I get. I think about death and I just feel empty."

"At church they teach us about Jesus and heaven and hell. I think that it's all bullshit. They're just trying to scare us so that we follow the rules."

"I think that there has to be some explanation for everything. I guess we won't find out until we die."

Bob was the only person that I discussed these topics with. He helped fill a void in my life that existed since Sheryl died.

Twenty-Six

SOMETHING HAPPENS TO BOYS when they enter 7th grade, and I was no exception. We become silly, annoying, and impulsive, and spend time comparing our penises with the other boy's. A big group of us spent time doing this in Vinny's basement when we otherwise would have been playing outside. We were fascinated, obsessed, curious, and proud of our *schwances*, and they were constantly on our minds. We had no inhibitions about them, and would proudly whip them out and put them on display. If it wasn't against the rules, we probably would have walked around all day with no pants on.

In September, 1963, I entered 7th grade at Grand Avenue Jr. High School. Shore Road and Winthrop Ave. elementary schools were both combined into Grand Avenue, which was about three miles from my house. I rode to school each day on a school bus that stopped at the corner of Navy Place and Legion Street. The boys spent most of the twenty minute trip taunting and mocking each other, an activity that I was good at and enjoyed. I had mentally collected dozens of insults, dating back to summers in the Catskills, and even had some original ones. When someone insulted me, I stood by them and shouted out to the other kids, "Ladies and gentleman, behold! Here is living proof that a person can live without a brain!"

When someone had a long insult, I interrupted and said, "Wow, keep talking. Maybe someday you'll actually say something intelligent."

Other times I talked in a sympathetic and sincere voice and

said, "I really admire your courage. You are brave enough to come to school every day looking like that."

The 9th grade boys rarely interacted with us younger ones, but when they did, we respected them. They gave many of us younger boys nicknames. They stood over us, with their hand on our head, and decreed that from this day forth we would be known as, whatever name they made up. I had a very short brush cut in 7th grade, and one day Neil, a big 9th grader, came to me and rubbed my head. "Your head is like a fucking peach," he said. "From now on, you are to be known as *Fuzzy*." And on that bus, I was.

Grand Ave. was a big two story school building, and there was bedlam in the halls between classes. There was a group of older boys, who had failed so many times that they were now 15 or 16 years old. They were called the "Hoods." They terrorized the younger and smaller boys. Their typical ways of victimization included standing on top of the stairs and spitting down on kids, suddenly pushing someone down the crowded stairs, grabbing loose leaf notebooks and emptying the pages into a crowded hall, randomly punching someone in the stomach, and pulling your shirt open and making the buttons pop off. Their leader was a 16 year old huge bully named Bob Conroy. If you "tattled" on them, they got even. They all lived in my friend Bob's neighborhood, and if you were outside walking at night in their presence, they were likely to grab you, and draw a mustache and sideburns on your face with a magic marker. Bob Conroy actually had a real mustache and sideburns.

Some days, especially when we had homework that we wanted to do together, Bob and I went to his house after school. During the time periods that he was allowed to see me, I was invited to dinner after his mom got home. His mom liked the fact that I wanted to eat all of the vegetables that she would serve with the meal. I also pretended to like the bottled water that she made us drink.

In October, I was walking home from Bob's house after dinner and found myself surrounded by Bob Conroy and his henchmen. They were brandishing magic markers. I had to think fast. I looked around, and noticed that I had nowhere to run. I considered screaming, but that would label me a coward. I suddenly remembered that Bob Conroy was in my Home Economics class, the one we all had to take, with Mrs. Mahoney.

"Hey, aren't you in Mahoney's class, too?" I asked. "I can't believe how fat she is. I heard that she fell in the Grand Canyon and got stuck. She's so fat that the post office is going to give her own zip code."

They all stared, but there was no reaction. I pretended to be banging on an imaginary microphone, like I saw them do in the Catskills, and said, "Is this thing on? What's the matter with you? This is funny stuff."

I continued, "She is so fat, that she leaves footprints in the concrete. Air force planes pick her up on their radar."

Finally, Bob Conroy starts to laugh, and his henchmen join him.

"Say some more," he requests.

"She's so fat, that her thighs applaud when she stands up. Our gym class is going to start running around her for exercise, instead of the track."

Now they are all in hysterics. Conroy hits me on the back and says, "Hey kid, you're alright. You can go, but the next time we see you, have some more jokes."

I thanked him and ran home. I immediately called Bob and told him what had happened.

"Your neighborhood just isn't safe anymore," I said.

The weaker teachers became the unwitting targets of our 12 year old sense of humor. Señor Rodriguez had the unenviable task of teaching a classroom full of 7th graders "Introduction to Spanish." Ramrod, as we called him, was short, fat, had a bald head with curly, unkempt gray hair on the sides, and had thick black glasses balancing on the tip of his ruddy nose. He always wore a tight sports jacket and his stomach hung out over the top of his brown pants. Each day, Ramrod acted out the same ritual. First, he'd stand in the hall outside the door, and glare at us as we walked into class. Then, when we were all seated, he'd burst into the room and throw his overflowing briefcase on the front desk so that it made a loud noise. He'd finish by shouting, "Callate!!!" at us- Spanish for, "Shut up!"

A couple of boys began to make loud farting noises that coincided with the banging from his brief case. Everybody laughed. I thought that we could do better. A few other kids and I arrived early to his class, and we examined the front desk before he came in. We noticed that there were screws attaching the legs to the desk. The next day, Tom brought in a screw driver, and we loosened the screws enough so that the desk was wobbly but still standing. Ramrod stuck to his ritual, threw his briefcase on the desk, and the desk came crashing to the floor. Everyone laughed so uncontrollably that the Principal had to come in.

Doc Steubens was our Math teacher. He always wore a suit jacket, and spent almost the whole period writing on the board with his back towards the class. We found it enjoyable to shoot spit balls through the plastic tube from an old Bic pen, and attempt to get them to stick to the back of his jacket. Doc Steubens was oblivious to what we were doing. I became quite good at this, and one day had a big spit ball loaded and ready to launch. I inhaled, blew as hard as I could into the plastic tube, and watched as Doc Steubens turned around just as the spit ball had begun its flight. I was caught red handed and couldn't talk my way out of the situation. For the first time in my school career, I was sent to the office. I prayed that my other teachers wouldn't see me.

Twenty-Seven

WE WERE TRACKED BY ABILITY in our social studies, English, math and science classes. The three levels were called: Advanced, Intermediate, and Applied. We were all mixed together in either French or Spanish, and in Gym, Home Economics, and Shop, which we had on alternating days. Valerie, the girl who had hit me in the testicles during a fire drill in first grade, sat next to me in Social Studies. I hadn't seen her since Winthrop Ave. She was beautiful looking and very outgoing. She scared me to death. She invited me to make out with her in the back of the library. I blushed and couldn't think of anything to say.

When I wasn't fooling around, I thoroughly enjoyed the academic part of school. Mr. Swanson was our Social Studies teacher, and we learned about American History. He also had us do research projects on controversial current events. I was assigned the topic, "Should the United States be selling its surplus wheat to the Soviet Union?" President Kennedy was in favor of this, but it was causing a great deal of controversy.

I wrote letters to different places asking for information, including the White House. About a month later, I received a big envelope from Washington, D.C. It contained several pamphlets and letters explaining the President's point of view. The letters were signed by President Kennedy. I read and reread all the information. I showed them to Mr. Swanson. I felt chills every time I looked at them. They were addressed to me and came from the White House. When I was done with my project, I hung the letters on my bedroom wall.

Mrs. Ritter was my English teacher and her class was the last period of the day. She was a big, stern, austere woman, and she never smiled. She assigned a great deal of reading, and often gave us surprise quizzes. We also had to complete many writing assignments, and one of her favorites was the five paragraph persuasive essay. She gave us a topic, and we had to develop three facts to support our opinion. I loved arguing a point of view, and felt more comfortable stating my opinions in writing.

Mrs. Ritter had given us the topic, "Describe the world's greatest problem," and our job was to write a well developed five paragraph persuasive essay for homework. I always tried to be unique, and my essay opined that the world's greatest problem was that it was controlled by human beings. Human beings had polluted the earth, we had created nuclear weapons that could destroy every living creature in the world, we had a history of waging violent wars against each other, and we had upset the balance of nature. I developed these ideas and said that any other problem was a problem created by human beings. Sometimes Mrs. Ritter liked my ideas, and sometimes she didn't. I eagerly awaited her reaction.

The next day Mrs. Ritter announced that she wanted to share one of our essays with the whole class. She then began to read mine, with no commentary. Everyone laughed at the thesis statement, "The world's greatest problem is that it is controlled by human beings." The class became more serious when she proceeded to read the rest. I still didn't know what she thought until after she was done reading and praised me for my creativity. It was like receiving manna from heaven.

In November, we had been assigned a particularly long and difficult story to read for homework. When we got to class the next day, Mrs. Ritter announced that she was about to give us a quiz on the reading. Everyone groaned. Just as she was about to distribute the paper for the quiz, her intercom phone rang. We watched her listen, and saw her burst into tears. We had never seen Mrs. Ritter show any emotion before. She walked up to her desk, sat down, and we stared at her as she tried to compose herself. Finally, she announced, "President Kennedy has been shot."

No one knew how to react. We all sat in stunned silence. A little while later, the principal announced over the loud speaker, "President Kennedy is dead." If he said anything else, I didn't hear it. I was overwhelmed with the same dread and emptiness that I felt when Sheryl died.

On the way out of school, some kids were laughing, others were crying, and others were saying unbelievably stupid things.

"Oh my God. Who is going to be president now?"

"LBJ, you moron," I thought. "How could you not know that he is the vice-president?"

"Maybe you could be president," someone said to me. "You're smart."

"Do you think that school will be closed on Monday?"

"Does this mean that we're going to have a nuclear war?"

"Do you think that the Russians did it?"

I sat by myself on the bus.

"It's okay, Fuzzy," someone said. "My dad said that he was a terrible president, anyway."

It felt like the world was about to end. If a great president could be murdered so easily, then what was going to happen next? I had memorized lines from his inauguration address and that night they echoed in my head.

"The torch has been passed to a new generation of Americans." I was part of that new generation.

"Let every nation know, whether it wishes us well or ill, that we shall pay any price, bear any burden, meet any hardship, support any friend, oppose any foe, to assure the survival and the success of liberty."

"Let us bring the absolute power to destroy other nations under the absolute control of all nations."

"Let both sides seek to invoke the wonders of science instead of its terrors. Together let us explore the stars, conquer the deserts, eradicate disease, tap the ocean depth, and encourage the arts and commerce."

"If a free society cannot help the many who are poor, it cannot save the few who are rich."

"The energy, the faith, the devotion which we bring to this endeavor will light our country and all who serve it, and the glow from that fire can truly light the world."

I pictured the enthusiasm and intensity with which he said these lines. I had been filled with hope and optimism every time I heard him speak.

Two days later we watched Jack Ruby shoot Lee Harvey Oswald on TV. The world was becoming darker.

Twenty-Eight

THE TV SCREEN TURNED ALL black, and eerie music flowed out of the speaker. An ominous voice declared, "There is nothing wrong with your television set. Do not attempt to adjust your picture. We are controlling the transmission...For the next hour sit quietly and we will control all you see and hear. You are about to experience the awe and mystery that reaches from the inner mind to -the Outer Limits!"

This was the introduction to the TV show, "The Outer Limits." It aired Monday nights at 7:30, and on Tuesdays, Bob and I could not wait to see each other and to have the opportunity to discuss and debate what we had watched. The science fiction plots explored ethical, philosophical, "what if" situations and tapped into the fears of thoughtful teenagers. Issues of the 1960's, such as racism, nuclear holocaust, and biological engineering, were explored and portrayed in futuristic formats. Each week there was a different episode with a different story and cast.

One episode told the story of a time traveler who went back in time to stop the birth of an inventor whose bacterium turned humans into mutants. Another dramatized a professor who discovered a way to speed up evolution. He applies his discovery to an angry coal miner. The miner grows a sixth finger and oversized brain, and intends to use his newly developed power of telekinesis to seek revenge on his tormenters. Instead, he evolves to a level of consciousness that doesn't include the concepts of love and hate. We also began reading authors such as Ray Bradbury who wrote about similar topics. Bob was the only person that I discussed books with, but everyone seemed to want to talk about television and music.

In December, before Christmas vacation, the conversations on the bus seemed even livelier. Debbie excitedly asked me, "Have you heard them yet? Have you heard them?"

"No," I replied.

"I can't believe you haven't heard them yet. You know so much about music," she said.

Everyone was talking about them, but I hadn't listened to the radio for a few days. I did when I got home that afternoon. The opening chords were like a rush of adrenaline. The energy, the exuberance, the joy with which they sang. My jaw dropped. If there was anything else like this, I had never heard it before. It was unique and familiar at the same time. After hearing all the superlatives, I expected to feel disappointed. Instead, I felt elated. The music was a wave of uninhibited, raw sensuality designed to pull us all out of our malaise.

I called Bob. "Have you heard, *I Want to Hold Your Hand* yet?"

"Yeah, and you should hear, *She Loves You!*"

Our love affair with The Beatles had begun. They became the main topic of conversation at school. We all collected their records, magazines, and posters, like we boys had collected baseball cards. The girls argued about which Beatle was better looking. Boys argued over who was more talented. We all added words like, "gear, boss, and fab," to our vocabularies. We awaited the release of their new records, and excitedly watched them on the Ed Sullivan Show. We discussed the meaning of their lyrics. Except for a few nonconformists, we were all connected by our infatuation with all things Beatle.

Twenty-Nine

DAD WAS NOT AROUND MOST of the time during my 7th grade year. There were even some nights that he didn't come home. Mom now had a full time teaching job at Shore Road, and tutored after school to earn extra money. There were still bill collectors who came to our door. Grandma still contributed her social security check to our household budget. I knew that we didn't have much money, and didn't ask for much. However, when I needed clothes, or money for a new Beatles record, Mom and Grandma gave me what I needed.

A few days a week after school, we had the opportunity to participate in intramural sports. I chose flag football, basketball, and baseball. I stayed with the violin, took lessons and played in the Junior High orchestra. Our music teacher, Mr. Vinson, was very discouraging. He told me that I was talented, but that I had to make a choice between sports and music. He frequently urged me to quit the orchestra. Bob was in the orchestra, and I loved playing the violin, so I ignored Vinson's requests. I even learned to play several Beatles songs on my violin. In April, we had a spring concert, and played excerpts from *The Sound of Music*, one of my favorite musicals. I was amazed at how incredible we sounded. Mom and Grandma both cried and told me how *farklempt* they felt from the music. Dad was home and came too. He told me that I sounded out of tune.

After the concert, we attended the 7th grade academic awards assembly. I had worked very diligently in my classes, and had a 97 average. I had earned grades in the high 90's in all of my classes except for Spanish, which was still in the 90's. I was the recipient of several academic awards, and felt very proud. But, on the way home, I was angrily attacked by Dad.

"Why did Albert Frankenstein and Bobbie Blake win more awards than you did?"

"You could do better if you applied yourself more."

"Why did you do so poorly in Spanish?"

"How could you go out in public wearing that tie with that shirt?"

He always found a reason to be angry at me. I was feeling so satisfied and important, having earned coveted academic awards, and he found a way to disparage me. I finally realized that there was nothing I could do that would ever please him. I remembered what it was like when I was little, and Dad would be bursting with pride as he walked with Sheryl and me around Brooklyn. He showed me his love then, but it seemed that I had no hopes of seeing it again. I felt empty and dejected. I also realized that no one was going to protect me from him. Mom and Grandma were as helpless as I was. I was scared. Sometimes, I thought about killing myself.

I understood that I needed to find my happiness somewhere other than in my family. And I was. I was involved with preparing for my Bar Mitzvah, which would be in July, and went two nights a week to the Temple for lessons. I particularly enjoyed my classes at school, all the activities that I was involved in, and the time I was spending with my friends. When I forced myself, I could feel important, capable, and accepted.

Then, suddenly, as it had happened several times before, I was unexpectedly told some devastating news. I did not see it coming.

"Your father has been spending time in Houston, Texas. The Weiner department stores have offered him a high paying, secure job there as a buyer of children's clothes. They are one of the best chains in Texas. He'll be making a lot of money. We'll all be moving to Texas in July right after your Bar Mitzvah."

I felt like I had been shot through my heart.

"What about all my friends?"

"You'll make new ones."

"I don't know anyone there!"

"We need to stick together as a family."

Now I knew why I had heard Mom and Grandma arguing at night. I looked to Grandma for support. "This is what your Mom wants to do," she said. "She's trying to save her marriage." Grandma loyally stood by any decision that Mom made.

I begged Bob, Vinny, and any friend that I could think of. "Please talk your parents into letting me live with you!" No one would take me in.

During April break, we all flew to Houston for a week long "vacation." It was my first time on a plane, and I was livid. I felt like I was caught in an undertow and being pulled in a direction that I didn't want to go. My life was out of my control. Everything was being disrupted because Dad couldn't keep a job in New York. I knew that he had bill collectors and detectives after him. From that point on, I called him Eli. I did not want to think of him as my Dad. On the plane I recalled all the times that he had hit me and verbally abused me, and now he was forcing me to move to Texas. This was the place where JFK was killed. I knew that nothing good would come of this.

A group of well dressed people representing Weiner's met us at the airport. We were taken to a fancy hotel. It was 100 degrees and humid outside. Eli gave me some stiff, scratchy, expensive new clothes to wear for our meeting with his new bosses. They talked with thick Texas drawls, and, in my mind, emanated phoniness. I could see past their fake smiles and feigned over the top hospitality. They acted the way Eli did around other people, but I knew what was lurking inside of them. I could not be any angrier, and glared at anyone who tried to talk to me. Back at the hotel, Eli grabbed me and told me that I was embarrassing him. That was his favorite thing to say to me. I looked in his eyes with such a feeling of hatred that he backed down. I wished that I was powerful enough to strangle him the way he choked me.

The Weiner's people tried to show us a good time. We went to the Six Flags over Texas theme park one day, and to a beach resort in Galveston. We ate at fancy restaurants, and were served grits with every meal. They showed us the sights of the city, including the Houston Astrodome, scheduled to open the next spring and already being called, "The eighth wonder of the world." Knowing that I was a Yankee fan, they informed me that the Yankees would be playing an exhibition game there when it opened.

I was introduced to Wayne, the son of one of Eli's coworkers. Wayne was a year older than I was, and he was big, tall and blonde. He spoke with an accent and in an unctuously charming manner to the adults.

"Yes sir. Pleased to meet you, ma'am. I trust that y'all will enjoy your stay in our great state of Texas. I will watch after Jeffrey and ensure that he has a good time. I will introduce him to my friends. I am certain that they will love him."

"What a nice young man," Mom observed.

Wayne took me to the pool behind his big house. He looked at me and said, "You little Yankee faggot. You are one ugly bitch, and we will eat you alive here. Why don't you go back to the other faggots in Jew York."

He tried to push me into the pool, but I managed to resist. He tried to push me again, and I thought, "Oh my God. He's another Eli."

I felt my body filling up with rage and hatred. I was not going to be bullied. I reached up, grabbed him by the throat, and spoke as intensely and menacingly as I could.

"I am from New York, and I know how to fight. If you try to mess with me again, I will fucking kill you. I am not going to take your shit." I squeezed his neck even harder and whispered maniacally, "Do you understand? Do you fucking understand!?"

He looked scared, so I let go.

"Calm down, little guy. I was just messing around. No offense."

We spent to rest of the afternoon together. I knew that this wasn't going to be the last time that I had to protect myself.

I was taken to Wayne's house the next day, and we were

driven to a pool at a fancy country club that his family belonged to. There were dozens of young, beautiful girls lounging around. I marveled at how smooth and confident Wayne acted around the girls, whereas I felt awkward and shy. Being from New York, I was a curiosity to them. They were fascinated with my accent, and asked all types of questions.

"How can y'all stand living in New York? Aren't all of the kids brats?"

"Isn't it really cold?"

"What's it like shopping at Macy's?"

"Aren't y'all afraid to walk on the streets at night?"

Wayne whispered to me, "Watch this." We all went into the pool, and he cornered a girl against the side. He talked to her for a few minutes, then pinned her with his body, put his hands against the wall on each side of her shoulders, and kissed her. She resisted at first, and then they kissed for a few minutes. He then swam away towards me.

"That's how y'all kiss a girl. Why don't you try it," he said.

I was sweating profusely just thinking about it.

After we flew back home, all the kids were noticing how tan I was.

"Where were you?"

"We went south for the vacation," I said. I felt embarrassed to admit that we were in Texas.

Thirty

WHEN WE GOT BACK HOME to Bellmore, the big event was The 1964 New York World's Fair. It opened in April in Flushing Meadows, Queens. For us, it was just a short train ride away. The admission was only $1.00 for kids, and I went several times with different groups of friends.

In the center of the fair stood a twelve story stainless steel globe called the "Unisphere." We witnessed the many optimistic predictions for the future, including computer terminals and keyboards, and video telephones. Several of the exhibits included moving seats that transported you into different worlds. The GM Futurama took you past demonstrations that depicted life in the future. The Space Park included full scale models of spacecraft, while Dinoland surrounded you with life size replicas of dinosaurs. The Ford Motor Company introduced several models of its new sports car, the Ford Mustang. A section of the Fair offered different sandwiches from around the world.

Next door to The World's Fair sat the newly opened Shea Stadium. The Mets played baseball there, and it was also the home of the NY Jets football team. It was easier and quicker to get there than Yankee Stadium, and we attended several Met games that spring. In May, we had spent the day at the Fair, and had good seats for a Mets game against the Cubs that night. During the 7th inning stretch I stood up and looked at the various people who were sitting in the surrounding seats. I saw a familiar looking man wearing a Mets baseball cap and a Mets sweatshirt. He had two tremendous men sitting on either side of him and I was glad that I wasn't sitting behind them.

"Isn't that Tony Bennett sitting in the row behind us?" I asked my friend Stan.

"Nah, he wouldn't be sitting with the regular people," he said.

"I am sure it's him. Do you think that he'll give me his autograph?"

Before he could answer, I walked up and said, "Mr. Bennett, I love your music. Would you please sign my scorecard?"

"Sure, kid. What's your name?"

"Jeffrey."

"To Jeffrey, Best Wishes, Tony Bennett." It was the first autograph I ever received.

The other big event was my upcoming Bar Mitzvah. A Jewish boy has several responsibilities at his Bar Mitzvah, which takes place on a Saturday, the Sabbath, near his 13th birthday. He is required to read that week's section of the Torah. The Torah is the five books of the Jewish Bible, and is written in Hebrew on parchment scroll. It is read in the original Hebrew language. The Bar Mitzvah boy's reading is preceded and followed by the chanting of an Aliyah, a Torah blessing, by a family member. Another responsibility is to chant a section from the Haftorah, readings from the Prophets. Other tasks include leading the congregation in responsive readings, and making a speech about what it means to be Jewish and a Bar Mitzvah boy.

Preparation includes learning all of the Hebrew, and learning the melody for the prayers and the chants. I had lessons with the Temple's cantor. The cantor, or *Chazzan*, leads the congregation along with the Rabbi and concentrates on the musical and singing aspects. Our cantor had a beautiful, operatic voice. It was intimidating working with him because I had a very limited singing voice. He found a way to cut down on the range of the notes that I would have to sing, and came up with music that I could handle. This was a tremendous relief for me, and I found it to be very mystical and fulfilling to sing.

In the spring, we all continued to listen to and talk about The Beatles. A so-called "British Invasion" was happening, and other groups from England also dominated the airways. We "grooved" to The Rolling Stones, The Animals, Gerry and the Pacemakers, Peter and Gordon, The Searchers, and The Dave Clark 5. We all knew more information about these groups than we did about the subjects we were studying in school. We bounced up and down to the beat, and sang along with the melodies from our 45 RPM records. We clapped our hands to the rhythms, smiled, and overflowed with warm feelings towards each other. Bob and I were successful in terms of figuring out how to play many songs on our violins and rejoiced triumphantly after performing a melody. When the music was there, a primal, jubilant rejoicing occurred, and any negative emotions were squashed.

The baseball intramural season had just come to an end, and our PE teacher Coach Millhouse had called me into his office. Coach Millhouse was a huge muscular man with a big square jaw and a face that resembled Dick Tracy. The story was that he had played college football in Denver, and was drafted by the Denver Broncos. He blew out his knee the first summer while practicing for the Broncos, and never had the opportunity to play professionally. He was very tough, but had a sense of humor. He pushed us, but didn't berate kids the way that Mr. Deluca did at Shore Road. Most of us liked him, and when he called you into his office it usually was a good thing.

"Goldstein," he said, "I notice that you have a great deal of speed and a great attitude. I am starting a football team for 8th and 9th graders next year, and I am picking the kids that I want to try out. You have a great shot at it, but you're small. I'd like you to start lifting weights, drinking protein shakes, and come back to school in September with more muscle. With your speed, and some bulk, you'd be a great running back. What do you say?"

You didn't say no to Coach Millhouse. I would be ecstatic to play football. "But no," I thought. "I am being dragged to Texas and won't be here next year."

I couldn't bring myself to tell him this. I was still secretly hoping that something would happen and I wouldn't have to go. I just said, "Thank you for picking me. I would love to play football."

Nothing I said was a lie. I walked out of his office with tears in my eyes.

Thirty-One

MY PARENTS WERE DETERMINED to throw an extravagant Bar Mitzvah reception. They booked the Huntington Townhouse, the Mecca for gaudy and garish events. I was able to decide which friends would be invited, but little else. I was fitted for a tuxedo, and had to spend time posing for pictures. An artist was commissioned to paint a big portrait of me in my tuxedo. Eli posed with us for all the family pictures, as if he were a loving father.

I was hoping that Milton and Shirley and my cousin Jackie would be invited, but there were always feuds going on, and this one coincided with my Bar Mitzvah. Milton's younger brother Richard got married six months earlier, and Jackie was invited to the wedding, but I wasn't. They explained that they didn't want any kids there. Jackie was 6 months older than I was, and in their minds, not a kid anymore. Jackie's two younger sisters weren't invited either. My family was livid, and refused to attend the wedding. They, in turn, refused to attend my Bar Mitzvah.

I had very few relatives attend. Eli's parents, the "other grandparents," did not attend, nor did any of Eli's three sisters or their families. None of Grandma's siblings attended. I especially liked her older brother Sigmund. He is the one who came to America first from Poland, and sent back money for the rest of the family to come. He had become very wealthy in the world of finance, and had been all over the world. His arms were full of marks from all the vaccinations he had to receive to travel to faraway places. He had visited us several times when

I was growing up, usually when we were together with Milton and Shirley. He told fascinating stories. He always gave me a fifty cent piece, and gave Jackie a silver dollar. "That's because she is older," he said. This also angered my family.

Phil and Barbara Nelick, relatives that I had never met, did attend. Phil's mother was my Grandpa's sister and she died during his birth. His father immediately remarried and did not want Phil to know that his wife was not Phil's biological mother. Phil's father never told him about his birth mother. Phil, years later, noticed that his mother's last name on his birth certificate was, "Wegbreit." He asked his father about this, and found out that he had relatives that he was unaware of. Phil managed to contact Grandma, and to meet his long lost relatives. I met him for the first time at my Bar Mitzvah. He gave me my favorite present, a Polaroid camera.

My Bar Mitzvah service was held at the Merrick Jewish Center. I hit all of the right notes, correctly pronounced all of the Hebrew, led the responsive readings with confidence, and delivered a successful speech. I felt like I was in a trance and that everything was flowing in a positive direction. I performed even better than I thought I could, and actually enjoyed being the center of attention. I happily soaked in all of the praise after the ceremony.

Eli had to do an *aliyah* during the service. He always seemed so poised, but was visibly nervous with a shaky, almost inaudible voice during his prayer. I was surprised, but thought that he probably felt uncomfortable in the House of God.

After we left the Temple, we all drove to the Huntington Townhouse, which was about twenty minutes away. There was a band at the reception playing music that none of us liked. The adults were drinking and dancing, and a group of us kids played a ball game outside with a plastic ornament from one of the tables. My friend Louis managed to steal a drink, and I had my first taste of alcohol.

A local tradition was for the Bar Mitzvah boy to kiss a girl and to smoke a cigarette. Someone smuggled a cigarette outside, and we took turns taking puffs, laughing and coughing. When we were done with the smoke, I was instructed to find a girl and to kiss her. Fortunately, before this could happen, we were all called inside so that the band could force us to participate in stupid dances.

At the end of the evening, I was given envelopes with savings bonds in them as gifts from Eli's business friends. My festive mood then turned to despair as I realized that we soon would be boarding a plane bound for Houston, Texas. I felt the undertow, and I couldn't escape.

Grandma and Family at Bar Mitzvah

Jeff, Keith and Michele at Bar Mitzvah

Part Three
TEXAS

Sometimes
I am drowning
Squirming
Treading, Treading, Treading
To catch a breath

Sometimes
I am aching
Sweating
Restless as an evil empire
Twitching, Twitching, Twitching
To dissolve

Sometimes
Voices
Echoing in my skull
Shoot daggers through my heart
Bleeding, Bleeding, Bleeding
On my soul

And sometimes
I am enveloped by a vision
Gleaming, Glowing, Purging
And I am home

Jeffrey Goldstein

Thirty-Two

OUR HOUSE ON NAVY PLACE was all packed. I had wrapped small towels around my precious record collection to make sure that it survived the trip. I stared at our house for the last time and felt as if we were leaving Sheryl behind. It was now going to be inhabited by a young doctor and his family. Someone else was going to be sleeping in my room on my bed. We weren't taking our furniture. What if Sheryl banged on the wall at night? I wouldn't be there. I wouldn't be able to walk down the block to Vinny's house anymore. I wouldn't be able to call Bob whenever I felt like it. I couldn't go to Newbridge Park to play ball. I wouldn't be able to take the train to Yankee Stadium or Shea Stadium. I wouldn't be playing football at Grand Avenue. I felt like I was dying.

The Weiners paid for our moving van and plane tickets, and we were on our way to Houston. I took my baseball glove with me on the flight. It comforted me to wear it and to intermittently bang it with my fist, like I was about to catch a fly ball. I was determined not to cry. I listened to Beatles songs in my head. I hummed my Bar Mitzvah prayers to myself. I missed my friends already.

It was unbearably hot and humid when we arrived at the airport. We were driven to the Jamestown Apartments on Stella Link Drive. Our street was made up of eight groups of different apartment complexes, all with different names. Our complex was only a few years old, and we had a three bedroom apartment on the second floor. We had air conditioning, a dish washer, and a garbage disposal, amenities that we didn't have in Bellmore. The living room had sliding doors that opened to a balcony. Keith and I would share a big bedroom, Grandma and Michele shared another one, and Mom and Eli had the master bedroom. They had a separate bathroom. There was a room with washing machines and dryers on the first level. The middle of the complex had a big swimming pool.

Our apartment was filled with big boxes that needed to be unpacked. The first week or so, while Eli was at work, I babysat for Keith and Michele. Mom and Grandma were out shopping or running errands. We now had a 1961 white four door Chevy Impala. It was the first car that I had ever seen with air conditioning. It was usually too hot to be outside, and Mom didn't want me to take Keith and Michele to the pool which didn't have a life guard, so we were stuck in the apartment. I was concerned that we weren't getting enough exercise, so I made up a game which consisted of me chasing Keith and Michele around the living room. I also read books to them. A sound mind in a sound body. I asked Mom to buy me a pull up bar, and spent time doing pull ups, pushups and sit ups. I felt like I was in prison.

When Mom was home, I went outside to the swimming pool in hope of meeting someone. I discovered that all eight apartment complexes had their own pools. One day I spent time at each one in an attempt to meet other kids. The only people who seemed to use them were old men or women. I *did* end up with a super tan.

After a few weeks, we found out that there was an encephalitis epidemic in the area. A thirteen year old girl who lived in our apartment complex was gravely ill and in the hospital with encephalitis. It was spread by mosquito bites. Mosquitoes were very attracted to me, so I asked Mom to buy some bug spray. After she came home, we saw a mosquito flying around the kitchen, and I sprayed it. I also sprayed the rest of the apartment to be safe.

When Eli came home, he smelled the apartment and was enraged. "We have air conditioning. We don't need to be filling the air with bug spray," he shouted.

I told him that I did it to kill a mosquito. He grabbed me, and I wrestled myself free. He came after me, and I faked one way and broke the other way, as I did so many times playing football. I used my speed and agility to run past him and out the door. I had no shoes or socks on, and was hot and thirsty. I walked around for a few hours not knowing where to go. I didn't have the Dorfman's house to go to. A few more hours went by, and I heard a police siren. I jumped into a garbage bin and pulled down the lid. A few rats scurried away. I was feeling sick from the heat and the smell, and was dying of thirst. After about an hour, I climbed out.

"Come here boy," a cop shouted and he grabbed me. "What are y'all doing worrying your parents like that?"

"He will kill me. My father is crazy and if you bring me home he will kill me."

"Y'all mind your father, boy. Y'all scared him to death."

"Please don't take me home. He will kill me!"

"Y'all belong with your parents, boy."

I was taken home, and Eli charmingly thanked the police, hugged me, and said how happy he was that I was home safe and sound.

"Y'all mind your father now," they said and left. I took a deep breath.

Eli lifted me up. He always seemed one level of anger away from killing me, and this time it looked like he may have reached that level. Except this time, I hit his arms away from me, looked him in the eyes, and proclaimed, "Don't you ever, ever, ever lay a hand on me again, or I will kill you! And you leave Keith and Michele alone also!"

That's what I wanted to do. That's what I wished I could do. But when he grabbed me, he was too strong and I froze. I got slapped around, choked, punched in the stomach, and verbally berated, but I didn't cry. He ended up again with his hands around my throat and I feared for my life. I promised myself that I would get strong enough to fight back. He pummeled me for what seemed like an eternity, and eventually grew tired, and stopped.

The next morning, I was all itchy and realized that I had several mosquito bites. I showed Mom and she went crazy. She immediately drove me to the doctor.

"We have to wait to see what happens. There is nothing we can do," he said.

"What do you mean we just have to wait!?" Mom screamed. "There must be something you can do."

He said that my appointment was over, and left the room. The nurse told us that if I started to develop a fever, we should call.

I just hoped that whatever happened wouldn't be too painful.

Family in Texas

Thirty-Three

ONE WEEK WENT BY, then two weeks, and luckily I was still healthy. I was exercising with my pull up bar, and getting stronger so that one day I could defend myself from Eli. I still hadn't made any friends. I spent time walking around the apartment complexes, sitting and reading by the pools, and hoping to meet anyone my age.

At the end of July I was swimming in our pool and was surprised by two boys who walked up to me and asked, "Are you that kid from New York?"

Doo wah, doo wah, doo wah ditty, yes I am the boy from New York City, I sang, paraphrasing and combining several songs from the radio.

They both laughed and introduced themselves. The tall boy, who looked like a bear was Bruce Rabin, and the short tan boy with the jet black wavy hair was Barry Holstein. We talked for a while, and I learned that Barry's father owned the Jamestown Apartments where I lived, and Bruce's father owned several of the other complexes on the block. They had heard that a family from New York had moved in, and being big Yankee fans, they wanted to meet me. I told them that I had been to Yankee Stadium many times, and they asked me questions about New York.

We all seemed to connect and to feel comfortable with each other very quickly. I asked them if they played baseball, and they said that they did, but that football was the big sport in Texas. They had a football with them and I explained how you could play with three people, like we used to in Bellmore. I got my sneakers, and we played in the big field outside the apartment complex. They were both good athletes, and even though it was oppressively hot, I felt as if I had just been released from prison as I ran around during the game. I was sweating and breathing hard, but glowing and alive. They seemed to want to play as much as I did, and I laughed for the first time ever as a resident of the state of Texas.

We were all thirsty and bought drinks from the vending machine in the apartment lobby.

"Drink up," I said. "The money is probably going to your families."

They asked me if I wanted to see where they lived. They pointed across the big field that we were playing on to a hill with huge houses about a mile away. They invited me to walk there with them. It was extremely windy and the air was full of dust. A few hundred yards away, a middle aged man in a business suit was walking in the opposite direction towards the apartments. I said, "This is how we greet people in New York," and I looked at him and gave him the finger. To our surprise, he began shouting and chasing us. We ran as fast as we could, laughing all the way to Barry's house.

Barry's house was a huge three story mansion. His family had a live in house keeper, a gardener, and a cook. There were tennis courts in his yard, a basketball court, beautiful landscaping, and a big swimming pool. I found out that Barry and Bruce were also Jewish, and had both had their Bar Mitzvahs earlier in the year. They both had baseball card collections, and record collections, but Barry had a big expensive stereo system, as opposed to my cheap little record player. They also read books and seemed to be intelligent. Bruce had to go home for dinner, and they said that they would come by to meet me at the pool in the morning. I ran home singing and smiling.

We spent the next few weeks playing football, listening to records, talking about girls, and just walking around. I had slowly become comfortable with the heat and humidity. Stella Link Drive, the road that contained all the apartments, was a dead end street. At my end were the big fields where we played and walked to Bruce's and Barry's houses. About two miles away across the fields in the opposite direction you could see the Astrodome being constructed. The other end of Stella Link Drive crossed a big avenue with stores and strip malls. Everyone called it "The Avenue." It didn't have a name as far as we all knew.

Around the corner on the Avenue was a big drug store with a counter and soda fountains named "Sam Houston's." Everyone called it "Sammy's." "Sammy's" was very kid friendly and we spent time sitting at the "pop" fountains talking and browsing through the paperback books. Bruce showed us a book called *Candy*, about a young naïve voluptuous girl who finds herself in all kinds of sexual situations that are described in graphic detail. We read the good parts together, giggled, and blushed if anyone looked at us. There was a juke box, and we played our favorite Beatles songs, drank milk shakes, and whispered about the girls who came in.

I asked my new friends several times if we could set up a big baseball game or football game. I told them about Newbridge Park and the big games that we played there. It occurred to me that I never saw Bruce and Barry with any other kids. Eventually, Bruce looked at me and said, "They don't like Jews in Texas. Sometimes they treat us like Niggers."

I was shocked. "Is everybody like that?" I asked.

"No, but you have to be careful." I was stunned by his use of the word "nigger." They were not comfortable with the topic, so I changed it.

Thirty-Four

IN JULY, THE BEATLES NEW album called *A Hard Day's Night* was released, with a movie scheduled to come to the theaters in August. Bruce, Barry and I each bought copies and listened to it until we knew each word of every song. We sang at the top of our lungs and frenetically danced around to the music. We listened to the new records on radio station KILT. I found out that west of the Mississippi the radio station call letters began with a "K," instead of a "W". Even though KILT was a rock and roll station, they sprinkled in local Texas songs. *In Fort Worth, Dallas, or Houston, Or in San Antone, There's a little girl a waiting, And she's all alone, In Beaumont, Lubbock, or Austin, Or in El Paso, She waits for me I know.* Everything had to be about Texas.

I wrote long letters to Bob regularly. Among other topics, I wrote about which songs were popular in Texas, and what the Billboard rankings were. We compared how the Beatle's records were doing in Texas versus New York. Bob and I were both very excited if a Beatle's song hit number one in either place, as if we had something to do with it. We all were eagerly anticipating their first movie.

Finally, in August, Bruce's house keeper drove us to downtown Houston to see *A Hard Day's Night*. It felt like we were going to see them in person. We waited in line, and found good seats. Eventually every seat was taken. The theater manager came out and told the girls not to scream during the movie. He said that we all paid to get in and deserved to hear the music. As the movie began, the excitement among the kids was palpable. The girls all squirmed and giggled, and if they made too much noise, an usher came over and threatened to remove them from the theater. My buddies and I tapped our feet, bobbed our heads up and down, and softly sang the words. We occasionally looked at each other and smiled. It was a religious experience.

Suddenly, the Beatles started singing *Can't Buy Me Love*! It was our absolute favorite song from the album. We even sang it when we played football. I secretly played it on my violin in my apartment. We couldn't help ourselves. We stood up and sang along as loudly as we could. Three ushers came running over and made us sit down. We continued to sing softly, and slapped each other's hands at the end of the song. Bruce's house keeper had to listen to us enthusiastically singing out of tune all the way back home. We were radiating the glow felt by people who had just experienced a rapturous occurrence together.

The next day, the three of us were playing football, and Barry remarked that I was really good. He told me that there was a combined eighth and ninth grade team that played tackle football and that you got to wear helmets and pads and play other schools. He and Bruce were going to play, and said that I should play, too. He asked me which school I was going to. I didn't know. They then explained how it worked.

"The schools in Houston were all tracked," he said. "You get assigned to a school based on your test scores. We go to John J. Pershing Junior High School because we have the highest grades. There are four junior high schools, and Pershing has no niggers or spicks."

I told them that I didn't like the terms niggers or spicks, and they just shrugged their shoulders. That was what they were called in Texas. I should get used to it.

"Well, in Texas, we're kikes, they said."

I repeated that I thought it was wrong and would never use those words no matter where I was.

Thirty-Five

A FEW DAYS LATER I FOUND OUT that I was going to go to John J. Pershing Junior High School. They accepted me based on my grades and test scores in New York, and probably because I was white. It was a ten minute drive away and I could take a public bus down the Avenue to get there. Mom drove me there to fill out papers and to register. I signed up to be in the orchestra, and was given a tour of the school. I received my schedule, which was very different from my old school. On Monday through Thursday everyone had ninety minute blocks with the core academic courses, English, social studies, science and math. In the middle of the day we were assigned a ninety minute block that contained different lunch periods, and gym classes. On Fridays we had science labs and all of our electives, including shop, home economics, a language, and music. Orchestra would be part of my day on Fridays.

I called Bruce and Barry, and found out that we had no classes in common, not even gym or lunch. They told me that football practice was about to start and they invited me to come along. I went with them on a Monday morning and met the coach. No one could tell me his name. He was just called "Coach." He had a crew cut, was tall and muscular, wore a baseball cap that said, "Houston Oilers'" and had sunglasses that hung around his neck on a lanyard.

"Y'all pretty small, boy," he observed with his deep drawl.

"I played football back in New York, I am really fast, and I will work hard," I countered.

"Jew York, huh. These kids are gonna rip ya a new one. If ya have the balls, come to the practices, but I cain't promise any game time," and he walked away.

Barry and Bruce smiled at me as if I had earned some sort of victory. They explained to me what the practices were going to be like, and what to wear. Mom took me to a store on the Avenue to buy the necessary equipment. Practices were going to start a week before school did, and there were going to be two a day, one in the morning and one in the afternoon. I could get a ride with Barry and Bruce if I walked over to their houses. I was excited, but scared. Eli had told me that he was the starting quarterback on his high school team. I yearned to share with him that I would be playing football also, but remembered what it was like when I was in Little League and said nothing.

Practice was the most intense physical activity that I had ever done. We did running, conditioning, agility, weightlifting, flexibility, hitting, and tackling drills in the oppressive heat and humidity. We had a water break every half hour. I was exhausted, but many of the other players still had the energy to harass me. I was growing my hair long, like the Beatles, but no matter how much I combed it, it was bushy. When I had my helmet off during the breaks, other boys would pat down my hair and say, "Where are the horns, kike!"

This was my first experience with anti-Semitism. I was tackled with extra force, punched, kicked, and scratched. I was bruised and bleeding at the end of every practice. We all had to share our gym locker with another player, and my "locker buddy" was Clay Darling. He was a big ninth grader, and he was relentless. He was pissed that he had to share his locker with, "a yankee faggot kike who looked like a spick." He had endless energy in terms of pushing me, slapping my head, and verbally abusing me.

"Why don't y'all do us all a favor and quit the team and move the fuck back to all the other faggots in Jew York," he'd implore.

I was afraid to answer back, but was determined to stay with the team. I pushed him back one day, and he retaliated with such a powerful shove that I flew across the locker room. Everyone laughed.

"The Jews killed Christ!" someone shouted.

"The Texans killed Kennedy," I retorted and walked away.

We ended up mostly practicing in groups according to our positions. The linemen, defenders, receivers, and running backs, my position, spent much of the time with each other. I was gaining respect as I proved that I was fast, quick and difficult to tackle. Some other kids would praise me, but never the coaches. Clay was a linebacker, and we only practiced together during scrimmages. I took pride in the fact that he had trouble tackling me, but when he did, I got bruised.

Right before school was about to start, we spent part of a practice competing in contests. One of the events pitted all the running backs against each other in a 100 yard dash. I had no idea how I would fare against the other backs, even though I was confident about my speed.

Clay rested his arms on my shoulders and said, "Jew boy, if y'all win the race, I will stop picking on you. If y'all don't win, I will make your life even more miserable."

We all lined up at the goal line at one end of the field. There were about ten of us running backs, a combination of eighth and ninth graders of all different sizes. I kept thinking about all the races that I had won when I was younger, and felt even faster now.

"On your marks, get set, Go!"

Three boys got off to a better start. I dug down as deep as I could, felt all the parts of my body working together, tapped into all the hatred that I felt towards Eli and for Clay, heard the terms nigger and kike in my head, and passed the other kids at the last minute. I turned around, found Clay in the crowd, and gave him the finger.

Thirty-Six

SCHOOL STARTS EARLIER IN THE year in Texas than in New York, and during the end of August, 1964, I began eighth grade at Pershing Jr. High. Mom joined a car pool with four other mothers, and I would be driven to school in the morning and ride the Avenue public bus home after football practice. The four other kids in the carpool were girls. I sat in the middle of the back seat surrounded by sweet smelling, smiling, arousing, sexy, young females. Lynn Camby's mom drove us the first day of school. Mrs. Camby drove with her body halfway turned towards the back seat. She was fascinated with me.

"Y'all have such beautiful hair, sweety. I love your eyes. Girls, would y'all look at his eyelashes. What a sharp dresser."

She didn't stop talking.

When I managed to say anything it was followed with, "What a lovely accent. All the girls at school are going to fight over him, aren't they ladies? He is such a cutie."

I kept turning redder and redder and the girls just laughed.

"Y'all have a great first day at school, Jeffrey. Y'all are so cute. Welcome to Texas."

We were dropped off in front of the school. Dozens of kids were milling around a big paved area that contained benches and had trees growing up through the concrete. The side of the school had a student parking lot with dozens of other kids. In Texas you were able to get a driver's license at age 14, and many ninth graders drove cars or motorcycles to school. We still had fifteen minutes until school started, and I walked around feeling anonymous. Finally, I was called over by Barry and Bruce. They were standing with a few girls. I was introduced.

Bonnie Gladdin was a few inches shorter than I was, had dirty blonde hair tied into a pony tail, and a scattering of freckles on her nose. She was wearing a miniskirt, had smooth sexy, tan legs, and her toes were turned slightly inward accenting the curves of her body. She flashed an incredible smile and leaned her body towards me when Bruce said my name. I was smitten.

The boys were all dressed in blue denim jeans and knit shirts, but I had turquoise jeans and a green dress shirt that I had purchased in New York. I chose a shirt that had tight short sleeves so that I could show off the muscles that I had developed working out for football.

"Where did y'all get those groovy clothes?" was the first thing Bonnie asked.

"I took them from a homeless person sleeping on a park bench back in New York," I quipped. "Luckily he was my size." I was attempting to imitate the sense of humor and nonconformist attitude that the Beatles displayed at their press conferences. It was working because everyone was laughing.

"What's it like in New York?" Bonnie asked.

"Not as good as it would be if you lived there."

"How did y'all get to Texas?"

"We made a left at Louisiana," I replied.

I continued to make her laugh until school started. I walked into the school, looked around at all the different looking and strange sounding people, and felt like an alien. We had a ten minute homeroom period prior to our first class, and the other kids stared at me as I sat down. "Boss clothes," a boy said. "Where'd you get them?"

I gave a straight answer. "Macy's"

"Idn't that in New York?"

"Yes, we just moved here."

"Welcome to Texas!" he said. "Nice to meet ya."

"Not everyone here is an asshole," I thought.

I went to my morning classes, social studies and math. I learned that the topic for the year in social studies was Texas history, as opposed to the United States history we learned in New York. Ninety minutes seemed like a long time for a class, but the teachers seemed interesting. The most salient thing about my classes was the girls. Beautiful girls clad in miniskirts. Everywhere I looked I saw legs. If I felt bored, I would drift off into fantasy. It was heaven for a newly pubescent boy. Some of the nubile nymphs actually smiled when they caught me gazing at them.

After lunch and gym class, I had science and we were given a list of the topics for the labs on Fridays. English was my last block of the day. In English, we sat in assigned seats. Sitting to my left was Bonnie Gladdin! What a delicious way to end the day. I enthusiastically raised my hand to answer any question posed by the teacher. I would have done anything to have Bonnie smile at me. At the end of the day we talked until I had to go to football practice. I loved the way that Bonnie leaned her body towards me and smiled when I talked. The look on her face reminded me of the look of approval that I saw on my parents' faces when we lived in Brooklyn.

My good feelings from the day ended quickly during football practice as I immediately became a kike again. I wondered how these kids got to go to the same school as everyone else that I had met. I was determined to be a good football player and I was becoming more and more immune to the taunts. I rode the bus down the Avenue after practice with other football players and girls who had stayed late for cheer leading practice. The girls were wearing their short cheer leader dresses, and I had more beautiful scenery to focus on.

Thirty-Seven

ON FRIDAY I HAD MY first day of orchestra and brought my violin to school. Most people ignored it. The ridicule and derisive remarks from some kids, however, were even worse than in football.

"Look at the fag-got with the vi-o-lin!"

"It's a girl with a dick carrying a vi-o-lin!"

"Hey homo, use that bow to fuck ya-self up the ass!"

I was shocked. I never anticipated this type of reaction. Word got around, and during lunch Coach found me and yelled, "Are you freaking crazy! Y'all cain't come to school with a faggot fiddle. Y'all might as well wear a sign that says, kick me in the balls. What are y'all thinking? A football player with a vi -o -lin? Make a choice, boy. Be a man or a faggot."

After lunch I had orchestra. I was the only boy there except for the percussionist. The teacher was Mr. Harrison. He was a tall, potbellied hunchbacked man with a circle of gray hair around his head. His face was long and sad looking and he resembled President Johnson. He was holding a viola and had tremendous hands. I wondered how he could play with such huge fingers. When he talked, he oozed warmth and kindness. I lit up as he told us the music that we would be learning for our first series of concerts. We were going to work on different classical music pieces by Mozart and Brahms, "Maria" and "Tonight" from *West Side Story*, a musical that I was in love with, "Til There Was You" a song from *The Music* Man which was covered by the Beatles, and "And I Love Her," a Beatles song from *A Hard Day's Night*. My jaw dropped. I wanted to be a part of this. He handed out some sheet music, and we all began playing together for the first time. I wanted to be part of this even more.

He seemed very approachable, so I went up to him after class and explained what had happened. I told him about what Coach had said. I said that I wanted to play football and be in the orchestra.

"This is a conundrum," he said. I looked up the word when I got home.

I thought about it and asked, "Maybe I could leave my violin at school, and just practice here. Then I wouldn't have to carry it back and forth in front of the other kids."

"Hmm. I have a better idea," he said. "I have some extra violins. You can take your violin home, practice there, and use one of ours at school. I think that you should be able to play football if you want to. I apologize for the ignorance of the cretins in this school."

At last, someone who agreed that I could do both. I called Mom, she drove to school before football practice, I ran out and put my violin in her car, ran back into school, and went to practice. I also looked up the word cretin when I got home, and realized that Mr. Harrison was the opposite.

Thirty-Eight

BETTY WAS A STAR. The Avenue bus was her stage. She was a legend, and I had heard the stories about her. Betty only rode on the bus once or twice a week, and finally, I had the opportunity to catch her performance. It was Wednesday after practice, and the football players and cheerleaders were boarding for their trip home.

The bus had bench seats, with their backs lined up against the side under the windows. The people sitting on the seats faced the inner aisle. The passengers who stood held on to one of the four metal poles that were spread out in the middle of the aisle. Betty was always the last person to enter. The boys excitedly whispered to each other, "She's here! She's taking the bus today!" The doors closed, and we pulled away.

The sound of the engine revving signaled the beginning of the show. Betty, with her short cheerleader dress hiked up even higher, voluptuously shook her body and strutted up and down the center of the bus, stopping intermittently to twirl around a pole. She made eye contact with as many boys as possible and inquired in a slow sensuous voice, "All the seats are taken. Where will I sit? I need a lap to sit on. Whose will it be?"

All of the boys sat upright and cleared off their laps. They smiled and looked at Betty as she smoothly slithered up and down the aisle with her hips undulating, and looking like a sleek tiger on the prowl. She would shake her butt over a boy's lap, act as if she was about to sit, and purr, "That doesn't look comfortable enough. Where will I sit?" She continued her dance until every boy was aroused, then chose the lucky winner and slowly sat. Making sure that everyone was watching, she would salaciously cross and uncross her legs, and bounce up and down as the boy under her would look as if he was about to pass out. When her inner sense of timing told her to move on, she got up, danced around again, and found another lucky lap to stimulate.

I was totally engrossed in her act. I remembered the stripper that I had seen in the Catskills, and imagined Betty taking off her clothes. I was so absorbed with watching her, that I didn't notice that I had missed my stop. I got off at the next one and ran for about ten minutes down the Avenue to get to my street.

I could not stop thinking about Betty and wanted to call Bruce and Barry to tell them about the show. Maybe I could convince them to take the bus one day so that they could watch. Maybe Betty would sit on my lap sometime. When I finally walked into my apartment, Mom was animatedly yelling and pacing back and forth. Once in a while Grandma joined in the screaming. Then they saw me and shared.

"He's gone! Your father is gone. He left us stranded!"

I realized that Eli hadn't been home for a while, but was shocked to hear that he was gone.

"He was fired from his job and he left Texas. I have no job. We have no money. They want to repossess the car."

Reality set in and I lost it, "What the fuck!' I shouted. "He moves us to Texas, and then he leaves! Why the hell did we move down here!"

I ran to my room and slammed the door. I was afraid I would hurt someone. I punched the wall and watched as my fist crashed through the sheetrock.

"How could he do this to us? Is this man completely soulless?" I put another hole in the wall.

A few days later, Mom called the "other grandparents," Eli's parents. Mom begged, "Please tell me where Eli is. I have no money and I have no job. Eli brought us here and we don't know anybody. I have three children to support. They are your grandchildren. They are Eli's children. Please show us some compassion."

Grandma got on the phone and pleaded, also.

"You'll have to work this out on your own," Eli's mother said. "We have no idea where Eli is."

We later found out that Eli was living with them in Brooklyn.

Mom went to see the local Rabbi. She asked the Rabbi for some help. The Rabbi said, "You married the man. You have to deal with it."

Mom had to park the car in a different spot each day. Grandma talked to her sister, Aunt Esther, and told her our situation. We lived on Grandma's social security and donations from Aunt Esther and Uncle Max for a while. Images of becoming homeless and starving to death on the street paraded through my head. Eli had abandoned us. Eli had fucking abandoned us! He left us in Texas! I was so enraged that I thought I would burst.

"Does he hate us that much that he is leaving us all with nothing?" I screamed at Grandma. Guilt began to radiate throughout my body, as if it was a revelation. "Is it all my fault? Did he leave because of me?" I went into my room and hid, like I was a criminal.

As the days passed, I became restless and perpetually agitated. On the weekend I suddenly left the apartment and ran to the Avenue. I wandered down the side of the road and absorbed the impact from the power of the cars and buses speeding by. Eli was gone, but his voice screamed in my head. "You are worthless! You embarrass me! You can't do anything right!" I saw Mom's agonized face and heard, "You should have died! The wrong person is alive!" I was crushed by the incredible guilt and emptiness that grew out of Sheryl's death. I saw myself jumping into the road and being crushed by the traffic. The tears flew from my eyes as I abruptly ran back to the field behind our apartments, stopped and screamed. Until I was hoarse. Until I had no energy left. Until I became aware of people watching. And I went home.

For a while, we were all fighting with each other almost any time that I was at home. My bedroom wall became full of holes from my fist. The joy had been sucked right out of my life. I was snapping at everyone. I had a perpetual scowl on my face at school. I felt totally powerless. One day I was standing with Bruce and Barry outside the school at the end of football practice. A group of other kids walked by and did their usual mindless taunting, "Look at the faggot Jew boys all standing together."

"Don't say anything," Barry warned, but I exploded, "Where the fuck are we? Is this Nazi Germany? What the hell is wrong with all of you?"

"This is Texas, Jew boy! If y'all don't like it, go the fuck back to Jew York!"

"Yeah, fucking Texas, where evolution works in reverse," I said. "The land where blacks are niggers, Mexicans are spicks, and Jews are Kikes. They kicked all the ignorant people out of all the other states and sent them to Texas! I'm sick of you all! I fucking hate you!" I ran towards the assholes.

They raised their fists and made a move towards me. One of the coaches intervened. "Calm down and go get dressed!" He sent the kids to the locker room and told Barry, Bruce and me to wait outside. He said nothing and then told us to go home about five minutes later.

I finally explained my situation to Bruce and Barry. I told them how Eli had disappeared and that we had no money. They slapped me on the back and told me that everything would work out. "Easy for a couple of rich kids to say," I thought as I got on the bus. When I got home I wrote a long letter to Bob.

Thirty-Nine

I BEGAN TO LET MYSELF ENJOY school again. English became my favorite class. Bonnie sat next to me, we read interesting stories, novels and poems, and did a great deal of creative writing. I always had enjoyed social studies, but did not want to learn Texas history. The history of Texas seemed as obnoxious as its present.

A few weeks after Eli left, we read the poem *Invictus* by William Ernest Henley. I totally identified with the message it conveyed and felt inspired by the words. The first verse was:

> *Out of the night that covers me,*
> *Black as the Pit from pole to pole,*
> *I thank whatever gods may be*
> *For my unconquerable soul.*

And it ends:

> *I am the master of my fate:*
> *I am the captain of my soul.*

I wanted to have an unconquerable soul. I wanted to be the master of my fate and the captain of my soul. I did not want to be the victim of any cretin who called me a kike, or of any bad situation created by Eli. We learned that William Ernest Henley had contracted tuberculosis when he was 12, and had to have one of his legs amputated below the knee when he was 17. He did not give in to his disability, and led an active life. I could conquer the obstacles in my life, too.

It seemed as if my newly created positive attitude was leading to better circumstances. Mom went to an employment agency, and a few weeks later she was hired to fill a teaching opening in an elementary school. The school was over forty minutes away, so having a car was a necessity. The Weiners had given Eli our car to use as a company car. When he was fired, they wanted it back and were attempting to repossess it. Mom kept hiding it, but decided to talk to the Weiners, and they stopped trying to take it. Since Mom was now working, she wasn't able to be part of the car pool anymore, but the other mothers agreed to let me continue to ride with them. I was able to sit in a car surrounded by pretty girls each morning, and to be embarrassed by Mrs. Camby once or twice a week. Most importantly, my fears of starving and being homeless were now alleviated.

Bruce's family was now inviting me to join them for dinner at fancy restaurants, and to go to the movies with them. Bruce, even though he wouldn't admit it, had apparently told his family about my situation. They even asked me to accompany them during a long weekend in October when they all went to visit Bruce's oldest brother at Rice University. I was taken on a tour of the campus, and spent time in a fraternity house. Everyone acted with intelligence and civility. One of the male students that I met actually played the violin, and was able to talk about it openly. There were many Jewish students, and no one called them kikes. There were students from all over the country, including New York City. I had the opportunity to see that other environments existed in Texas. I pictured myself attending Rice University when I was older.

In English we were reading more poetry and several times each of us was given a poem to memorize and to recite in front of the class. At lunch I sat with three other boys from English; Brandon, Marshall, and Wayne. We had fun changing the words of the poems so that they still fit the rhyme and meter of the original, but became funny and obscene. I had transformed the poem *The Raven* by Edgar Allan Poe into a representation of adolescent immature humor which I called, The Porcupine. We all laughed so loudly when I read it to the group that we caught the attention of the lunch monitor. In a raucous noisy room full of loud eighth graders, we managed to catch her attention with our unrestrained merriment several times.

I was assigned the poem, *Stopping by Woods on a Snowy Evening* by Robert Frost. I liked the poem, and I liked the fact that Frost had read a poem at President Kennedy's inauguration, but we still had fun butchering it. We were silly, 13 year old, pubescent, immature eighth graders sitting in a group in a noisy cafeteria during our lunch break. Frost's lines: *My little horse must think it queer, To stop without a farmhouse near*, became: His hairy horse must think he's queer, When he sticks his dick into its rear. We chortled so boisterously that tears were rolling down our faces. I was afraid that I would wet my pants. I struggled to contain my giggling on the way to science class.

In English, I was hoping that I wouldn't have to recite my poem that day. I laughed to myself every time I thought of the line about the hairy horse. The other three boys recited their poems without incident. A girl read her poem and then it was my turn. I was in control until I said, *"My little horse."* I looked at Wayne and burst into hysterics.

"Jeffrey! Compose yourself," said the teacher.

"I am sorry," I said and started over. This time I couldn't get a word out without breaking into laughter. Everyone else in the class had now joined in. Miss Brewster was livid.

"Jeffrey. Go get a drink of water, and when you come back, you'd better be ready to show respect for your poem and to read it correctly."

"Yes ma'am," I said. While I was out in the hall, another kid read his poem. I decided that I wouldn't look at my friends when I went back. I had a paper clip in my pocket, and I unraveled it so that I could poke myself in my hand if I started to laugh. I took several deep breaths. I recited the first few lines out loud. I felt in control.

I went to the front of the room. I was about to laugh and I dug the paper clip into my hand. It hurt. I began the poem, my lips quivered, and I took several deep breaths. I tried to talk again, and the laughter uncontrollably exploded from my gut. I was bent over in pain. My eyes were tearing. I couldn't catch my breath. I was in grave danger of wetting my pants. The whole class was roaring. I started hiccoughing. My face was contorted into strange expressions. I began to cough. Brandon was slapping his desk. Miss Brewster was silent, but I could see her chest heaving up and down. Someone farted. I walked out of the room, went to the boy's room, and continued to laugh. As I stared at my happy face in the mirror, I saw my smile slowly fade with the realization that there was no laughter at home.

Forty

WE HAD BEGUN TO PLAY football games against other schools during the middle of September. Barry, Bruce and I continued to practice with determination and intensity and seemed to be improving our skills. Since we played different positions we only had the opportunity to talk to each other before or after practice. It was a common occurrence for us to share with each other the fact that even though we were doing well, none of us were receiving any praise or any other feedback from the coaches. I had participated in a few scrimmages in which I seemed to be unstoppable, with no one being able to tackle me. Other players had praised me, but the coaches said nothing. At the games, it became obvious that we were not going to get any playing time.

After the third game, we decided to go up to Coach and to ask him what we needed to do to get onto the field. Bruce posed the question and Coach responded by screaming, "Shut up and go get changed."

"At least he didn't call us Kikes," I said.

I was getting more muscular, feeling in great shape, and mostly enjoying the practices so I wasn't that upset at the fact that we apparently had no chance of getting into a game. "We'll definitely be starting next year when we're in ninth grade," I said.

At the far end of the parking lot of my apartment complex, where the big fields began, stood one lone basketball hoop. Jack was about six foot four inches tall and a fellow resident of the Jamestown Apartments. He was a junior in high school, and a star of the varsity basketball team. Jack didn't play any fall sports and most days after school he spent hours doing drills and shooting baskets at the one hoop. I was fascinated by basketball and when I had nothing else to do I watched Jack practice.

Jack was driven and most of the time he didn't even notice me. He eventually invited me to join him. Jack never even asked me my name, but he seemed to enjoy coaching me. He taught me the correct form for dribbling and shooting, and how to stand and to move on defense. We talked about nothing other than basketball, and I drank in all of his advice. Dribbling and shooting had a cathartic effect on me, and I was a quick learner. Jack beamed with pride at my every improvement. He told me that football was the only interscholastic sport that an eighth grader could participate in, but there were basketball intramurals. The coaches sometimes watched, and if I played well, I would have a better chance of being chosen for the ninth grade team.

The football season ended at the end of October. When I handed in my uniform, Coach said, "Y'all hung in there, kid." I decided to spend my newly created free time after school practicing basketball. Bruce and Barry joined me occasionally, but they didn't like basketball as much as I did. There were still a few weeks before the varsity season started, so Jack continued to give me lessons. When he went in for dinner, he let me use his basketball and gave me drills to practice. I would take 20 jump shots in a row from different spots, practice layup after layup, and do dribbling drills. I wanted to improve and to impress Jack. He continually reminded me that since I was short, I would have to work extra hard. After about an hour, I'd walk up the stairs to Jack's apartment, and return his ball. He'd normally open the door just a crack, grab the ball, and close the door without saying a word. I had the feeling that something was going on in his apartment that he didn't want me to know about.

It sometimes was extremely windy outside. Jack and I

would shoot the basketball and watch the wind divert the arc of the ball. Jack told me that shooting in the wind was good practice because we learned to adjust our form to the conditions. On a particularly windy day in November, I was practicing by myself after Jack went up to dinner. He specifically had admonished me to take care of the ball. I was practicing my jump shot when a tremendous gust of wind blew the ball onto the fields. I chased after the ball, determined to get it back. All of a sudden, the skies turned black, the winds escalated, and it started to pour rain. I continued to run after the ball with the winds at my back and my vision obscured by the sheets of rain. I was not going to let Jack's ball get lost. I sprinted as fast as I could for over ten minutes, and finally caught up to the ball near where the Astrodome was being completed. I began my trek back to the apartments blinded by the wind and rain.

As I pushed on, tightly gripping the basketball in the same way that we were taught to cling to a football to keep from fumbling, I heard a deafening roar of thunder. Then the sky lit up with bolts of lightning followed by even louder blasts of thunder. I looked around and realized that I was still in the middle of nothing but flat fields for as far as I could see. I remembered what we had been taught in third grade, and I hunched over the basketball and curled up into as small a figure as I could make, as close to the ground as I could get. I heard the continuous booming of thunder and felt the heat from the lightning. My body was shaking and I was overflowing with fear, but I fought off my urge to get up and run. I kept my position until the storm finally passed about ten minutes later. I was soaked and my teeth were chattering when I knocked on Jack's door. He said nothing, grabbed the ball, and closed the door. I never saw the inside of his apartment.

Forty-One

INTRAMURALS BEGAN IN DECEMBER and we had games every Tuesday and Thursday after school. I was assigned to a team with seven other eighth graders. The gym teachers kept the time and officiated the games, but the teams had to coach themselves. Bradley and I emerged as the two players who knew the most and played the best, and we became the unofficial captains. Bradley and I ran plays that I had learned from Jack, give and go and pick and roll combinations, and we won most of our games. I enjoyed having authority with the team, and Bradley and I became friends. He lived near my apartment and we played one on one and practiced our skills on days that we didn't have intramurals. I continued to be amazed that the weather was still warm enough for us to play outdoors.

The big ballyhooed school wide-event in December was the Winter Cotillion to be held before Christmas vacation. The students voted for a ninth grade boy to reign as the King, another to be honored as a Prince, and a ninth grade girl to serve as the Queen, with another girl to be honored as the Princess of the Cotillion. As part of the election two eighth grade boys were to be voted in as Dukes, and two eighth grade girls were to be chosen as Duchesses. Everyone, including the teachers, was glowing with anticipation.

The first Friday in December we had an extended homeroom period. The teacher explained that each of the ten eighth grade homerooms would vote and chose one boy and one girl to be nominated to run for Duke and Duchess. We would vote with a secret ballot and then the teacher would tally up the votes. During lunch an assembly was planned and the entire student body would vote for students from the home room nominees. The winners were to be announced at the end of the day and they would become the King and Queen and their court for the Cotillion.

As the teacher was handing out the ballots, a girl shouted, "Let's vote for Jeffrey! He's cute!"

I turned bright red and didn't want any part of this. I voted for another boy whose name I picked at random.

Before lunch, I was summoned to the auditorium. I was told that I was nominated by my homeroom, and I was required to introduce myself at the school wide assembly. I turned even redder than I was before, began to perspire, and at the same time my mouth became totally dry. I tried unsuccessfully to manufacture some saliva, and felt my tongue sticking to the roof of my mouth. Each of us nominees had to stand in front of the auditorium, talk into a microphone and tell everyone our name and say that we wanted people to vote for us. I felt like I was about to die. I fought the desire to run away. This was the scariest thing that I ever had to do.

Everything was a blur. I felt panicky as I saw the auditorium fill up with hundreds of rowdy kids. We sat on the stage in the order that we were going to speak. I kept trying to conjure up some spit. I cleared my throat to see if I still had a voice. The back of my shirt was drenched with sweat. All of a sudden, it was my turn. Eli's insults always overpowered my other thoughts when I had to do public speaking. I forced myself to walk to the microphone. After what seemed like a thirty minute pause, I managed to say, "My name is Jeffrey Goldstein and I would like you to vote for me to be the Duke."

I walked back to my seat in a daze. After the assembly, Barry and Bruce were slapping me on the back and smiling. "This will really make you popular with the chicks. Good job."

I still felt like I was going to vomit.

In the hall, as I was walking to my last class, a beautiful girl in a mini skirt and cowboy boots grabbed my arm. She had long, flowing light brown hair and dark blue eyes. She stood in front of me, and I backed up until I was touching the wall. She came closer, pressed her breasts against my body, and lifted her thigh up until it was wedged into my crotch. She leaned her face into mine until our noses were almost touching. I could smell her spearmint gum scented breath as she spoke.

"I voted for y'all. Y'all are so cute. Where did y'all get those clothes?"

I couldn't even think of answering. I had stopped breathing. She pressed her body even closer, brought her lips next to mine as if she were going to kiss me, and pulled her head back again. I thought that my penis was about to explode.

"Well, I hope y'all win, Jeffrey. See ya at the Cotillion." Then she floated away. It took a few minutes, but I managed to peel myself off of the wall, and limped to my last class.

At the end of the day the winners were announced and thankfully I wasn't chosen

Forty-Two

MILQUETOAST WAS ONE OF our vocabulary words in English, and it was the perfect word to describe the personalities of the other kids in the orchestra. They were all good musicians, and it was a great experience playing with them, but it was torture trying to talk to them. Trudy played the viola, she was very pretty, talented and intelligent. She seemed to always be in a good mood and smiled most of the time. However, Trudy talked like an elderly woman. My Aunt Esther had more personality than Trudy did. Horace, the only other male, didn't even know anything about the Beatles. He heard their songs for the first time when we played them in orchestra. Fortunately, we practiced intensely when we were together and there wasn't much time for socializing.

A few weeks before our winter concert, Mr. Harrison announced that we needed to have an extra practice after school to help us prepare. I asked if we could avoid Tuesdays and Thursdays since those were my basketball days. Everyone agreed, no one was involved in anything else anyway, and we rehearsed on Wednesday. I left the violin with Mr. Harrison and left school to catch the Avenue bus. Outside the school, I was suddenly surrounded by four boys.

"We saw y'all in there with that faggot fiddle. We don't like queers around here. Y'all need to have some of that faggot shit knocked out of you!"

They came towards me. I realized that this time I couldn't get out of this by telling jokes. I was not going to be very successful fighting back. It was extremely unlikely that anyone

Caught in the Undertow

was going to help me. They all looked very focused and intent on causing me bodily harm. The biggest boy grabbed my waist. I did a spin move to break away, like I had learned in football, dodged the other kids, and ran away. I streaked across the road, in a direction that I had never been before. When I looked back, they were right behind and coming after me. I picked up my speed, sprinted down another street, turned a corner, jogged through backyards, jumped over a fence, ran down another street through some more yards, and found myself in downtown Houston. I kept running. Finally, I looked around and did not see my pursuers anywhere.

Unfortunately, I had no idea where I was. I asked a few passersby if they knew where the Avenue was, and received shrugged shoulders and quizzical expressions in return. I asked some other people if they knew where Pershing Junior High School was, and received similar responses. I began to get scared. Nothing looked familiar. I walked up and down different streets and couldn't find any recognizable landmarks. I saw a policeman, but turned around. I remembered my last experience with Houston's finest.

I only had a small amount of change in my pocket, which I was going to use for the bus. I found a bus stop, waited for one to stop, and a crowd of commuters pushed their way through the doors.

"Does this bus go to the Avenue?" I asked.

"Which avenue?" replied the bus driver.

"It is just called the Avenue," I said.

"They all have names," he snapped back. "These people need to get home," and the bus pulled away.

I wished that I had learned the local geography better. I only knew how to get to school by going down the Avenue, and how to walk to Barry's and Bruce's neighborhood. I had never paid attention to anything else. I felt alone and frightened I walked and strained my eyes trying to find anything that I could recognize. People rushed past me, knowing where they were going, and I felt chills. I passed a bum who asked me for some change.

I recalled a recurring nightmare from when I was a small boy in Brooklyn. I would wake up covered with sweat and feeling panicky because I had dreamt that I had been abandoned in a strange city. I was crying for my parents, and everyone ignored me. I was overwhelmed with the sensation of déjà vu. But this time I wasn't dreaming.

I kept on walking and felt tears in my eyes. I thought of Eli and how much I hated him. I seethed and cursed the state of Texas. I turned my head back and forth searching for anything that could give me a clue as to where I was. I saw the movie theater where we watched *A Hard Day's Night*. I had no idea how we got there that night. I passed a Weiner's Department Store and walked faster. I thought of President Kennedy and how he was murdered in Texas.

"This is hell!" I screamed in my head. "Texas is where you are sent when you go to Hell! I am not going to die here!"

I saw a gas station. It occurred to me that people sometimes go to gas stations to get directions. A teenage boy was pumping gas. I sheepishly asked him to tell me how to get to Pershing Jr. High School. He pointed me in the right direction, and after a twenty minute walk, I was there. I was tired, hungry and thirsty, and had to go to the bathroom. The building was locked, so I peed on a bush by the side of the school.

I went to the Avenue, and luckily a bus came about ten minutes later. I finally made it home.

Mom was home and was angry. The superintendant of the district where she was working had called her to his office after school. She was told that the school district had investigated her background and discovered that she owed an incredible amount of money.

"That's my husband's debt, not mine," she replied to him.

"He's still your husband, and it's your debt also" he responded. "We can't have someone working here who disobeys the laws."

"I have three children to support. He deserted us and left us with nothing. I have no idea where he is. I need this job or my family has nothing," she pleaded. "I had nothing to do with the money he owes."

"Aren't you all Jewish?" he asked. "I thought that Jewish men were better than that."

"Well, I married the one who isn't."

The superintendant relented and told Mom that because she had a good reputation as a teacher, he would let her stay. But, she had to take a class in Texas history before she could come back next year.

"Hopefully, we won't be here next year," she said.

This was the first indication I received that maybe we could move back to New York.

Forty-Three

I WOKE UP, LOOKED IN THE MIRROR, and noticed there was one. The next day a few more appeared. A few days later they had spread all over my face. I didn't recognize myself. Suddenly I had acne. Zits. Pimples. I was ashamed to go to school. My face looked like the before picture in a *Clearasil* commercial. I made sure that I had a seat next to the window in the morning car pool. I turned my face as far away as I could from the girls as we drove to school. I felt hideous. I refused to look anyone in the eyes and didn't raise my hand once in class. I didn't look at any girls in fear that they would look back. The Cotillion and the Winter Concert were two weeks away and I felt like a mutant. In gym a boy looked at my face and said, "What happened, did y'all eat a nigger?"

In English, I sat with the side of my face leaning against my hand so that Bonnie couldn't see me. I left as quickly as I could when the bell rang. The next morning my complexion was worse. I asked Mom to buy me some *Clearasil* and whatever pimple medicines she could find.

It was Mrs. Camby's turn to drive. She looked at me and said, "Jeffrey, y'all should wash your face with some brown soap. That'll clear it right up, sweety."

The girls in the car then turned and stared at me. I blushed so brightly that my zits were temporarily overshadowed by my bright red skin. I again attempted to conceal my face at school. When I finally returned home, I scrubbed with the acne soap that Mom had purchased and covered the pimples with *Clearasil*. My situation was aggravated by Eli. He wasn't there, but his voice echoed in my head. Eli had constantly denigrated me for being too skinny, being too short, not combing my hair correctly, or for wearing the wrong clothes. I could hear him telling me that the pimples were my fault and that I should hide my face in shame.

By the next week, I would check the mirror in the morning and declare it either a "clear day," when the pimples diminished to the point where there was more unblemished skin than there were pimples, or a "zit day," when my acne was the salient feature. On the clear days, I felt full of confidence, raised my hand in class, and looked directly at people. On the zit days, I felt self-conscious, ugly, depressed, and tried to be invisible. On either type of day, I was too embarrassed to talk to Bonnie. I believed that if she saw any pimples, she wouldn't like me anymore. I avoided her and quickly walked away whenever she tried to talk to me.

"Are y'all angry at Bonnie?" one of her friends asked me. "Is something wrong?"

"No," I answered and walked away. I didn't want to say that what was wrong was that my face had become a pimple farm.

Barry, Bruce and I had been practicing our dance moves in preparation for the Cotillion. We watched *American Bandstand* at Bruce's house and imitated the teenagers on TV. I taught them the dance moves that I had learned in 6th grade, and we became experts at a new dance called, "The Freddie." The British band, "Freddie and the Dreamers" had popularized these new steps, and we played their records and could adeptly perform in rhythm with their songs. We were eagerly awaiting the opportunity to display our talents at the Cotillion.

Our Winter Concert occurred on one of my zit days. I rationalized that I was too far away from the audience while sitting on the stage for anyone to see my face. The spectators were comprised mainly of parents, anyway, and they would all be focused on their own kids.

The day of the Cotillion arrived and I had a semi zit day, semi clear day. I decided not to go, but Bruce talked me into attending. I got dressed up in my new shirt and tie, and could not take my eyes off of all the pimples on my face. I went to Mom's room, surreptitiously fled with her flesh colored *Cover Girl Makeup*, and covered up the blemishes. Mom caught me putting on her makeup and told me that I didn't look that bad. She said that she had acne that was much worse when she was a girl, and that she quickly outgrew it. It felt good to hear her talking nicely to me, but I still was embarrassed. I self-consciously went outside and waited for Bruce and his mother to pick me up.

The gym was buzzing with fancily dressed teenagers. The student council had colorfully decorated the walls, and there was punch, food, and most importantly, the music that we liked. Many kids just stood and watched, but we proudly asked girls to dance. We were excited about showing off our skills. I only danced with girls that I considered plain. I was too embarrassed to let an attractive girl see my face. I especially did not want to get close to Bonnie.

All of a sudden, *Do the Freddie* by *Freddie and the Dreamers* started to play. Barry grabbed Bruce and me, and we lined up and performed our routine. I got swept up in what we were doing and had no time to be scared. A crowd gathered, watched us, and then started to clap their hands to the music and to whistle and holler. I started to sweat, and felt the makeup run down my cheeks. Everyone applauded when we finished, and I quickly grabbed a napkin from a table and wiped my face. Barry, Bruce and I slapped hands.

Bonnie walked over. "Y'all were excellent!" she exclaimed. "Please dance this next one with me."

It was, *Sealed with a Kiss*. A slow one. I turned red, perspired, held her, and danced. The song seemed to last forever. I couldn't let her see my face. When it was over, I turned my head, said thank you, and walked away. I did not dance again at the Cotillion.

Caught in the Undertow

Bruce's family invited me to their house for a New Year's Eve party. It was to be held outside by their swimming pool. My first New Year's Eve party was going to be outside in 70 degree weather. It didn't seem natural. I kept thinking about all the books that I had read about the after effects of a nuclear holocaust.

I walked over around 8:00. The backyard was huge. There were men dressed in tuxedos serving food and drinks, music was playing, people were dancing, and crowds of guests were noisily laughing and talking. Bruce's brother was there with a big group of his college friends. There were college girls dressed in bathing suits. I couldn't take my eyes off of them.

Bruce found me and whisked me into the house. He had stolen some beer and wanted to share. I took a sip. The taste was strong and bitter. I scrunched up my face and forced myself to drink more. I let out a tremendous belch. Bruce laughed. He already had drunk a whole can, he said. I managed to finish my can.

We spent the rest of the evening swimming, annoying the girls by trying to splash them when we jumped into the pool, drinking more beer, singing to the music, and doing whatever else we could to get the attention of the girls in the bathing suits. They mostly laughed at us and I realized that they had drunk much more beer than we had.

Right before midnight, we all gathered around a TV and watched the countdown from Times Square in Manhattan. I realized that Eli was probably somewhere in NYC. My stomach churned at the thought of him. Bruce asked me if I had ever been there when the ball dropped. I never had. At midnight, couples kissed and we watched and laughed. It was now 1965. I was invited to sleep over, and we went to bed around 4:00 feeling slightly drunk.

Forty-Four

AFTER WE WENT BACK TO SCHOOL in January, Barry and Bruce informed that they had girl friends and that they were, "Going steady." They urged me to find a girl friend so that we could all go on big dates together. They were going bowling with their dates on Saturday night.

I had a crush on Bonnie. I yearned for her to be my girlfriend. But every time I even thought about asking her, I turned red and perspired. I was determined to go out with her, and started practicing what I would say.

"Would you like to go out with me and my friends this weekend?" I wrote the words down, and then said them over and over again in my room. I tried saying them to a mirror in the bathroom, but got fixated on my pimples. I went back to my room, and spoke the same words over and over and over. I was confident that no matter what happened, those words would come out. I called her up on the phone, but lost my nerve and hung up when she answered. I decided to ask her in school at the end of English class.

The next day, I repeated the words to myself for the entire period. Every time Bonnie looked at me, I smiled. Finally, the class ended and I turned to her. She looked at me, I started to talk, but nothing came out. Eventually I asked, and she said, "Yes."

"Great, Me, Barry and Bruce will come by your house at 7:00 and we'll all go bowling."

"Groovy," she said.

Bonnie said yes! Bonnie was going to go out with me! Bonnie was going to go out with ME! Bonnie Gladdin! BONNIE

GLADDIN! This was the greatest moment of my life! I was ecstatic. I was bursting at the seams. When I got home, I ran to Bruce's house, but acted cool and nonchalantly told him. We were all going bowling on Saturday.

Saturday finally came, and I started getting ready. I took a shower, borrowed the razor that Mom used on her legs and shaved off the few hairs on my upper lip. I covered up my zits with her makeup, and splashed *English Leather* on my neck. I picked out my coolest clothes, put *Brylcreem* in my hair and combed each one until it was just right. I brushed my teeth and rinsed my mouth with mouthwash. I practiced smiling in case my nervousness made me look unhappy. I put handkerchiefs in my pockets to use to wipe off the sweat if I started to perspire. I rehearsed my bowling approach. I thought about how sexy Bonnie was, and felt excited, then scared, then insecure, then excited again. I WAS GOING OUT WITH BONNIE!

I met up with Bruce, Barry and their dates and we all walked to Bonnie's house. Her parents invited us in and asked me some questions. I was so nervous. I smiled and politely answered, but had no idea what I said.

I walked next to Bonnie as we started our fifteen minute trip to Regal Lanes on the Avenue. I tried to be witty, and the more that Bonnie laughed, the more comfortable I felt. It seemed very natural being with her. I even dared to hold her hand. I felt all tingly and warm inside as we walked side by side and casually conversed. At the bowling alley, when we weren't bowling, we sat together on the plastic benches. I put my arm around her, and she put her hand on my knee. Sitting so close to Bonnie was the best feeling that I had ever felt in my life.

While Bonnie was bowling, Barry called me over. "You're going to kiss her later, right? If you don't kiss her, she'll think that you are a faggot."

This became all that I could think about. I had never really kissed a girl before. I felt like someone had just punched me in the stomach.

"Do I keep my lips together or apart? Do I use my tongue? What if my breath smells? What do I do with my hands?"

I tormented myself with these questions. I had never talked about this with anyone before. My warm, tingly feeling was replaced with anxiety.

We started our walk back. Barry and Bruce walked with their girlfriends to their houses, and I took Bonnie to her house. We held hands the whole way back. We finally arrived at her front door. She turned towards me and smiled. I looked back at her. I knew that she was waiting. She held both of my hands. I had to make my move. I closed my eyes, lunged towards her with my face, felt my forehead hit her nose, and heard her scream. I opened my eyes and her nose was bleeding. I panicked and ran home as fast as I could. I was mortified.

I told Mom to tell Bruce, and then Barry that I wasn't home when they called. On Monday, I expected to be the laughing stock of the whole school. But no one said anything. I thought that Bonnie was going to be livid, but she just smiled at me in English class. After class she said, "I am going to have to teach y'all how to do that right."

Bonnie wasn't angry at me! She wanted to see me again! I was in love.

The next weekend we all went out again. This time we walked to a movie. I put my arm around Bonnie, slowly moved my head towards hers, and we kissed.

"This is what you do with your lips," she whispered. "This is what you do with your tongue."

"I think that I would like to practice some more," I said.

I now had a girlfriend. I didn't obsess over the number of pimples on my face anymore. We walked through the halls at school holding hands and announcing to the world that we were a couple. I had to endure her long winded phone calls once or twice a week, but felt special that she was calling me. Each weekend the whole group went out. We usually walked around or went to someone's house. Sometimes we went to a movie or bowling. We practiced our kissing. The year 1965 started out very nicely for me.

Forty-Five

ENGLISH CLASS CONTINUED TO PROVIDE us with the opportunity to be creative. The class was divided up into various groups of three or four students, and our assignment was to act out an interview with a character from one of the books or stories that we had read. Our group was to interview Odysseus from, *The Odyssey*. I had the idea, after hearing it done on the radio, to use prerecorded snippets from songs as answers to the interview questions. We brainstormed a large list of questions and answers, and decided that I would play the role of Odysseus and mouth the words to the songs during the interview. The other members of the group would take turns asking questions. Since I had a tape recorder and the biggest record collection, we met at my apartment after school to record the answers.

Question: "Odysseus, what did they tell you about your wife, Penelope, while you were gone?"

Odysseus: "She loves you, yeah, yeah, yeah,"

Question: "What did you think when you were wandering at sea for ten years?"

Odysseus: "I get around."

Question: "How did you feel when your trip was finally over?"

Odysseus: "I was glad all over."

We came up with over five minutes of questions and musical answers. Everyone laughed and I reveled in the merriment. It continued to be glaringly obvious that none of these good interactions ever happened at home. And sometimes I felt so empty.

Houston had a major league baseball team called the Colt 45's, and in the spring they were going to be renamed the Houston Astros. They were scheduled to play at the newly constructed Astrodome. For the first time in history, a baseball game was going to be played indoors. The air conditioned Astrodome was being touted as the Eighth Wonder of the World. It was supposedly an engineering marvel. There was constant talk about the new stadium on TV and the radio. The first game slated to be played was a pre-season exhibition game against the New York Yankees. My New York Yankees. One of my favorite parts of New York would be joining me in Texas.

The game was already sold out and it was impossible to get a ticket. I thought about sneaking in, but realized it would be impossible. The Governor of Texas, John Connally, was chosen to throw out the first pitch. Governor Connally was already present at a bigger historical event. He was riding in the car with President Kennedy when the President was assassinated. Connally was wounded, also. The Mayor of Houston was going to be there, and President Johnson and his wife were scheduled to attend. Obviously, there was going to be massive security at the game.

I dreamed about watching the big event. I had seen the Yankees many times at Yankee Stadium, but if I were sitting there watching the New York Yankees at the first game at the Astrodome, it would be the highlight of my life as a baseball fan. Texans would not be able to appreciate the event as much as I could. There was no way to make it happen, however. I hoped that it would be on TV, but then thought about when Eli attacked me for watching the All-Star game on TV. I hated the fact that he so unexpectedly entered my thoughts.

In March I was at Bruce's house and we were listening to the newest Beatles album. His father came into the room and announced, "Even though the game was immediately sold out, I was able to acquire a set of tickets to opening day at the Astrodome. Would you like to go?"

"You are so lucky," I said to Bruce before he could answer.

"I was asking you, too, Jeffrey," said his dad.

I was incredulous. My jaw dropped. I thought that I was dreaming.

"I want to go more than anything in the world," I finally replied. "Thank you!"

April 9, 1965. Bruce's father sat with a group of his business associates, and Bruce and I sat with a group of their kids. We were sitting at the Astrodome for the first baseball game ever played indoors. The Astrodome was spectacular. Each section of seats was a different color. There was the biggest scoreboard ever built and it even had a name, "The Astrolite." The seats were cushioned like the ones in a movie theater, not the typical hard wooden seats that were found at other ballparks. When you looked up, the stadium was covered with a huge glass dome. Instead of the usual hot dogs and cracker jacks, they were selling all kinds of fancy foods. Bruce's dad purchased little steaks for us. The temperature was maintained at a constant 72 degrees. We watched the Yankees take batting practice. Mickey Mantle was attempting, unsuccessfully, to hit the domed roof.

The Yankees starting lineup was announced. Mickey Mantle was going to lead off for the Yankees, instead of hitting in his usual cleanup spot, so that he would go down in the record books as having the first at bat in the Astrodome. Mickey Mantle then proceeded to have the first base hit at the Astrodome. A few innings later Mantle hit the first homerun ever at the Astrodome. My favorite Yankee made baseball history, and I was there watching!

The game lasted 12 innings with the Astros finally winning. After the game, Bruce's dad took us to the first level and we waited outside the door to the Yankee locker room. Elston Howard, Joe Pepitone, and Tom Tresh signed my scorecard. I did not stop smiling the rest of the night, and probably slept with a smile on my face.

Jeffrey Goldstein

A few weeks later, Bruce and I attended the season opener against the Philadelphia Phillies. There were twenty-one NASA Astronauts in attendance and all of them threw out an opening pitch. We were lucky enough to attend five other games. A family, and a father, other than my own, had rescued me temporarily from my abyss.

Forty-Six

As THE SCHOOL YEAR WAS winding down, Mom talked about moving back to New York. She didn't know if we could get our house back, or how we would get there. I refused to take the idea very seriously. It didn't seem to be possible, so I never talked about it with anyone else. I was enjoying my relationship with Bonnie and my friendships with Bruce and Barry. I wasn't as intent on moving back as I was before. Besides, I enjoyed the absence of Eli.

Barry and Bruce left for two weeks to attend a youth camp near Dallas as soon as the summer began. Bonnie also left with her family to visit relatives in Los Angeles. We all promised to see each other in two weeks. The next day Mom broke the news.

"Your father is arriving on Wednesday and we're going to drive back to Bellmore. We're finally going back home."

The toxicity called Eli was returning. I felt sick. My saliva suddenly tasted like metal. It had been nine months since I had to worry about being physically abused. It was nine months since I had to fear for my life in my own home. My body pulsated with rage, fear, and anxiety.

"Where are we going to live?" I asked.

"We're working on that. We won't be able to get our house back for a while."

"When are we leaving?" I inquired.

"In a few days. We will pack as quickly as we can, and then start our trip."

It then occurred to me that I wouldn't have an opportunity

to see Bonnie or my friends before we left. I felt myself being pulled away by forces out of my control. Every time I thought that my life was improving, I got punched in the head. I went to my room and paced back and forth.

"How will I let them know what happened?" I thought. "They'll come back and look for me, but I'll be gone. I'll never see them again. They'll never know what happened."

I racked my brain. I was tormented. What was I going to do?

I wrote a letter to Bruce explaining the situation, and asked him to tell Bonnie and Barry what had happened. I ran over to his house. His house keeper answered the door.

"Master Bruce is away," she said.

"I know," I responded. "Please give him this letter when he returns."

I wrote down his address so that I could write him when I got back to Bellmore. I was overwhelmed with an empty sick feeling. Just like it was with Sheryl, I never had the chance to say goodbye. I also knew that I would never see any of them again.

For the next few days, Mom was worried that Eli wouldn't show up. Our lease was up, she resigned from her job, our possessions were packed, and we had no choice but to move. Wednesday morning, however, right on schedule, Eli walked through the door. I felt nauseated. He lifted up Michele and hugged her. He hugged Keith. He stuck out his hand to me. I grabbed it with a vice-like grip and glared at him.

"You better not fuck with me," was the message that I wanted to convey.

"You got bigger," he noticed. "But you're still too skinny."

He was still about four inches taller than I was, and at least one hundred pounds heavier. I yearned to tell him about football, about how well I had done academically, about my girlfriend, and that I had been working out. I wanted to tell him about the Astrodome. But I knew that he would be brutally critical. I wasn't ready for his verbal abuse. I knew that no matter how strong I got, he intimidated me and I still felt helpless around him. I wanted him to love me, to approve of me, to stop making me feel so worthless. When I looked at him, I felt fear, anger, and loss. We were going back to New York, but not on my terms.

Part Four
LONG ISLAND REVISITED

Blue black rippling flowing waters
The current runs rapidly past the white brown rocky shore
Cold wailing winds
The chirps of seagulls
Gliding
Then swiftly flying
Graceful and beautiful
Hungry and foreboding
I strain my eyes
Turn my head
And lie back
Falling into earth's bed
The vast indifferent dome of the sky above

Suddenly
A gull dives straight down
And plucks a fish from the water

I stare at the blue black rippling flowing waters
And I complacently smile

Jeffrey Goldstein

Forty-Seven

THE NEXT DAY, WE BEGAN our trek back to New York. My head was swimming with thoughts of my friends, and with an aching for Bonnie. Eli was driving, and I was sitting in the back seat next to the window. All six of us sat in our air conditioned 1961 Chevrolet Impala. This was the vehicle that started out as a company car for the Weiners. This was the vehicle that Mom had to hide so that it couldn't be repossessed. It seemed ironic that it was now on its way to New York.

Eli tirelessly did all the driving, and we travelled for about twelve hours each day. Each night we'd stay in a cheap motel. We got into a routine in which we'd eat breakfast at the motel and then stop for lunch and then for dinner. We also did some quick sightseeing and visited attractions such as Lookout Mountain in Tennessee, and Tupelo, Mississippi, Elvis's birthplace. I took pictures at each stop with my Polaroid camera. I spent the time in the car alternating between looking out the window at the ever changing scenery, and reading. Everyone was very quiet.

I was looking forward to discussing books and ideas with Bob. I had written him a letter and he knew that we were coming back. I had just finished *The Golden Apples of the Sun* by Ray Bradbury, an author we both liked. I began to read and to write more poetry, and was enjoying *The Spice Box of Earth*, a collection of poems written by Leonard Cohen. I especially liked the fact that Cohen wrote about topics that I had never seen expressed in poetry before. His writings were vastly different from anything we had read in school. He explored sexuality, religion, philosophy, and relationships. These were subjects that I wanted to write about. I spent a morning as we were driving through Louisiana writing this poem:

I Wish

I wish
I could write
A poem
Which contained
Every destructive thought
Every feeling of anger
Every feeling of hate
Rage
Guilt
And self-pity
Every useless thought
That has ever passed through my head
So that I could take this poem
And burn it

Then
I would write a poem
In the sky
With the clouds
And the world would see it
And smile

Our trip, fortunately, was peaceful and uneventful. No one did much talking, and I enjoyed my time reading, writing and seeing the countryside. I followed our progress on a map, took pictures and collected postcards from each state that we had passed through. I slowly became excited about returning to my old life in Bellmore, and going back to 9th grade at Grand Avenue Junior High School. I had great stories to tell my friends.

Caught in the Undertow

The turmoil started when we arrived back on Long Island at the end of June. A doctor and his family had a lease to rent our house on Navy Place. It was a one year lease with an option to stay for a second one. They refused to move out until the end of the second year. We hired a lawyer, but nothing could be done. We now had nowhere to live. Everyone was extremely tense and angry. I thought about sneaking into the house at night with a group of friends, and scaring them out. I felt that it was our house and they had no right to be there.

We stayed in a motel for a while, and then moved into a tiny apartment in a town called Freeport. Freeport was two towns west of Bellmore, but unlike Bellmore, it was very impoverished. There were almost no Black families in Bellmore, and Freeport's population was almost all Black and Hispanic. It was considered an inner city area that was dangerous to walk through. Our apartment was part of an old dilapidated house. We had a tiny room, which served as a combination living room and kitchen, a bathroom the size of a small broom closet and a little bedroom with just one big bed. All six of us had to sleep in the same bed. We would crawl over each other to get in and out of bed. Rats and cockroaches ran through the house, and howling wild cats woke us up each morning. Grandma would get up and throw pots of boiling water at the cats to scare them away.

Our apartment was four blocks south of Merrick Road. The first opportunity that I had, I walked up to Merrick Road, and took the bus on the short trip through Merrick and then to Bellmore. Bob lived three blocks north of the stop, and I joyously ran to his house. I was greeted by his mom. She looked at me and engaged me in a long conversation. I was self-confident and articulate as I told her stories about Texas. I put a positive spin on our varied experiences, and framed our time there as being a one year adventure. I had the opportunity to see new places and meet different people.

I was saying all these things for my own benefit. I felt that if I could focus on the good experiences, the bad ones would lose their impact. I wanted to have more control of my thoughts and emotions, and at least I was in charge of what I shared. I wanted so desperately to be happy.

Bob's mom was impressed. "You are so much more mature," she observed. "You left here a boy, and you are returning a man!"

"At least for now, Bob will be allowed to see me," I thought.

Bob and I spent the morning talking and catching up. He said that if we couldn't move back to Bellmore, his parents would let me stay at their house so that I could go back to the same school. I felt hopeful for the first time since we returned. I was invited to stay for lunch and dinner, and Bob's mom was again impressed by me when I excitedly ate all the vegetables that she served.

Riding the bus back to Freeport that evening, my mind was flooded with thoughts about Bonnie, and memories of Bruce and Barry. I felt awkward about the way that I left them, and was angry that I had no control over the situation. I wondered if they thought of me and if they missed me. I was thrilled, however, to be back with Bob, and I wished that I was able to combine both worlds. I wrote the following poem during the trip back to our apartment:

Ambivalence

Happy but yet sadly so
I'm on a bus again
Going down another road
Away from loyal friends

Goodbyes I did not want to make
Too soon I had to go
I feel that I have no control
Caught in an undertow

Forty-Eight

ON JULY 1, 1965, I had my 14th birthday. Mom took me to Robin Hoods and we purchased a barbell, two dumbbells, and 100 pounds of weights. I set them up in the corner of our tiny living room/kitchen. There wasn't much room to use them, but I managed to work out in the morning before I left for the day, or at night when I returned. Bob also bought weights, and we set them up in his basement. We read books and publications about weight training and exercise, and particularly paid attention to a periodical called, *Strength and Health*. This was published by a man named, Bob Hoffman, who was a famous health enthusiast. Hoffman owned the York Barbell Company, and we voraciously devoured all of his articles about nutrition and muscular development. Bob and I began to gain muscle weight and to greatly improve our strength and physiques. We worked out several times a week in his basement while listening to music and talking about books. Bob's mom was thrilled that we wanted to eat healthier foods.

Sometimes when I was working out in our apartment, Eli was home eating breakfast or dinner. There was nowhere else for me to put the weights, so I was forced to listen to him rant about me for the whole time that he was there. He denigrated everything about me from my voice, to my looks, to my faggot friends, to my personality. I became the focus of everything bad in his life. I became adept at transforming my anger into energy that I used to train even harder. I tried as hard as I could not to internalize what he was saying, but it was a losing battle. He wore me down.

Several times a week, I took the bus to Bellmore and walked down to my old hangout, Newbridge Park. The first time I went back I saw a "continuous" baseball game. Many of the same kids I had played with before were there. I didn't think that they would recognize or remember me. But David, who was two years older, saw me and screamed, "Goldstein's back! Hey, guys, Goldstein's back! Goldstein, get on your horse and ride!" It felt so good to play ball with them again.

Newbridge Park had three basketball courts, and there were constant pickup games being played. I began participating, and felt confident due to my experiences in Houston. A boy named Butch was always there. He was a few years older, and a basketball fanatic. He was considered the best player, and an expert on rating the other players. If Butch disapproved of you, you weren't allowed to play in the competitive games on the first two courts. Those players were relegated to the far court which was reserved for the "scrubs." After I had played a few times, Butch gave his assessment of me.

"Goldstein has a good jump shot and he's very quick to the basket. He needs to develop his left handed layup."

I was allowed to play with the good kids on the upper echelon courts.

Sometimes Bob came with me when I played baseball or basketball, but he played tennis. We found time to meet up during the day to lift weights and to talk.

After July started, I realized that I still hadn't been back to Jones Beach. Bob wasn't allowed to go there, so I got in touch with Vinny. We used to ride the bus there. Vinny informed me that his family now belonged to a "Beach Club." I learned that the rich families of South Bellmore and South Merrick, when they didn't want to mingle with the common people at Jones Beach, now joined exclusive beach clubs with names such as The Malibu, The Sands, and The Lido. These were located on the south shore of Long Island west of Jones Beach and there were private sections of beach area reserved for members only. They had their own cabanas and pools. Vinny belonged to The Sands.

Members of beach clubs were allowed to bring a guest. Vinny didn't have many other friends, so his parents were happy to bring me along. I had a golden brown tan from my time in Houston, had worked diligently on developing my muscles, had new stylish bathing suits from Texas, and felt very confident walking without my shirt along the beach. There were plenty of pretty girls our age, and I smiled at anyone who looked back at me. Members were allowed to walk along the ocean from one club to another, and Skinny Vinny and I checked everything out. He was skinnier than ever and wore a sweatshirt.

A group of girls walking along the shore in our direction smiled back at us. We stopped and talked about school and music, and I told them about Texas. A girl named Andrea invited me to see her beach club called The Catalina, and the two of us walked off. Andrea was from the village east of Bellmore, called Wantagh. We swam in her pool, and then went to her cabana to dry off. As we were standing and facing each other, I kissed her. I put my arms around her and kissed her again. We did this for about five minutes, and then she said that it was time for her to meet her parents and to go home. Maybe we'll see each other here again, we said. I savored the feeling of having had my first New York kiss.

I found Vinny again and boasted about the kiss. He looked at me but said nothing. He usually said nothing, and I remembered why I hadn't called him sooner. After that, I found other kids to go to Jones Beach with, and never returned to a beach club.

That night I thought of Bonnie. I still missed her. I wrote a poem in the style of the sophisticated ones written by Leonard Cohen.

Jeffrey Goldstein

For Bonnie

*We kissed on hot Texas nights
Enjoyed the pleasure of our mouths
Here in New York
Your taste remains*

Forty-Nine

WE STILL NEEDED TO FIND a place to live in Bellmore so that we all could return to the same school district. We kept looking, but were not having any success. Mom's friend Carla, who was also an elementary school teacher, told Mom about an opening that had just come up for a third grade teacher at Fairfield Elementary School in Massapequa. Carla recommended Mom, and she went to an interview. She was soon offered the job. We were all relieved that Mom would be working.

A week later we received more good news. Bob's mom found out that her aunt, who lived in Bellmore, had planned to move out of her house. The house would be vacant on August 1. A deal was worked out in which we could rent the house for a year, and then the house would be put up for sale. Our old house on Navy Place would be available to us at that point. We now had a place to live, if we could survive our stay in the tiny apartment in Freeport. I would be able to go back to Grand Avenue Junior High.

We moved on August 1. Our new temporary home was a small ranch house on a street called Park Place, which ran off of Merrick Road. At the corner of the block there was a 7/11 Store. We were located in the older blue collar section of Bellmore, and I was now only five minutes from Bob's house. We decided that after school started, when the weather was nice, I would ride my bike to Bob's house and we would walk to school from there. It was not considered cool to ride a bike to Junior High. In eighth grade, I was told, only one person, Roger Jackson, ever rode his bike to school. He was still a legendary athlete and supposedly never rode in a bus or car. He always ran or rode his bike to wherever he was going. I wanted to be known as an athlete also, and often thought about Roger and was inspired by him when I worked out.

Our house had three small bedrooms, and I shared one with Keith. The room was big enough for me to have my weights in it, along with two beds and a desk. My set of weights kept growing and I now had a weight bench to do bench presses with. If Eli and I were home at the same time, I read, worked out, or listened to music in my room.

A few weeks after we moved in, Eli invited some of the men that he worked with and their families to a barbeque in our back yard. Over the years, Eli had brought home different groups of friends from work. The people changed as his jobs changed. This group included three boys who were my age. Eli brought them over and told me to introduce myself and to "Play some ball" with them. I asked them if they liked football and we chose teams for a two on two game in the yard. I automatically hated them because they were associated with Eli.

During the game, I could not be touched. They weren't very athletic, and every time I had the ball, I scored a touchdown. I made use of my speed and football skills and reveled in the satisfaction of running past them or faking them out each time I carried the ball. Sometimes I teased them by slowing down and letting them almost catch me, and then exploded away like a bolt of lightning. It felt like I was making a fool of Eli.

As we continued to play, it occurred to me that Eli was watching. I looked over and saw his face. Staring at me. I cringed. Even when he wasn't saying anything, his voice was in my head. The sound of it infuriated me. Paralyzed me. I felt his hands around my throat. "The game's over," I said and went into the house.

Eli found me in my room. "Get back out there! You're making me look like a fool!" he yelled. I walked out the front door and went to Bob's house. We talked as we pumped our muscles in his basement.

"I read that girls really dig guys with a "V" shape," said Bob.

"I know," I replied as I struggled under a heavy barbell. "But there's more to it than that. Look at Roger Jackson. He's solid muscle and his body is the widest "V" I've ever seen, but the girls stay away from him."

"Yeah, he's just weird."

"Exactly. They like a good personality, too. You have to be funny, like the Beatles."

We continued to lift and laugh until it was time for Bob to eat dinner.

My happiness turned to dread as I slowly walked home. Eli was going to be in a bad mood. I snuck in the back door, silently entered my room, sat at my desk and read.

Fifty

BOB AND I KEPT ADDING to our collection of weights as we got stronger. I had a bench, and in order to do all the lifts that I wanted, I needed squat racks. I priced them at Robin Hood's, and they were too expensive. So, I decided that I would make my own. I got two old buckets, bought some cement, and took the two bars that had support stands on top of them off of the weight bench. I used all these parts to make squat racks which I could use for a variety of exercises. Eli always had been extremely skilled using tools and had the ability to build just about anything. He had no patience in terms of sharing his expertise with me and berated me for being useless in these areas. I was so nervous around him that I couldn't even hammer a nail while he was watching. The look of disdain on his face, and the anticipation that he would erupt and either verbally or physically attack me, deterred me from ever trying to build anything at home. I therefore felt extremely proud of my creations.

Our living room, dining room, and kitchen were part of one big room that had very little furniture. My bedroom became too small to exercise in, and after my squat racks were completed, I moved all the weights and equipment to an empty corner of the living room. My mini gym was now complete, and Bob came over to lift with me.

"I can't believe that summer's almost over," he said. "School starts in just a few days."

"I can't wait to get back to Grand Avenue," I replied. "I really missed it when I was in Texas."

"I guess that it will be a chance for us to dazzle the girls with our muscles."

That night, after Bob left, I was listening to the radio and working out again in my little corner of the living room. The rest of the family was sitting and watching TV in a little room that we used as a den. Eli suddenly walked into the house. We never knew if or when he would decide to come home. He demanded dinner and Mom silently served him some food and went back to watching TV. I tried to ignore him. In the middle of his meal, he went into one of his rants. These had become a regular feature of my existence at home. His words overwhelmed and inundated me and sucked me down with the force of a tsunami.

"When you answer the phone, you sound like a girl. I can hardly understand what you are saying. If one of my friends call, it is embarrassing. I told them that my oldest kid is a son, not a daughter. You have the worst voice that I've ever heard. Do me a favor and don't answer the phone anymore. No matter what you do, you are worthless. A boy in kindergarten is stronger than you. My friends have sons that they can be proud of and I have one that I am ashamed of. Are those supposed to be squat racks? It looks like a monkey made them. I don't know how you can be so retarded when it comes to tools. If I let you use mine, you'd probably cut your hand off. And you eat like a girl. No wonder you're so skinny. When are you going to do something right? Look at your hair. I should get some scissors and cut it myself. I don't know what I did to deserve a son like you. I am so fucking ashamed of you. I can't even look at you. Or listen to your voice."

I kept on working out. I was not going to give him the satisfaction of leaving the room. He kept attacking, I ignored it, and put my energy into my bench presses. Finally, he finished eating. "I gotta get the fuck out of this house," he mumbled as he left. His words burrowed deep into my psyche. Each one like a dagger cutting away a piece of my self-confidence. As hard as I tried to build myself up, he had more power to bring me down. I was becoming stronger physically, but felt more and more helpless and broken. He hadn't tried to hit me in a while, but his venomous tirades hurt even worse. My physical bruises healed, but I couldn't seem to recover from the psychological ones.

Fifty-One

SEPTEMBER, 1965, I WAS IN 9th grade at Grand Avenue. The halls were full of friendly, familiar faces and I knew that I belonged. I recalled my feelings from my first days at school in Houston, and smiled at the difference. Several of my former 7th grade teachers saw me and welcomed me back. Mrs. Ritter actually came over and gave me a hug. Girls walked by and smiled at me. Boys slapped my hand. "How was Texas?" someone asked. I joked around, laughed and prayed that no one would be able to see the insecurity and feelings of worthlessness that were festering in my guts.

When we signed up for our classes over the summer, I decided to take Latin to fulfill my language requirement. I had developed a love for words and wanted to increase my vocabulary. I realized that many English words were derived from Latin roots. I spent time reading each night, made lists of new words and memorized their definitions. I read sections of the dictionary and studied the words and their etymologies. I looked up the definitions of any unfamiliar words that I heard on TV and added them to my list. I had started doing this when I looked up the meanings of *conundrum* and *cretin* after Mr. Harrison used them in Texas. I was also intrigued by the sound and the rhythm of words. I analyzed words in songs and poems. I kept a small pocket notebook with me and wrote down lines that came into my head during the day in hopes of using them in future poems.

Like battered leaves that cling to trees trying to survive a howling wind.

I wrote that after being verbally abused by my Mom.

And I complacently smile

I intended to make that the last line of a poem about my life.

Taking Latin was enhanced by the fact that our teacher was a twenty-four year old dark skinned, sexy woman with long black hair named, Miss Vela. She wore short miniskirts and tight sweaters that accentuated her breasts. Her face was beautiful and glowing, and her voice was gentle and soothing. She tried to act tough by referring to us by just our last names, but we were all in the class because we wanted to be and there were no discipline problems. She was a creative teacher and she knew how to make the content fun.

Gallia est omnis divisa in partes tres

All Gaul is divided into three parts. Those were the opening lines of *The Gallic Wars* by Julius Caesar, which we read in the original Latin. We also read *Julius Caesar* by Shakespeare in English that year. I was totally enjoying the academic part of school.

My ability to actively participate in a class by talking and answering questions, however, varied according to my level of self-esteem around a particular teacher. Mr. Proctor, my Science teacher, had an angry, bitter, derogatory demeanor and I felt choked off when I tried to speak in his class. I enjoyed the subject matter and earned grades in the high 90's on all the tests, but I could not find the courage to raise my hand to answer a question. In contrast, I especially felt comfortable in Mr. Meyer's class. He was a warm, cheerful, nurturing Social Studies teacher, and my hand was the first one up each time he asked for a response. Kathy, a very intelligent but shy girl, sat behind me. Kathy was overweight, had stringy, unkempt hair, and was afraid to look people in the eye.

"Stop raising your hand so much," she would whisper. "You're drawing his attention to me." Mr. Meyer sometimes would then notice her and ask, "Kathy, what do you think?"

Kathy would blush and stammer, and then kick the back of my chair when he wasn't looking. The look of approval that I received from Mr. Meyer was temporary redemption from the guilt of being alive that was instilled in me by my parents. This outweighed my empathy towards Kathy, and I continued to raise my hand.

I will break the wrists of hands that choke my throat and keep me in this Hell!

I wrote this down in Science class and shared it with Kathy in Social Studies. I explained to her how I felt around Mr. Proctor. She blushed and looked away.

I also signed up for Orchestra. Bob was in it, as well as some of my other friends. I felt like I had improved in 8th grade and was excited about demonstrating my progress to Mr. Vinson, whom I hadn't seen since the end of 7th grade. His first words to me were, "A ghost from the past has returned." We had individual tryouts so that he could assign us to different spots in the hierarchy of the orchestra. It was my turn to play for him. I was wearing my usual attire, a tight short sleeved knit shirt. As I held up my violin and bowed the strings, he tapped my proudly developed bicep with his baton.

"You are too strong to play the violin," he said.

"It doesn't affect my ability to play at all," I replied.

"You can't mix football and orchestra."

"The coach doesn't mind."

He let me be part of the orchestra but made me a second violin, even though we both knew that I was better than that. Nobody in this school gave me a hard time for playing the violin, except for him. My joy in playing motivated me to withstand his idiocy. I never expected that being in orchestra would become such a challenge. But, most of the other things happening to me didn't make much sense either.

Fifty-Two

ORCHESTRA WAS THE ONLY CLASS that Bob and I had in common. We ended up with the same lunch period and sat together each day. Bob had three friends from the blue collar, Gentile, old section of Bellmore who also sat with us. They were extremely immature and annoying, acting like we did in 7th grade. But if I wanted to sit with Bob, I had to be with them.

Theo Shultz had a long oval face and dirty blonde hair. He was very German looking with thin lips that were frozen in a perpetual smirk. He was my height and was naturally incredibly muscular even though he never exercised. Bob always complained that it was unfair that we worked so hard to develop our physiques while Theo did nothing. Theo was always restless and looked like he was moving even when he was still. I avoided sitting next to him because he would always be stealing my food or punching me in the arm.

Jann Zieback was well over 6 feet tall with a big head and a big white smile. He had curly brown hair that fell over his forehead and a thick neck. Jann worked out like we did, and had broad shoulders that were magnified by the huge woolen sweaters that he always wore. He was the only one of the three of them who read and had any intelligence. He had a cruel sense of humor and seemed sadistic to me.

Pat O'Conner was the dumbest of the group. He had vacant eyes, little ears that stuck out from the sides of his round head, and hunched over shoulders. He was always emitting a nervous, staccato, guttural laugh. He stared at you and tilted his head like a dog when you talked to him.

Wendy and Joanna, two extremely plain looking and unpopular girls from Bob's neighborhood, eventually began to sit with us. Theo, Jann and Pat mocked them and persisted in telling them to sit somewhere else. I just wanted to talk to Bob and watched all of their interactions totally dispassionately. Jann gave Joanna the nickname, Seahag, and soon that's what everyone called her.

"Why are you friends with these clowns?" I asked Bob.

"You have to get to know them," he said.

After a few weeks of the girls sitting with us and the Three Stooges harassing them, I was asked to write a song to scare them away. I refused. "But you are so good at writing shit like that," Theo said. "They deserve it. We have told them a million times to sit somewhere else."

"Then you do it," I said.

"You're the best at it. It'll be fun."

"I'll think about it."

When I got home, it occurred to me that I had been commissioned to write a song, just like The Beatles had been for several movies. I felt flattered, but didn't want to be too cruel. Seahag had two syllables and I tried to think of a melody that I could put words to. I looked up and saw my sister, Michele, and decided to use the song, *Michelle* by the Beatles. It took about five minutes to write something and then I rewrote it so that it wasn't as crude. I brought it to lunch the next day and everyone agreed to sing it to Seahag and Wendy.

Seahag's a drag
We all wish that she would disappear, to the stratosphere
Seahag, dishrag
Her clothes look like they came from a grab bag, so rag tag
Annoying and vexing and humdrum
She makes us feel so glum
If she would walk away with joy we'd be overcome
Why can't she see
We're begging on our knees, Set us all free, Let us be

We all sang it, everyone laughed, and I looked at the girls nervously expecting them to be upset. Instead, Seahag walked up to me, put her hand on my shoulder, smiled and said, "I can't believe that you wrote that for me. You must really like me. Thank you," and she kissed my cheek and they walked away.

"Holy shit! She's so dumb that she doesn't even know that we just hosed her," said Theo.

"No, you're so fucking dumb that you don't know that she hosed us," I replied.

I filed away in my head that I wanted to be able to react like that to the people who denigrate me.

Fifty-Three

MOST MORNINGS I WOKE UP gasping for my breath. I was stressed and agitated and even the air seemed to be rancid. When I left my room I was entering into a hostile environment. There was a great deal of screaming. I often yelled at Keith or Michele and told them to get away from me. Grandma would protect them by taking them into another room. Most of the fighting was between Mom and me.

"You make fun of the Dorfmans, you're not even worth the ground that they walk on!" she'd screech.

Whatever she said, I heard it as "You should have died instead of Sheryl!"

"I hate you!" I'd scream back. "You are a horrible mother!" We'd verbally attack each other until one of us left the room. Usually, I didn't even know what she was saying or what I was saying. We were both drowning in our own rage and trying to throw some at the other person.

Many nights Eli didn't come home, and when he did, he would often leave saying that he had to go make a long distance phone call at the corner 7/11. Nobody talked about it, but it was obvious that Eli was having an affair. He was becoming less and less of a physical presence in the house, and more of a toxic psychological one. I asked Grandma, "Why did Mom get back together with Eli?"

"She was hoping that he changed," she said.

"He's a monster! He'll never change."

"Your Mother doesn't want to be alone."

"He's having an affair."

"Your Mother wants to work it out. She wants to give him another chance."

"He is a monster and he's made our lives miserable."

"Your Mother needs a husband. She knows what she's doing."

I felt sick to my stomach. The undertow was becoming even stronger.

A few weeks later, my parents threw a party at the house. As if nothing bad was going on. Many of their old friends from Brooklyn were there, and I interacted with some of them before going to bed. There were more than twenty people there and it was noisy. I had trouble sleeping. Around midnight, I left my room to go to the bathroom, and heard my name being mentioned. Eli was talking about me to a group of men. I stood by the bathroom door and listened. He was bragging about me. He told them about how good my grades were at school and about what a good athlete I was. He told them that he had spent hours and hours playing ball with me. He told them that he had bought me weights and about how strong I had become. He showed them the squat racks that "he helped me build." I was so infuriated that I cried.

This asshole had never said a kind word to me, he continually verbally abused me, many times he had almost beaten me to death, he had disrupted my life over and over again, and now he was taking credit for what I had become. I had at times contemplated suicide because of him. He had absolutely nothing to do with anything good about me. I accomplished all these things on my own. I wanted to run out there and tell those people the truth. I wanted to expose him for the fraud that he was. Why wouldn't anyone acknowledge the fact that he had beaten me? Why are they believing all of his lies? Why couldn't someone see what was really going on in my house!? I couldn't stop sobbing. Hearing him talk like that hurt me more than his abuse. He was talking like the father that I always wanted. He was bragging like someone who was proud of me. Why couldn't he really be like that? It was all a fraud. A mockery. He pretended to have a happy family while he was cheating on his wife. Why didn't these people see him for what he really was? I hated him. And I wanted him to love me.

As I drifted off to sleep I cried. I cried because I was angry. I cried because I was sad. I cried because I was empty. I cried because I was alive. And I cried because I realized that no one was going to help me. I was on my own.

Fifty-Four

ALL OF THE STUDENTS AT our school, starting in 7th grade, were put into one of three academic tracks based on our test scores and teacher recommendations. I was in the advanced track. We had more homework, difficult tests, and a challenging curriculum, and we also had smaller classes and the best teachers. We didn't have classes with the other students except for gym and music or art.

The second track was called "intermediate" and was the regular curriculum. Many very intelligent students chose not to work as hard and took the intermediate classes which also were challenging. It was expected that everyone in advanced and intermediate would eventually go to college.

The third track was called "applied". These classes were filled with the worst students in the school and with the "Hoods". The Hoods smoked in the bathrooms and the boys had slicked back hair. They all seemed to be trying to look like James Dean, while the rest of us were trying to look like The Beatles. Tony D'Angelo, who sat near us during lunch with his greaser friends, looked like a 1950's version of Paul McCartney. Bob and I joked that we would be getting laid every night if we looked like that. We imagined that the Hoods were shagging each other all of the time, anyway. They were all at least a couple of years older than the rest of us, having failed so many times. Some of the girls were pretty, but they reeked of cigarettes and hairspray. As they did when I was in 7th grade, the hoodlum boys terrorized the younger, smaller and weaker boys, but usually left the normal 9th graders alone. Having made a group of them laugh when I was in 7th grade, I still had a reputation and they would point at me in the hall and say, "He's funny". I enjoyed the fact that I had their respect.

Alfie Gelfand was in all of my advanced classes, even though he was on the lower end of our hierarchy in terms of his intelligence. Alfie was grossly overweight, his huge belly hung over the top of his pants, had a face full of pimples, and his mouth was located to the left of his nose. He could never seem to keep his shirt tucked into his pants or to keep his shoelaces tied. It seemed like every hair on his head grew in a different direction, and he spoke with a nasally twang. Nevertheless, he was always smiling, and everyone loved him. I was usually feeling extremely insecure, and began observing the kids who exuded confidence in an attempt to figure out how to get some of my own. Some boys were very athletic or good looking, others emanated power and authority, some dressed impeccably and had perfectly coiffed hair, others were musically or artistically talented, and there were kids who were superbly articulate and outspoken. I couldn't figure out what Alfie had.

One day, I noticed it. Alfie was totally comfortable in his own skin. He accepted himself and was at ease with what he was. He was down to earth, cheerful and unpretentious. He looked everyone in the eyes and smiled. Alfie would give a stupid answer in class, laugh and the teacher would laugh. He was an average athlete, but the coaches would keep him on the team and slap him on the back and encourage him when he messed up.

In the shower after practice, we all noticed that Alfie had huge fat feminine breasts. If someone made fun of him, he would say, "Hey, I'm a 40 D-cup. I can feel myself up whenever I want. You want to cop a feel?"

He walked down the hall with the prettiest girls at his side, one under each arm. "Hey, Jeff, check out my harem!"

In English, the topic of virginity came up in one of the short stories we were discussing. "I don't want a virgin, I want the broken in model," Alfie quipped. No one else would have gotten away with saying that.

I wanted to escape from my situation and was beginning to form a vision for myself. I imagined the qualities that I wanted to have and how I wanted to look. To me, Alfie was the quintessence of poise and self-confidence. He became my role model.

"First you conceive it, then you achieve it" became my creed. I daydreamed about my future. I pictured myself growing up and being a good father, a good husband, and being a member of a loving family. I wanted to have enough self-confidence to be impervious to the Eli's of the world.

My vision wasn't coming to fruition in my sports career. I allowed most of my coaches to have the same effect on me as Eli did. When they criticized me, my body stopped working. I became awkward and clumsy. Eli's words became a self-fulfilling prophecy. This was the most frustrating occurrence of all. When I participated in sports away from school, I often heard, "Why don't you play like that in practice?" "Wow, Coach should see how good you are!" "Why are you trying to hide your skills?" Newbridge Park was the place where I was loose and unencumbered. After the school football season ended, we had a big pick-up game with members of the high school varsity team. I was chosen to be one of the running backs. Some of the varsity players outweighed me by over 100 pounds. When they tackled me, I had trouble getting back up. During the game, however, I had a group of huge older kids blocking for me. By running through the holes that they set, I was able to score several touchdowns. After the game was over, we were all talking and joking around and I said, "I've never run behind such enormous linemen before. It was like the parting of the Red Sea."

"That must make you Moses," someone laughed. The high school kids called me Moses whenever we played after that.

Ricky Kaufman set up a phone tree to call people to come and play games at the park after practice and on weekends. During Thanksgiving vacation we were having a cold snap and it had snowed. "Come down to the courts for some basketball and bring a snow shovel," the voice on the phone said. It was about 20 degrees and windy, but I didn't want to jeopardize my membership in the group, so I said that I would be there. About ten of us showed up, we cleared the snow off the clay surfaces, and played for over two hours in the biting wind that blew off of the ocean. The swirling salt air hitting our exposed skin stung us like needles. *Like battered leaves that cling to trees trying to survive a howling wind,* echoed in my head. It was impossible to play with gloves on, and after the games were done, my hands were frozen white, cut and bleeding.

"Good job, Moses," Ricky grinned at me. The camaraderie and approving looks quickly enabled me to forget about my aching hands and numb feet. When I went to the park, I was able to leave Eli home.

Fifty-Five

WE WERE ALL SITTING at lunch a week before Christmas vacation when Wendy and Joanna, AKA Seahag, approached.

"Would you all like to come to a Christmas party at my house?" asked Joanna.

"Fuck off," replied Theo.

"I'll go," I said. "Just tell me your address.

"Would you like to come Christmas caroling with us, too?"

"With my voice, if I go door to door singing, I'd probably get arrested," I said.

"They're skanks," snorted Theo. "Why would you want to go there?"

"Must be the same reason that I spend time with you."

Joanna's house was about 1/2 mile away from my house in the old section of Bellmore. She lived on Hughes Street, the street where the famous, radical comedian Lenny Bruce grew up. He was the most famous person to come out of our home town. I walked there by myself. It was an old, white, two story structure with a tiny yard.

"I am so glad that you came," Joanna said as she let me in. "We're all in the den."

There was food and music playing and a group of kids that I didn't know. Her parents and about ten other adults were listening to different music in another room. We were all talking when Joanna's older brother brought in a bottle of vodka and a pitcher of orange juice.

"You mix them together and you have a screwdriver." He filled a big glass with ¼ vodka and ¾ orange juice. "Who wants this?" I volunteered. I slowly swallowed it down and Joanna had the next one. I had never had hard liquor before. Eventually, most of the kids had a drink, also.

Soon, I was giggling and singing and unaware of any self-consciousness. The whole group was uninhibited and laughing. "Let's all tell the first dirty joke that we heard when we were little kids," someone said.

I thought of one first. "A couple just got married and they're on their honeymoon. The husband takes off his shirt. 'What happened to your back,' asked the wife.

'When I was a boy, I had bacteria,' said the man.

He then takes off his pants. 'What happened to your leg?' asked the wife.

'When I was a boy, I caught knee-monia,' he said.

Finally he takes off his underpants.

'Oh my God, what happened there?' she exclaims.

'When I was a boy, I had prickly heat!'

Everyone was in an uproar.

I walked over to Joanna, kissed her on the lips and said, "You're not so bad." We then went into a duet of *I've Got You Babe* by Sonny and Cher. Everyone was hysterical. I noticed that there was a window that opened up onto the roof.

"Let's go sing on the roof," I suggested.

"It's freezing outside."

I grabbed her hand and we climbed out. We sang Beatles songs into the night sky at the top of our lungs. I was pulsating with pleasure. People were shouting at us, and we sang louder.

"You're going to fall," yelled her brother.

"I'm not coming in until we finish our song," and we almost slid off from laughing so hard.

We eventually climbed back in, and sat next to each other on her couch to warm up. I put my arm around her, and delighted in the feeling of her body pressed against mine. I felt close and connected, but not in a sexual way. We sat and felt no need to talk. My mind was devoid of all thoughts and I was only aware of the sense of intimacy that I was experiencing. We sat and cuddled for almost 30 minutes. Around midnight her parents told us all to leave. I walked home still feeling content and glowing from the contact of our bodies. I realized as I approached my house that no one in my family had hugged me since Sheryl died. My eyes filled up with tears as I was overcome with a deep emptiness.

"You kissed Seahag!" Jann chortled at me during lunch after we returned to school.
 "Why, are you jealous?" I replied without looking up.
 "I'd rather kiss a dog," Theo laughed.
 "So that's why you all have dogs. I hope they're all female."
 "How can you make out with a skank like that?"
 "She's more girl than you guys will ever get. Hope you're happy with your dogs."
 I was proud of how quick witted I could be in banter with my friends, and disappointed with how choked off I was with Eli and his substitutes.

Fifty-Six

SOUTH BELLMORE AND SOUTH MERRICK were growing rapidly. Immense expensive new houses were being erected and rich professional men and their families were moving in. They had big, well groomed yards, and fancy, elite brand new vehicles parked on the wide driveways that lead up to their three car garages. I would often deviate from my run around the Park and jog through the different developing neighborhoods while gazing at the new structures springing up out of the former marshes.

I was especially curious about the new high school on South Bellmore Ave. It was a tremendous three story edifice with huge areas behind it that were in the process of being developed into a football stadium, tennis courts and other sports facilities. It was scheduled to be open in September and would house grades 10, 11 and 12. My class, the class of 1969, would start as sophomores, and we would be the first class to go all the way through it.

All the students in Bellmore and Merrick were now attending Mepham High School, which was located in North Bellmore. The Hoods, however, went to Calhoun High School, located in Merrick. Calhoun was a "Vocational" school. The new school would be for all the non- Hood students in South Bellmore and South Merrick.

It was announced that the new school would be named John F. Kennedy High School. I would have the privilege of going to a high school named after my favorite president.

I still was spending money on more weights, books, and records. Mom and Grandma were still unselfish when I asked for something, but it was obvious that they didn't have much and it would be beneficial to me if I could have some other source of income. It had snowed during Christmas vacation, and I grabbed our snow shovel and walked around the neighborhood looking for work. Most of the houses around my block had a cement sidewalk running parallel to the street, a path from the sidewalk to the front door, and a paved driveway stretching from the road to the garage. It took me about 30 minutes to clear everything when there was a few inches of snow. I soon discovered some residents who were willing to pay me to remove the snow, and usually received a dollar for my efforts.

We received a great deal of snow during a storm in February, and after finishing up in my neighborhood, I ventured over to the new, rich looking homes in South Bellmore. Most of those families informed me that they had professional snow removal services, generally trucks with plows, hired to do the work. A few people agreed to utilize my services, and I charged two dollars since the removal required about twice as much time as the other houses I had been doing. On a Saturday, after I had done over ten jobs, I rang the bell at a residence on Lee Place, near the new high school. It was an impressive structure that consisted of several wings, three stories, a three car garage and the widest driveway and front walk of any place that I had been. Everything there was still covered with snow. A tall well-dressed man in his twenty's told me that he would pay me five dollars, but only if I completely cleared all the walks and the driveway. "What a great way to end my day," I thought. I was earning money and having a great workout.

As I was shoveling, I discovered that the walks were made out of different types of stone, instead of cement. Under the snow, there was a thick covering of glare ice. I removed all of the snow, and began chipping away at the undercoating. I raised the shovel high in the air, and using all the power in my muscles, I thrust the edge of the blade into the gray layer of frozen precipitation with the force of a jackhammer. I spent over an hour attempting to make a dent in the slippery frost, but made little progress. It was late, dark and cold when I rang the bell. My hands and feet were aching from the frigid temperature and my cheeks were wind burned and raw.

"I told you that you would get paid only if you totally cleared my walks, "the man said.

"Well at least pay me for clearing all of the snow."

"A deal's a deal."

"I've been out here working as hard as I could for over two hours."

"Get everything cleared off and you will be paid."

I walked home feeling tired and dejected. This time, at least Grandma realized that I was late. I wondered if anyone would notice if I never came home. There were very few positive interactions occurring at my house. I was overwhelmed with a sense of helplessness.

Fifty-Seven

EVERY FIVE WEEKS AT SCHOOL we had a "grading day" and all the students were given two copies of our grade cards in homeroom. In each class we were assigned seatwork for the first part of the class. While we were all completing the assignments, one student at a time would walk up to the teacher's desk and wait while they filled out the cards with our five week averages and a teacher's comment. We were scolded if we shared our grades with anyone else during class. I loved this day because I knew that I had earned high marks, and I usually received a smile from the teacher. I always acted very intense and worried about my grade and frowned after I received it, not wanting to let anyone know that I had done well. However, my high grades were no secret. In math class the grade was totally based on objective tests and I generally earned a 98, 99 or 100 average. In January, I knew that I had achieved a 100 average. I was walking away from the teacher's desk when Alfie asked in a stage whisper, "Did you pass?" Everyone, including the teacher, burst out laughing. I slapped Alfie's hand and again realized how much I admired him.

As in past years, English was the class where I had the opportunity to be the most creative. We had just finished reading a famous short story called, *The Lady or the Tiger*. The story took place in an ancient land ruled by a powerful king. When a person was accused of a crime, he was placed in a big arena that contained hordes of spectators sitting in the stands. The accused was forced to make a choice between two doors. One had a beautiful woman behind it, and the other had a hungry tiger. No one knew which one was where. If the accused chose the lady, he would be set free but be forced to marry her and spend the rest of his life with her. If he chose the tiger, he would be immediately pounced on and torn limb from limb. In the story, the king's daughter, a stunningly alluring, attractive princess, fell in love with a commoner. The king found out about their secret relationship, and sentenced the lover to the arena. The princess discovered what was behind each door, and signaled to her lover to choose the door on the right. The princess was conflicted about what to do, and the story ends mysteriously with the narrator saying, "I leave it with all of you. Which came out of the opened door-the lady or the tiger?"

Our assignment was to write a suitable ending to the story, and the best entries were to be entered into a contest with 9th grade students from other schools. I began my narrative with the princess crying and the king staring at her. For the next three pages, I focused on the torment felt by the princess and her conflicted thoughts. She was agonizing over her decision. She couldn't bear to see her lover married to another woman, but didn't want him killed either. She was angry at her father for putting them into this predicament. She weighs the pros and cons of directing her lover to one door or the other. I end it with the crowd screaming and the princess standing up. She wipes the tears from her eyes, turns her back on the king, and quickly walks away. "The princess will have to live the rest of her life thinking about her harrowing decision." I never reveal what happened.

I earned third place in the contest and my story was displayed at Hofstra University. School had definitely become my sanctuary.

Even though I was not capable of getting past my insecurities during sport teams practices, I was able to excel during gym class. In February, we all were required to perform on the climbing ropes that hung at least thirty feet from the ceiling. The gym teachers screamed at and humiliated boys who could not climb to the top. Most people climbed up by using both their arms and legs. Some were too heavy or weak to even pull themselves off the ground. All the weightlifting that Bob and I had completed enabled me to quickly climb to the top using only my arms. I was strong enough to hold my legs out at a 90 degree angle and parallel to the floor as I swiftly ascended to the top. I also showed off by holding a rope in each hand and climbing two at once. I enjoyed having everyone watch me as I displayed my strength.

We were also participating in a wrestling unit. I was easily capable of defeating anyone in my weight class, except for the boys who were on the school team and who knew all kinds of holds and moves. I did give them a good fight, however. One of the gym teachers, Mr. Johnson, was also the wrestling coach and he asked me to come out for the team. "I enjoy basketball too much," I said, but I was flattered that he wanted me.

My sense of well-being and contentment was torn away when I returned to our house. Eli still didn't come home many nights, and Mom was very angry. She was teaching and tutoring after school, and acted stressed and weary. Our screaming matches became a daily occurrence. When Eli did come home, his abusive language bludgeoned me as I limped into my room and slammed the door. I turned up my stereo, but could still hear the cacophony of his relentless, booming attacks. I took out a pad and pencil and cathartically composed a poem:

Reprieve

Like
A brilliant bowel movement
After
An eternity
Of critical constipation

Caught in the Undertow

The Relief
I Feel
When
You
Finally
SHUT YOUR MOUTH

Fifty-Eight

THE FULL ORCHESTRA REHEARSED three days a week, and the other two days we each had private lessons. On the lesson days, we were individually sent to one of several small, sound proof music rooms to practice until it was our turn to work with Mr. Vinson. On several occasions Mr. Vinson neglected to come to my room. I observed that when he was finished with everyone else he still would not join me. When he did, he was very disparaging and discouraging. I was still a second violin even though it was obvious to the rest of the orchestra that I had the talent and ability to be a first violin.

"What's his problem with me?" I asked Bob.

"He just doesn't like you," Bob replied.

"He keeps commenting on my muscles. You have big muscles, too," I observed.

"Maybe it's because your biceps are bigger than mine," laughed Bob. "I wouldn't worry about it. You have more people who like you than he does."

When we played our instruments, we put our sheet music on stands. On top was a rectangular flat piece of black metal with a small ledge on the bottom to hold the sheet music. This slid up and down a black pole which was attached to a metal base that consisted of three metal wings. The top was moved up or down to accommodate the height of the person playing and whether they were sitting or standing. The stands were heavy, old, and wobbly.

"My stand is stuck. Would you fix it for me, Muscles?" asked Ilene, a viola player. I was called "Muscles" by many of the orchestra members because that was my horribly salient feature, according to Mr. Vinson.

"Mr. Muscles to you," I replied. I turned around and grabbed the top of her stand which was stuck in the lowest position. It wouldn't budge.

"Come on, you're stronger than that!" she teased.

I put both of my feet on the base, grabbed the top with both hands, bent my knees, and yanked. The heavy metal top came flying off the pole and the sharp top edge hit me square in my forehead. Suddenly, blood was gushing everywhere. It splattered all over Ilene's dress and her viola. I pressed my handkerchief against the cut and it was soaked through in seconds. Bob walked me down to the nurse, and I was taken to the hospital. I received fifteen stitches and was told that I couldn't participate in sports or gym for ten days. That hurt more than the gash on my head.

I returned to school the next day with a tremendous bandage across my forehead and having to face the humiliating fact that my injury was sustained in orchestra. My hope that people wouldn't know how it happened was shattered when the first kid who saw me said, "Wow, how can you get injured by a music stand!?"

I decided to act like Alfie. "You have no idea how vicious those thing are," I replied.

"I hear that you were attacked by a music stand," smirked my homeroom teacher.

"They're ferocious when no one feeds them. Fortunately my attacker will be put to sleep."

"I didn't know that orchestra was a contact sport," laughed another teacher.

"Yeah, well, that's why I have to do so much weightlifting."

All day long I received the taunts, and I responded by making fun of myself or the situation. The other people laughed with me instead of at me. I felt respected instead of insulted. If only I could do this with Eli and his surrogates.

Fifty-Nine

ON THE FIRST FRIDAY EVENING in June, Grand Avenue Jr. High School scheduled a Moving-Up Day Ceremony to honor the 9th graders who were about to graduate. I walked over to Bob's house and rode to the school with his parents. The boys were required to wear a white shirt, a dark tie and black dress pants. I found a tight, short sleeved dress shirt to wear that showed off my muscles. Mrs. Petrocelli commented on how nice Bob and I looked. I didn't wear ties often, and Bob had to help me put it on.

The program included academic awards, speakers, and performances by the orchestra. I was a member of the Junior Honor Society, and our assignment was to direct the parents and other guests to their seats. As ushers, we also handed out a booklet called, *Grand Horizons, 1965-1966*. The cover consisted of the title, and artwork by one of the students. Inside there was the schedule of events for the evening, brief biographies about all of the teachers based on interviews done by members of the school newspaper, and statements from each of the more than three hundred 9th graders about their interests and plans for the future. Bob's statement said, *Bob played in the orchestra. He collects coins and hopes to major in science.* Mine said, *Jeff enjoys sports and music. He hopes to major in English and law.*

I loved interacting with the parents and helping them find their seats. Several people congratulated me for my academic successes and gave me other compliments.

"My daughter Judy takes Latin with you and she says that

you are the star of the class. Boy, Latin is really going to help you all do well on the SAT's."

"You must be lifting weights. How much can you bench press?"

"I hear that you've earned a 100 average in math a few times. Good work!"

"You are really friendly. Thanks for your help."

It felt liberating connecting with adults in a positive manner and I was feeling at ease and self-confident. Everyone was smiling and warm. There were hundreds of adults swarming around the lobby by the auditorium and they were overflowing with benevolent energy. I turned to see the smiling stares from Mom and Grandma and walked towards them. I then realized that they were standing with Eli.

"Look at that shirt. How can you dress like that?" were his first words. I self-consciously turned and walked up to some other parents. The sound of his voice felt like a cannon ball hitting me in my stomach.

The orchestra sat up on the stage as the ceremony began. As we set up our instruments and sheet music, Ilene laughed and told me to be careful with the music stands. I told her that maybe I should wear my football helmet in orchestra, also. We played the *"Ceremonial March"* as the other 9th graders walked in. Then we listened to several speeches, and academic awards were given out. I received awards in Latin and English.

After the recognitions for achievement, the full orchestra performed. We played *Song of Brotherhood*, by Beethoven, and excerpts from the Rogers and Hammerstein musical, *The Sound of Music*. The sound of all the diverse instruments contributing harmoniously had a visceral, powerful effect on me and I felt pure joy as I played my part. My whole body seemed to resonate with the music. I pictured Mom and Grandma crying as they were enveloped in the sounds. I envisioned us all ascending to a happier existence. A myriad of colors radiated from the musical instruments and sparkled before my eyes. It felt as if time had stopped. As our last song ended, I was elated, but then experienced an emptiness and a sense of loss.

Jeffrey Goldstein

Mom and Grandma found me at the end of the evening and gushed as they spoke about the concert. As I let their blissful feelings rub off on me, I noticed Eli was walking over, and refused to let him inject any negativity into the evening. I turned away, found Bob, and rode to his house. We felt intoxicated after having performed some beautiful music, and soon improved our moods even more as we talked and absorbed the sounds from his stereo.

Sixty

By the end of 9th grade my record collection had increased to more than twenty albums and many more singles. Most of the money that I made shoveling snow, and then mowing lawns in the spring, went towards buying the vinyl. Listening to music was an enjoyable escape for me, either the radio was on or records were playing whenever I was working out or reading. I played songs for my brother Keith, who was now 9 years old, and told him information about the various groups and musicians whom I liked. I compiled music tapes which combined songs from the radio, from my records, or from albums which I borrowed. I tried to be creative by having the songs flow from one to the next. One tune would begin with the same chord or note that the previous song ended on, and I grouped songs together that were performed in the same key or with the same rhythm. One day as I was recording, Eli banged on my door and shouted, "Turn the fucking music down, idiot!" This recording became immortalized as the "fucking music" tape because you could hear his voice in the background as The Stones sang, *Satisfaction*.

In June, the school guidance counselors told us 9th graders that local homeowners were willing to pay students to perform various chores for them. I immediately jumped at this opportunity to earn extra money to purchase more records and more weights. The guidance office posted lists of the jobs available, and we signed up for the ones that we felt qualified to do. After each task, the homeowner would tell the school how we did, and if we received a favorable recommendation, we'd be eligible for more work. The first two weekends I was given assignments that were within biking distance of my house. I washed windows for one family, weeded a big garden for another, and moved heavy furniture and vacuumed at another home. The school received positive feedback about me, and I continued working and earning money into the summer.

After a few weeks, the families who requested work were all in North Merrick and too far away for me get to by bike. I needed a ride. Mom reluctantly drove me, but yelled and complained the whole way to the job and all the way back. "I work two jobs every day during the week so that you can eat and I don't have the energy to be driving you all over Long Island on my days off! You are so selfish!" She had the ability to keep this up as long as we were in the car. I wanted the money, so I was willing to put up with this and stared out the window while she screamed. Sometimes she could be just as angry and abusive as Eli.

One Saturday a man hired me to mow his lawn. The house was twenty minutes away, which meant twenty minutes of being screamed at. I surveyed the yard and told Mom to come back in two hours. The man of the house then informed me that I had to use his hand mower. I told him that his grass would look a lot nicer if I could use his power mower. He told me no, gave me a rake to use when I was done mowing, and went back into the house. The grass was a few inches high, and I struggled to cut it with the old mower with its dull blades. After two hours, when Mom came back, I was barely half way done. She yelled that she was not going to drive all the way home and back, and parked and waited. It took over four hours to finish. This time I decided that the enraged shrieking that I had to endure was not worth the money that I earned. I didn't ask her for a ride again.

The next weekend I was assigned a job at a house that was a twenty minute bike ride away. When I arrived, I was taken through the house to a raised wooden deck that was attached to the kitchen. There were a few cans of wood stain and a brush, and my task was to coat the top of the deck. It took over two hours to finish. The owner looked at the deck and asked me if I put a drop cloth underneath it. "No, you never told me to do that," I replied. We went outside to the yard, and he showed me that there was a marble patio on the ground below the deck and that stain had fallen through the spaces between the boards onto the marble stones.

"You're not getting paid until you clean this all off!" he demanded. It took me another two hours to clean it all off. This was my last job of the summer. I had worked hard, probably wasn't paid a fair wage, had to endure being yelled at, but I now had enough money to buy a guitar.

Sixty-One

On July 1, 1966, I turned fifteen. I combined the money that I had earned and the birthday cash from Mom, and we went shopping for my first guitar. I had played a guitar with Richard when Michele was born, and at various friends' houses. I knew some basic chords and how to read music from playing the violin. Mom took me to a music store in Freeport, and I strummed several acoustic ones that were in our price range. I picked up a tan one with nylon strings. My hand fit perfectly around the neck. I played all the chords that I knew and plucked out the notes to a few Beatles melodies. It felt perfect, like holding a new born baby. The sound and the tone were beautifully melodic. This was what I was looking for. We purchased some picks, a *Guitar Lessons for Beginners* book, a set of pitch pipes to use for tuning the strings, and still had some money left over. I had decided that I was not going to be in orchestra anymore when I started high school, so this was going to be my new method of achieving musical catharsis.

At the end of July we moved back to our old house on Navy Place. I was back in my former bedroom, the place where I was when Sheryl died. I was in the same room, lying on the same bed where Mom had ripped my heart out. I was next to the same wall but Sheryl was no longer on the other side. I looked at the same dresser that Eli threw me against resulting in my injury that required stitches. Repressed memories stormed into my head and it seemed like all the weights that I owned were piled up on my chest. I began to hyperventilate. I could hear

Eli and Mom yelling at each other. I spent the next few hours playing my guitar.

I had a tremendous amount of trouble falling asleep that summer. I heard Sheryl knocking on the wall. Mom's voice yelling, "You should have died instead of her!" reverberated in my head. I visualized Sheryl coming back to trade places with me. I felt guilty for being alive. I shook with fear, depression and a sense of worthlessness.

Many mornings I felt like I couldn't get out of bed. I wanted to die. After a while, it would occur to me that I didn't want to be this unhappy. I forced myself to think of the good things that I could do. I wanted to play sports, exercise, listen to music, make music, and see my friends. I would put on a record, force myself to smile and dance around the room. I took my transistor radio with me to the kitchen and moved my body to the beat as I ate breakfast. The negative emotions swirling inside of me often had the upper hand. Getting past the pain was a constant struggle. But it felt so good when I did.

I will break the wrists of hands that choke my neck and keep me in this Hell!

Sixty-Two

In September I entered the newly built John F. Kennedy High School as a sophomore. There were more than 800 students in my grade, the class of 1969. The school combined kids from three separate junior highs, so there were hundreds of pupils who were attending the same school for the first time. The building was immense. It contained three separate gymnasiums, a huge auditorium, a shooting room for a rifle team, a Driver's Education room with driving simulators, and three stories of classrooms. We were tracked academically in our courses again and I was in what was now called the "enrichment" level. Generally all of our classes were in the same area of the school.

Several of the good teachers from the junior high schools came up to teach at JFK. Coach Millhouse, the gym teacher and football coach at Grand Avenue, was now at the high school. We were a new school and needed to choose a nickname for the sports teams. The students were to vote for one of the two final choices: *The Kennedy Cougars,* or *The Kennedy Kingsmen.* People campaigned for their favorite. Coach Millhouse, who was very well respected, declared that he would go to another school if *The Kingsmen* won. We became *The Cougars.*

At the beginning of each school day, we all reported to homeroom. We sat alphabetically, and I discovered that there were four boys in my grade who had the last name of Goldstein. We found out that none of us were related in any way. Sitting next to me each day was Marcie Goodman. She was from a wealthy family and lived in one of the new homes in South Merrick.

Marcie's reputation had preceded her. In a school full of beautiful girls, she stood out as the sexiest and most desirable one. All the boys talked about her.

Marcie was a cheerleader and a gymnast. She would wear a new short skirt every day and tantalize us all with her smooth, moisturized legs. The scent of her long, flowing blonde hair filled the air as she glided by when she walked. Her eyes were bright blue and she would look at you with an alluring, disinterested, condescending gaze. Everything about her emanated, "I am special!" In class every boy always had at least one eye on Marcie. I was lucky enough to sit next to her in English as well as in homeroom each day.

One day in homeroom Marcie deigned to talk to me. "You really have a 'V' shape going, don't you?"

"If I work hard enough, maybe I can achieve a 'W' shape," I replied using my best Groucho Marx voice.

"Do you wrestle?" she laughed.

"No, I like basketball, but I'd be happy to wrestle with you," I quipped, knowing that I'd probably faint if I touched her.

"Ha, in your dreams," she retorted.

When I went home that night, I referred to my list of words and phrases and scribbled down a poem about the legendary Marcie and the ritual of her entry into a classroom.

> *She struts*
> *Swaggers*
> *To a ceremonious flourish of trumpets*
> *Sumptuous conspicuous thighs*
> *Devoured*
> *By the assemblage*
> *Of hungry, pubescent boys*
> *The pageantry of her presence*
> *Transcending*
> *The shackles of the classroom*

I thought about Joanna, who was now attending a Catholic school, and the mean poem that I had written about her. I remembered our bodies pressing against each other at her party, and her warmth wrapped around me as a pleasant memory.

Bob and I weren't in any of the same classes or lunch period. I now sat in the cafeteria with a group of boys whom I met playing sports. Shawn, Marshall, Levi, and Dave all had gone to Merrick Avenue Jr. High. They told me about their version of Newbridge Park called Merrick Park, and sometimes on weekends I rode my bike there to play ball. Most of the time I heard the same familiar refrain from them also. "Oh my God, why don't you play like that in front of the coaches?" I felt infuriated with Eli each time that was said, but I still wasn't capable of overcoming the power of his voice in my head.

One Sunday in September after an invigorating series of basketball games I asked the boys to tell me where exactly in Merrick they lived. They told me that they lived in the expensive houses in South Merrick.

"Isn't that near where Marcie lives?" I inquired.

"Yup, that's why we all have constant boners," Marshall replied.

"Remind me to never let you pee at my house," I said. "You'll get the wall all wet."

Each of us then took turns describing what we would like to do with Marcie sexually.

"When Marcie walks into a room, every boy gets a hard on," joked Dave. "What power she has. I wonder what that must be like."

"You wonder what it would be like to give a room full of boys an erection," I retorted. "I'm worried about you."

He punched me in the arm.

"You know, Marcie told me that she likes my "V" shape," I volunteered.

"Holy crap, she likes you!" exclaimed Shawn. "You should ask her out. We can all have vicarious pleasure through you."

"Mrs. Lang would like your use of 'vicarious'," I said. "But I have about as much chance of going out with Marcie as you do with Marilyn Monroe."

"Marilyn Monroe is dead."

"Exactly my point."

"Do you think that Marcie knows how much we all talk about her?" Marshall asked.

We all shrugged.

I enjoyed being accepted by this group from the wealthy section of the school district. They reminded me of Bruce and Barry from Texas, and I wondered if they realized how different my world was from theirs.

Jeffrey, age 15

Sixty-Three

ELI HAD BEGUN TO STAY away for several days at a time again. We never knew if he'd come home, and at one point we hadn't seen him in over a month. Mom called his parents in Brooklyn, and like they did when Eli abandoned us in Texas, they denied knowing anything about the situation. By November, Mom had tracked Eli down. He was living in Brooklyn with his girlfriend Anna and her two children. He apparently had been with her when he left us in Texas.

"So, he moves us all to Texas, leaves us there, and then goes to live with another woman," I yelled at Grandma. "Do you think that he's the father of those kids?"

"Who knows," she replied. "He should *gai in drerd arein!* Go rot in hell! He's *nisht gut,* no good!"

Mom proceeded to hire a lawyer and sued Eli for child support. He refused to pay. The lawyer said that there was very little that could be done to make him contribute any money. Mom eventually had to fly to Mexico by herself to get a divorce. Grandma worried the whole time that Mom was away. She looked like she was aging right before my eyes. Mom finally came home with tears, sadness and anger streaming from her eyes. A broken woman.

Eli would never come home again. Mom was now officially the sole breadwinner in the family. She had no husband. We had no father. Our family, as dysfunctional as it was, was now also incomplete. There was no more Eli.

At first, I was numb. His physical presence in the house had been diminishing, but he was always in my head, and there was always the possibility that he would walk through the door. Now, he never would. It didn't seem real. I couldn't even begin to process all of my emotions. I was agitated, distressed, and afraid. Eli was gone and all that remained were his hands around my throat and his angry voice in my head.

My relationship with Mom took a turn for the worse. She yelled at me with venomous words that flew from her mouth with the power of a gale force wind. She spewed out curses and insults. When I saw the look on her face and heard the tone of her voice, all I heard was, "I wish you were dead! You should have died instead of Sheryl! I hate you! You should be dead!" When I yelled back, Grandma would clutch her chest and shout, "You're giving me a heart attack. Stop yelling at your Mother!" I had no allies. No one to protect me.

One night before Thanksgiving I felt like I was the one having a heart attack. I woke up around 2AM with incredible pain in my chest. I was dripping with sweat and couldn't catch my breath. I was engulfed in an intense, terrifying sense of utter distress. I was positive that I was dying. I staggered around the living room trying to get enough air. The pain and my horror both escalated. I kept walking in circles around the room, gasping for air. Finally, I began to feel calmer and after about an hour, I went back to bed. No one had noticed what had happened, and I told myself that it was just a bad dream. I put the incident out of my mind.

Sixty-Four

BILL PETERSON LIVED DOWN the block from me on Navy Place. His father's name was Seymour, and everyone called him Sy for short. When we had first moved to Bellmore, and Eli would take me for a walk down the block, we'd sometimes pass Sy working in his yard. Eli invariably would sigh real loud and say, "Hey Sy, I'm saying your name. Listen, that's your name." Sy would glare back and Eli would continue to sigh. Sy became one of the many neighbors who hated Eli.

Bill didn't like to play any sports but we shared an interest in music. When one of us purchased a new album, we often went to each other's house to share it with each other and analyze the lyrics. Everything, according to Bill, was about sex. He could take any song and creatively explain the alleged sexual innuendos. When we were in 6th grade, he persuaded a group of ten of us boys to compare our penises in his backyard. He then wanted us all to walk down the block while exposing ourselves. We told him that if he did it first, we would follow him. It never happened.

After we entered high school, Bill regaled us with stories about all the girls he was "doing it" with. His tales included vivid details about sexual acts and female anatomy. He was always sitting with a girl on the bus or walking down the hall at school holding hands with a girl. We looked forward to and believed his stories. I wanted to do what he was doing. He grilled me about my experiences, which had only included making out and feeling breasts.

"All the girls think that you're funny and cute," he said. "I'm gonna help you get some."

Bill also was the first person that I knew who was "turning on" or smoking pot. "Grass" had become a major topic of discussion. The Beatles, Bob Dylan and The Stones had all admitted to using drugs, and older kids were supposedly smoking at their parties. "Girls want to have sex when they're high," Bill said.

Before Christmas, Bill found me at school. "I'm gonna take care of you," he promised. "Come with me to a party in Merrick. I'll get you high, and a girl named Shelly will be there. She's a nympho. She'll do it with anyone. You're sure to get laid. You just better know what you're doing 'cause she's hard to satisfy."

Bill gave me a crash course on how to pleasure a woman, and how to smoke pot. On Saturday night, we began our walk to South Merrick. "I'll put in a good word about you to Shelly. I won't be jealous if you bang her. I've already been there."

We arrived at one of the huge, expensive new homes in South Merrick. We went into a dark room in the basement. There were about thirty kids, the music was pulsating and there were strobe lights. I was hit in the face by the smell of incense and marijuana smoke. Soon, a group of us were sitting in a circle passing around a joint. I inhaled as much smoke as I could and held my breath for as long as I could, as per Bill's tutorial. I felt slightly light headed, but not much more. I was disappointed that I wasn't high. A buxom, pretty, brown haired girl smiled at me and then walked over.

She spoke with a sultry sexy voice. The words came out very quickly. "Hi, I'm Shelly. You must be Jeff. Bill told me about you. I've seen you at school. You're cute. It's pretty stuffy in here. Let's go for a walk."

Before I could even process what she had said, Shelly took my hand, and led me to the backyard. I hadn't even said a word yet. Before I knew it, we were making out. She gently pulled me down to the ground and we kissed while lying next to each other. I felt her big firm breasts. I rubbed her thighs. I inhaled her perfumed smell.

"You're a good kisser," she purred, and then she lifted up her dress. "I never wear any panties, just in case a guy's too shy to make a move," and she stuck her tongue in my mouth. I looked down and saw the female genitalia for the first time. I realized that I didn't really know what to do. I panicked. I pulled away.

"I need to get back inside," I said as I hurriedly ran to the house. I couldn't believe that I passed up this opportunity. I felt like an idiot. I didn't want to face Bill.

Later, I found Shelly. She was alone. "Please let me walk you home," I pleaded. She consented. We held hands, and when we got to her door, I started kissing her. While I had my arms around her, Shelly began rubbing my crotch. As soon as I was totally erect, she angrily pushed me away, went into her house, and laughed, "Now you know how I feel." As I stood there bewildered, I heard her door slam and the sound of the lock turning. It was a very long walk home.

Sixty-Five

CHRISTMAS VACATION HAD STARTED. It was eight o'clock in the evening. I was sitting on the floor of my bedroom, leaning against the side of my bed in a cross legged position, reading an engrossing detective novel and listening to one of my music tapes. Keith and Michele were downstairs watching TV. I was vaguely aware of Mom and Grandma. They were talking loudly in the kitchen, and gradually their voices escalated to the point where they were screaming. The emotional level of their bickering reached a tipping point and I was unable to concentrate on my book. I turned up the songs, but the tumult of the yelling hijacked my awareness.

My insides churned with fear and apprehension. I was transported back to the days after Sheryl died. I was falling deeper and deeper into a bottomless void and my brain throbbed with unending anguish. I felt helpless. I was in a black world with no parameters, no hope, and I felt vaguely responsible. My family was coming apart at the seams and I was driven by the urge to protect them. I pictured Sheryl's face and she was crying. I wanted to run out of the house, but the upheaval in my guts grabbed me and pulled me towards the hornet's nest.

I checked on Keith and Michele. They were expressionless and transfixed by the TV, ostensibly oblivious to the bedlam in the kitchen. I prepared myself for battle and entered into the war zone. The only word that I could discern from the explosions of their caterwauling was, "Eli!" "Eli this, Eli that, El this, Eli that!"

"Stop your screaming," I demanded. "You are driving me crazy!"

Mom turned all of her weapons on me. What I heard was, "YOU SHOULD HAVE DIED! YOU HAVE NO RIGHT TO BE ALIVE! YOU ARE EVIL!" My whole body convulsed with a series of emotions that all blended together indistinguishably. Then I heard her say, "YOU ARE NO BETTER THAN YOUR FATHER!"

I was paralyzed. He represented pure evil to me. I felt his hands around my throat and wanted to grab a kitchen knife and plunge it into my chest. I stood there frozen until something deep inside of me gave me the strength to fight back, "You are a bitch. I fucking hate you! Just shut your goddamn mouth! Shut it! I can't stand listening to you anymore!"

"Stop yelling at your mother like that! You're going to kill me!"

With my head spinning, we attacked each other until I had no more energy, and I went upstairs and collapsed on my bed.

I woke up from a deep sleep around 3AM. Again, I had an excruciating pain in my chest, I couldn't catch my breath and was soaked with sweat. My whole body shook as I paced around the living room attempting to catch my breath. I had no doubt that I was dying an unbelievably painful death. This time Grandma heard me. I eventually went back to bed and fell asleep.

In the morning, Mom came into my room acting scared and concerned, and ended up driving me to Dr. Gittlestein's office. Dr. Gittlestein was a chain smoker. There was a big glass ashtray in each room that was overflowing with cigarette butts. He always had a Marlboro in his mouth when he examined you. "At least I know what I am going to die of," he would laugh as he turned his head to the side to exhale the toxic fumes. I had no respect for him, but he was Mom's choice for the family physician. I described my symptoms to him, and he did a thorough fifteen minute examination.

"Are you taking any drugs?" he asked as he expelled smoke through his nose.

I felt insulted. "No," I replied. "I exercise every day and eat healthy foods."

"Well, I can't find anything wrong with you." He had the nurse come in to draw some blood. I heard him tell Mom that many teenagers these days do illegal drugs and that she should keep an eye on me. I thought about how he was killing himself with a legal drug. He had absolutely no credibility with me. Mom and I didn't talk on the way home. I still had no answers and was extremely worried about my future.

During the vacation, Mom was home all day and Eli's desertion hung over the family like a black cloud. I snapped at anyone who dared to come near me, including Keith and Michele. I was anchored in a malaise and felt too depressed to get out of bed. Several times, however, I found myself leaping out of bed and pacing the living room trying to breathe. The living room was the biggest area of the house and I felt the least claustrophobic there. Each time that this happened, I was certain that I was about to die. Finally, Mom took me to a Diagnostic Clinic on Sunrise Highway and I had a six hour long visit. They had state of the art machines, and I underwent every test available. A kind, young doctor, who didn't smoke cigarettes, interviewed me.

"Have you ever had hypertension?" he asked.

"I have a lot of tension," I replied.

"No, hypertension is high blood pressure."

"No, I've always had good blood pressure."

He asked questions about my past and my family during the breaks between the physical exams. I told him everything about Sheryl, Eli, Mom and what my life had been like. At the end of the day he offered to talk to me alone. The two of us went into a consulting room.

"You are in excellent physical shape," he said. "You obviously are very active and fit. You have nothing to worry about in terms of any physical illnesses. You have been experiencing what are known as 'Panic Attacks'. Panic attacks cause severe physical symptoms and they are extremely frightening. They often occur while people are sound asleep. In your case, there is no physical cause and I believe that your symptoms are brought about by stress and anxiety. You have been had some horrible experiences and that is why you are having this reaction."

"What can I do?"

"You need to deal with this psychologically. I am going to refer you to a psychiatrist. He is also a physician and he can prescribe you medicine to help with your anxiety and other symptoms."

"Am I mentally ill?"

"No, I think that you are a normal, intelligent young man who needs help dealing with an incredibly stressful situation. Dr. Birnbaum can help you control all the anxiety that you've been feeling."

"Will my panic attacks stop?"

"If you work at it, there's a good possibility that they will stop, or at least occur less often."

Mom had spent the day in the waiting room. He called her in and explained my diagnosis. He also recommended that we all go to family counseling.

On the way home I finally felt some optimism. There was a reason why I was having these horrible experiences and I was going to see someone who could help me. Mom agreed to set up an appointment with Dr. Birnbaum.

Sixty-Sixty

"THERE'S GOING TO BE A huge football game at the Park on Sunday afternoon," said Ricky on the phone. "There'll be kids from Merrick and all over. Be there at one."

During breaks in the game, I spent time talking to Sam Mowatt. I had just met Sam this year in gym class, and we enjoyed being around each other. We shared a passion for sports and music, and Sam had a dry, entertaining sense of humor. He referred to himself as, "The Mo," and would greet you by saying, "The Mo says hello." When we were playing basketball, if I jumped higher than he did for a rebound, I'd hear, "The Mo is below." After losing a game he'd look sad and say, "The Mo's feeling woe." The Mo had a big round face, with straight brown hair, and a big wide body. "I'm 5'10" tall and 210 pounds, the same size as Harmon Killebrew," he would tell anyone who would listen. Harmon Killebrew was a great homerun hitter for the Minnesota Twins and Mo's favorite player.

Mo was very intelligent but he disliked school and earned mediocre grades. He was well read and highly knowledgeable concerning politics and current events, and was a great conversationalist. During our timeouts from the football game, Mo spouted off facts and statistics about the Vietnam War. At the end of the afternoon, he introduced me to two of his brothers who had also participated in the game.

Robbie Mowatt was two years older and a senior and he had driven to the Park. Robbie was about four inches shorter than Sam, and had a very slight build. Craig Mowatt was one year younger than Sam, well over six feet tall, and muscular but thin. I was amazed by the difference in their appearances. I accepted Robbie's invitation to come to their house. Robbie had an old, run down, indeterminate model car with a filthy exterior. I noticed a metal hanger protruding from where the antenna should be. It was shaped to resemble a hand with the middle finger extended. Robbie noticed me looking at it.

"It represents my attitude towards the world," he explained.

"Or maybe it's the world's attitude towards your car," I said. "Is it safe?"

"Sure, if I can get it started, we can go anywhere."

I got in and sat in the back. The seat had springs and foam rubber sticking out and there was a hole in the floor covered with old *Newsweek* magazines. Craig got in on the other side and sank into his area of the rear seat. Sam slammed the door on the passenger side of the front and declared, "The Mo says it's time to go." It took over five minutes for Robbie to get the car started, and then we sputtered away. He turned up the radio.

"Seems like your obscene antenna works," I said.

"Enjoy your trip in our auto Mo bile"

The Mowatts lived in the poor section of Merrick that contained the old houses north of Merrick Road. They had a tiny, two story home that was covered with cracked and crumbling white stucco. There was one big maple tree in the front yard shading a brown lawn. The driveway was unpaved and full of uneven ruts. A weather beaten wooden shed sat in the backyard, and there was no garage. Mo told me that he had eight brothers and sisters. Robbie was the oldest kid. Mo, Robbie and Craig shared a small bedroom in the basement that barely contained their three beds. I met Mr. and Mrs. Mowatt. They both were short and plump and smoked cigarettes.

"My parents are from Syria," Mo said.

"You're not *Syri-ous*," I couldn't resist saying, and Mo laughed.

I asked Mo questions about his family and where he went to school before Kennedy High School. I found out that his parents were devout Catholics, and that all the kids were required to go to St. Mary's until they entered high school. When Mo was in 8th grade, he became a heavy drinker. The older neighborhood kids and he would play drinking games and consume huge quantities of beer every weekend. The parish Priest then took Mo under his wing and made him promise to stop drinking. Mo hadn't had a drink since then and now worked at the rectory every week so that Father O'Conner could keep an eye on him. Mo said that one of his younger brothers, who was now thirteen, was even wilder than he was. I was impressed with Mo's openness but shared very little about my background when I was questioned.

The Mowatt's had a basketball hoop on the side of their shed. After we all had some stale pretzels and tap water, Robbie, Sam, Craig and I played two on two. We bounced a slippery old ball on the hard dirt around the shed and competed until it got dark. Robbie then drove me home and I was invited to come back. I envied Mo for being part of a tight knit family and for having brothers so close in age.

Sixty-Seven

AFTER VACATION, I HAD MY first appointment with Dr. Birnbaum. Mom drove us to his office in Seaford, and I sat apprehensively in the waiting room and wondered what psychotherapy would be like. I was determined to become the person that I yearned to be, but felt extremely nervous about reliving all the bad things that had happened. I was also afraid that Dr. Birnbaum would say that I was mentally ill or that I really was evil. I pictured him looking like Eli and was scared that I would become choked off and not be able to talk. I looked over at Mom. She was restlessly reading a magazine and didn't look back. I knew that she was uneasy about me being here, and I was grateful that she arranged the appointment in spite of her trepidations.

After what seemed like an eternity, I was finally directed into his office. Dr. Birnbaum had grey and white thinning hair, was wearing a black turtleneck shirt under a grey tweed sports jacket, and had reading glasses hanging around his neck. He smiled even though his face still looked very serious, and shook my hand. I was directed to get comfortable on his couch. He sat on his swiveling desk chair and faced me. He had a pad of paper on his lap. His eyes seemed to be staring right through to my brain. He lit a pipe, took a few puffs, and began asking me questions. His demeanor and voice had a calming effect on me. I immediately felt that he sincerely wanted to help me, and was overjoyed by the fact that an older man was reaching out to me in a kind way. He deftly extracted my life story within the first thirty minutes.

"Jeffrey," he said as he lit up another pipe full of tobacco, "you have what is known as 'survivor guilt.' Your sister died, your Mother told you that you should have died, your Father reinforced your dysfunctional feelings by beating you and abandoning you. No one told you that Sheryl was sick. No one told you when she died. You were not allowed to go to her funeral. You were not allowed to grieve in a normal way. You have repressed some powerful and destructive feelings that have led to panic attacks and anxiety. I will help you become aware of your feelings and to lessen the pain and anxiety associated with them. You will need to come here regularly."

I was dazed and attempted to comprehend everything that he said.

"You look confused. You have had to live through some overwhelming experiences and now is the time to start the process of understanding what is going on inside of you. Are you all right with this?"

"I think so."

"I am also prescribing you a drug called valium. This will help you with your anxiety and help prevent the panic attacks." He scribbled on a sheet of paper and handed it to me. "Take two pills every day and make another appointment to see me."

"Did he blame everything on me?" Mom asked as we got into the car.

"He wants me to become aware of my feelings so that I can reduce my anxiety."

"You're going to hate me."

"I don't hate you. I love you and I want you to love me. You're the only parent I've got. But I know that I am extremely angry."

"I do love you. I wish that you weren't so angry. You don't know what it is like to lose a child. I say crazy things."

"I'm in pain too. I lost my sister. I loved her and never had the chance to tell her."

We were talking about things that we had never discussed. We were bonding. We were hopefully beginning a process of understanding each other. We both cried as Mom drove us home.

Sixty-Eight

I WAS SWEATING. I COULD FEEL the moisture drip down from my underarms and the drops appear on my forehead. My cheeks and nose were beet red. My throat was bone dry. I tried to swallow. It took four attempts before there was enough saliva to make it down my gullet. My mind was blank and my tongue was swollen. My shirt was wet and stuck to the middle of my back. I felt winded. I stared at the windows on the back wall.

"We're ready whenever you are," implored Mr. Weigel, my social studies teacher. I was standing in front of the class about to give my assigned oral report on Robespierre. I took a deep breath and trudged through it. I was on automatic pilot and not even aware of what I was saying.

I *was* aware of Eli. His words echoed in my head. *"You have the worst voice that I've ever heard. I am ashamed of the way you sound."* I became extremely self-conscious. Most of the time I didn't think about it. But in front of a class it was all I thought about.

After social studies I went to biology class. Mr. Carlson, a science teacher and assistant football coach, barked out, "Mr. Goldstein, come up here to the front of the class." He was standing next to a skeleton. He pointed to the thigh bone. "This is called the femur," he informed us. "Mr. Goldstein, please tell the class which muscles surround the femur." He sounded like he was about to perform a magic trick and that I was his assistant.

"The quadriceps are in the front and the biceps femoris muscles, or hamstrings are in the back."

Mr. Carlson continued to name most of the bones in the

human body and had me tell the accompanying muscles. I knew the names of the muscles from the time Bob and I had spent reading the *Strength and Health* magazines, and I had often discussed my weightlifting progress with Mr. Carlson during football.

"Wow, we can't stump Mr. Goldstein, can we? Let's give him a round of applause."

Mr. Carlson smiled at me and winked when I looked back at him. I wished that Mr. Carlson had been my father instead of Eli.

While waiting for English class to start next period I found myself staring at Marcie's legs. "Are you growing your hair long?" she asked.

"As long as I can. In sports you are not allowed to have it go down past your collar."

"We can have ours as long as we want," she laughed. "I can let it grow past my ass."

"Please don't cover up that beautiful tush," I replied.

"Ha, do you have a girlfriend?"

"Why, are you asking me out?"

"I don't have to ask," she said as she turned her head and all the beautiful blonde hair followed in waves and then fell perfectly into place.

Towards the end of the period, it suddenly overpowered me. A panic attack. I had no idea what had triggered it. I tried to slow down my breathing. I stared at my desk afraid to let anyone see my face. The bell rang and I hurried to the bathroom and hid in a stall until the next class started. I cupped my hands under the faucet and collected enough water to use to swallow a valium. I continued to breathe slowly and deeply and felt the symptoms subside.

"Where's your pass?" demanded Mr. Olson the hall monitor.

"I was sick. I don't have one."

"Did you go to the nurse?"

"No, I didn't have time."

"You seem all right to me. I am writing you up for skipping class. Be at detention today."

"But I was sick."

"If you don't show up today, you'll have it for a week."

Mr. Olson was in charge of the after school confinement. The room contained some of the few "hoods" who attended Kennedy High School instead of Calhoun High School. There were also some kids like me who got in trouble for being late to a class.

"What are you doing in here? You're such a goody two shoes," asked one of the hoods.

"I was caught doing drugs in the boy's room," I replied and took pleasure in watching his jaw drop.

"Shut up and sit down!" yelled Mr. Olson.

The detainees were ignominiously constrained to one of the desks facing the four walls of the stark room. Each desk had a partition on either side. A prisoner who looked away from his dungeon was pounced on by a waiting Mr. Olson. Those unlucky enough to be scolded twice were condemned to a second day of incarceration.

The hoods reveled in making Mr. Olson miserable. They farted loudly when he wasn't looking, tapped their pens noisily on the desk, and shot spit wads at each other. They were all going to spend weeks there, anyway, and wanted to be as disruptive as possible.

The sentence was ninety minutes. If the jailbird was involved in an afterschool activity or sport, which none of the hoods were, they would be very late. The miscreant then incurred the wrath of the coach or teacher when they finally arrived. Upon my liberation I slinked as unobtrusively as I could onto the late bus and went home. I didn't want to face anyone. I didn't want to be associated with the hoods.

Sixty-Nine

"Picture what happened. Relive it. Focus on your feelings. Describe them to me."

I sat on the couch with my eyes closed and re-experienced the horrible events. I viscerally conjured up the painful emotions and described them to Dr. Birnbaum during our weekly sessions.

"Be more vivid. Give me more details."

"What would you do if you acted upon your anger? Let your mind go. Fantasize. What would happen?"

I attempted to achieve stream of consciousness.

"What was going through your head when your father hit you?"

"What were you feeling when your mother yelled at you?"

He asked me about my dreams. He asked me about my fantasies. He asked me to describe the thoughts I had while masturbating. He wanted to excavate my innermost secrets. Nothing was off limits.

"This is the only way for you to have control. You must be aware of all of your thoughts and feelings."

I trusted him implicitly. He was always nonjudgmental. I shared everything and he explained my reactions in a way that made them seem normal, not evil. Sometimes the realization of the enormity of my situation was unbearably distressing. I often had to wrestle with my suicidal urges. When I ran into these rough patches, he increased my dosage of valium. It was very easy to take more.

Mom always waited and then drove me home. She seemed

very threatened by my relationship with Dr. Birnbaum, but still took me to every appointment.

Bill Peterson was sitting on his front steps with Skinny Vinny when we drove home after one of my weekly sessions in February. I hadn't seen Vinny in a while.

"Vinny, why won't you ever go to the Park with me anymore?"

"You guys are too good for me."

"You're one of the fastest people I know. You're still the 'Flying Vinny'. "

He shrugged and walked home. Bill stood up.

"Alright Jeffrey. You are still a double virgin. This time you will get laid. And this time you will get stoned. Stoned and laid. We have nymphos. We have some opiated hash. Party at Kaplan's house Friday night. You're coming with me. You are really going to come."

The festivities were only two blocks away. We climbed the stairs to a room in the attic. There was a hookah with six hoses attached to it sitting on a table.

"We're using wine instead of water and we have some seriously potent opiated hash," bragged Bill. "Start inhaling."

The liquid cooled down the smoke and I was able to hold huge amounts in my lungs for long periods of time without coughing. Bill grinned at me. I was supremely serene. It seemed as if I had just consumed one thousand valiums. I was calm, joyful, uninhibited and all of the chains attached to my body had melted away. Eli didn't exist anymore. I wished that I could always feel like this. The room began to pulsate and to oscillate. *Parsley, Sage Rosemary and Thyme.* Simon and Garfunkel were playing. I could see the words as they came out of the speakers.

"So that's what thyme looks like," I laughed. The room vibrated to the rhythm of my heart beats.

"Are you feeling it?" asked Bill. "Are you stoned? Smoke some more."

Caught in the Undertow

A beautiful girl grabbed my hand. Except it wasn't my hand. We were drifting through the kaleidoscope of colors with no clothes on. I was in front of her, behind her, inside of her, and attached to her. We were bobbing up and down like a ship on the ocean. We fell deeper and deeper into a swirl of pleasure as the music echoed and flashed around us. I woke up naked on the floor.

Bill walked me home. "Now you're a fucking man!" he said.

"I have no clue what just happened."

"You had fun!"

Seventy

THE SUN SHONE ON MY eyes and I pulled the blanket over my face. My body was pinned to the mattress by waves of depression. What day is this? I had to think hard. It was Saturday. I woke up during the night in the throes of another panic attack. I had taken another valium. "Why is my life so out of my control?!" I screamed in my head. "Why can't I get rid of these goddam emotions?!"

I was sitting at the kitchen table and eating a bowl of cereal when she started.

"You peed on the toilet seat. *You're worthless, you should be dead!*" over and over again.

"Leave me the hell alone!"

"*You are useless, you're not worth the ground that Michael Dorfman walks on!*"

I threw my spoon at her. Her screaming escalated and then Grandma joined in.

"It's a *shandeh un a charpeh,* a shame and a disgrace. You're killing me! Don't treat your mother like that!"

I was trapped. Being yelled at from both sides. I wanted to strangle my mother. And I wanted to hug her.

I ran into the bathroom, slammed the door, got dressed and ran out of the house. I found my way to Bob's.

"Hey, can you work out with me?"

"Sure, I'll meet you downstairs."

I went into his backyard and lifted open the two big white doors that covered the steps leading down to his basement. In the back, past the furnace, we had placed his weights, exercise equipment, and a radio. This was our refuge. We'd weightlift, listen to music, and talk. We'd reflect over topics such as philosophy, poetry, politics, sex and music.

You Really Got Me by The Kinks played on the radio.

"I figured out how to play that," I said.

Bob had started learning the guitar, also. "Show me later," he said.

We always did our squats first because it was our least favorite exercise. We then did rowing, curls, military presses, abdominal work and ended with bench presses, our favorite. Bob spotted for me and I could take risks and experiment with larger amounts. I was now bench pressing 180 pounds. The heavy barbell resting on my chest; my triceps, deltoids, and pectorals working together to push the barbell off my body; and the sense of triumph as I fully extended my arms into the air above me was an exhilarating experience. I was alive, vital, and powerful. I was in control. The camaraderie that I felt being with Bob, the intense exercise, and the rock music blasting in the background helped me transcend my insidious despondency.

Just as I extended my arms for the first repetition of my third set, we heard Mrs. Petrocelli shouting from the house.

"Bob, get up here. Now!"

"I just have to do some chores. I'll be back in less than ten minutes," He assured me.

I sat on the bench and read one of the *Strength and Health* magazines that he kept in the basement. Ten minutes went by, then twenty, and then thirty. A feeling of despair began to wash over me. Demons danced around inside of me and pulled at my entrails with plungers. My guts churned as the winds of rage blew through my brain. I was abruptly being transported back to when I was seven and Sheryl had just died. I sat there all alone with the visceral reaction that I had towards my parents. The anger was escalating and I was breathing faster and faster. Finally, he came back downstairs.

"I'm sorry," he said. "I couldn't get away from her."

"Why did you say that you could work out if you couldn't,"

I screamed. "I came all this way and I wouldn't have stayed if you told me that you had chores to do. I can't just start and then suddenly stop. What kind of friend are you?"

I totally lost control and continued to attack. The angry words just flowed out of me. All of a sudden, I realized what I was doing. I bolted out of the basement. "Oh my God! I sound just like my parents," I thought. I was humiliated. I had never let my rage out at anyone outside of the family before. As I ran, it took every ounce of strength that I could muster to keep myself from running in front of a car. "I *am* worthless!" I thought. "I should be dead!"

I slammed the door to my room. "My demons have taken over," I thought. I swallowed two valiums and fell on my bed.

Seventy-One

"WHAT WERE YOU FEELING when you yelled at Bob? Describe what was happening inside you. Who were you really screaming at?"

Dr. Birnbaum again probed and prodded and helped me to understand what was really going on with me. My deep rooted feelings that formed when Sheryl died were attaching themselves to current situations. I was actually re-experiencing the abandonment and pain that stemmed from Sheryl's death. He explained the concept of "emotional triggers". Certain words, situations or events caused me to physically and emotionally react in the same way as I did to the stimuli and events that followed Sheryl's death. My unconscious mind didn't know the difference between then and now.

I was annoyed with Bob but the intense emotions that overwhelmed me in his basement had nothing to do with him. I had to recognize and understand the origins of my deepest emotions in order to control them. I was feeling guilty over things that I didn't do. I didn't kill Sheryl. I had to accept what my parents had gone through, even though they had done awful things to me. Mom was overcome with incredible pain and grief, and I had to recognize that, and not personalize what she said. She was now dealing with all of her emotions brought on by a failed marriage. It was going to be an extremely difficult process. I was going to make progress and then have setbacks. I could never change the past, I couldn't change my parents, but I could learn to control myself.

Mom was in the bathroom standing in front of the mirror, brushing her hair and putting on make-up. She had a fancy dress on. "Do these shoes go with this outfit?" she asked Grandma. They both were smiling.

In the spring, Mom joined a group called PWP, Parents without Partners, or Predators with Penises, as I referred to them. She wanted to start dating. I was extremely ambivalent about this. I did not want a new man in the house. But she seemed to be much happier and the atmosphere in the house improved. Soon she was going out each weekend with a divorced man named Ronny. The family met him several times and sometimes he brought his nine year old son Jason along. Ronny seemed to be very uncomfortable around me. I felt relieved by the fact that he was not Eli.

Mom and Grandma acted much calmer. Several times I invited them into my room to hear a new record. Often Keith and Michele would join us. They always listened to the music and to my interpretation of the lyrics. When I could, I played along on my guitar. When the words were unintelligible, I tried to convince Grandma that they were singing in Yiddish.

"How would the Beatles know Jewish?" she would ask.

"Everyone knows Yiddish," I'd say. "It's the language of the world."

After we had listened to a new Beatles album one night, Mom wrote a short poem that ended with:

Listening to the Beatles superstars
Best night so far

We all were definitely trying. Mom was showing me positive emotions. Sometimes I actually felt like we were a family. At times we were calmly doing things together, we weren't fighting, and the black cloud called Eli had not debased our house.

Seventy-Two

BOB DYLAN'S VOICE WAS DRENCHING the room. *Once upon a time you dressed so fine, threw the bums a dime, in your prime, Didn't You!* There were about twenty kids from Kennedy High School milling around Shawn's basement. A few pairs of boys and girls were holding hands or had their arms around each other. Some people were bouncing up and down to the music but not really dancing. There was no alcohol, pot, or any other drugs in the room. I was invited by Shawn and didn't know many of the other guests. The conversations were pleasant and polite. This was the group of students that Mr. Carlson called, "wholesome".

"I heard that you were on after school detention one day," Marshall told me.

"Yeah, that hall monitor Olson. I was a minute late for class and he nabbed me. I had to miss practice," I said.

"He always finds you," Levi chimed in. "I had detention because of him, too. Sitting there all that time is a real drag."

"At least the hoods were amusing. They are ruthless. I thought that Olson was going to have a stroke," I said.

"I think that they like being there because it's good practice for their future in prison," said Levi.

"You got that right."

"I'm hungry," declared Shawn, "Let's order some subs."

"Who delivers here?" I asked

"There's a place called, 'Fat Frankie's' in North Merrick. We've ordered from them before. They have forty- nine types of subs," answered Shawn.

I smirked. "Let me call them."

Shawn dialed the number. "Fat Frankie's," said the voice on the other end.

"I hear that you have forty nine types of subs," I said. "I can't decide what to order. Can you name them for me?"

"I can't name all of them. We have the normal types and all different combinations."

"Normal is a relative term. Do you have tongue?"

"No, that's not a normal meat for a sub."

"It's normal for me. That's what I eat for lunch every day. How about pastrami?"

"No."

"Corned beef?"

"No, they're not your typical sub meats. We're not a deli."

"Are you aware of the huge Jewish population in South Merrick?"

"We do business with everyone. Do you want to place an order or not?"

"We have twenty one people here waiting to buy your subs. I just need some more information. Can you tell me at least ten types of subs, then?"

"We have ham, turkey, roast beef, salami, different cheeses, lettuce, tomato, and different toppings and combinations."

"How about liverwurst?"

"No."

"Sardines?"

"No."

"Gefilte fish?"

"No."

"Chopped liver?"

"No."

"Herring?"

"No."

"Knishes?"

"No."

"Blintzes?"

"No."

"Wow, you don't like anything Jewish. How about peanut butter and jelly?"

"No one puts those things in subs. Do you really want to order?"

"Yes, but I don't believe that you actually have forty nine types. We learned about false advertising in school. I could get you in trouble."

"You have one last chance to place an order or I'll hang up."

"Well, do you have pepperoni?"

"Yes."

"I'll have an all pepperoni sub."

"Pepperoni is a topping, not a main ingredient."

At this point everyone is listening and laughing. A girl I've never seen before is sitting on the floor right next to me. I make eye contact with her and she was staring and smiling.

"How about bacon?"

"We do have bacon."

"I don't eat bacon. How about spam?"

"No."

"You're really making this difficult. Do you have a menu?"

"Last chance to order or I hang up."

"Okay, I'll have a tuna, lettuce and tomato sub. I'm going to pass the phone around so that everyone else can place their order. Just one last question. Is Frankie really fat?" I laughed and gave Levi the phone before the man could answer.

The girl on the floor stood up and giggled. "You are so cute and funny," She said. "My name is Regina, what's yours?"

"Jeff. Do you know that Regina means Queen in Latin?"

"I went to Catholic school. What do you think?"

"Nice to meet you, Queen."

The sub delivery man arrived and rang the bell. "I want to meet the kid who made the phone call," he said.

I walked over. He shook my hand. "You really had us going. I wanted to see what you looked like. I'm Frankie. Your sub is on the house."

"Thanks, Fat Frankie."

"So, do you think that I'm really fat?"

I looked him over. "No comment. I'm sure that your mother loves you, though."

Seventy-Three

REGINA ROSATO INVITED ME to dinner with her family on Sunday.

"Do you think that your parents are going to be okay with a funny Jewish boy coming to Sunday dinner?" I asked. "They're going to send you back to Catholic school."

"They'll love you," she said. "Just be yourself."

"I don't think that being myself is a good idea, but I'll be polite and friendly."

She laughed, not quite understanding what I really meant.

Regina had a round face topped with very curly dark brown hair. Her dark eyes always seemed to be staring at me. She had beautiful clear skin, big breasts, a small waist, and muscular legs that filled out her short skirt. I kept thinking that I should be physically attracted to her, but I wasn't. I loved her admiring gaze and warm personality, and felt very at ease around her. It felt weird spending so much time with a girl that I had no sexual attraction for.

Regina lived in a big expensive house located down the block from Marcie. The Rosatos were one of the only Catholic families in an area inhabited by Jews. We sat at a big dining room table on Sunday with her two cherubic younger sisters and her parents. Her father said grace before we ate. A salad, vegetables, bread, and sliced ham were passed around. There was agreeable, cheerful conversation and everyone seemed to genuinely like each other. I observed the interactions as if I were watching a Disney movie. I was stunned by the contrast between the way Regina's family acted and the situation at my house. "I want to be part of a family like this," I kept thinking.

"What do you want to do when you grow up, Jeffrey?" her father asked.

"I don't know yet, but I want to feel fulfilled and challenged by my job."

"I hear that you do very well in school. You should be able to do whatever you want."

"Thank you. I enjoy learning and I can't wait to go to college."

I glowed from the positive attention that Mr. Rosoto gave me. Regina's younger sisters smiled at me and giggled. I wasn't physically attracted to Regina, but I was smitten by her family.

On weekends, Regina and I went to movies or just walked around and talked. I was invited to dinner on Sundays. We never did anything physically other than hold hands.

"Is it important for you to have a physical relationship with a girl?" Regina asked me one night as we walked and held hands.

"I've got to give the right answer," I thought to myself. I paused for a few seconds and replied. " A physical relationship is a natural way for a couple to express love for each other. They have to have strong feelings first."

"Do you have strong feelings for me?" she asked.

"Uh oh," I thought. "I really do treasure being with you," was what came out of my mouth.

"Then why won't you ever kiss me?"

I didn't know what to say so I threw my arms around her and kissed her lips. She hugged me as if she was never going to let go. "I guess that I can enjoy this," I thought.

Our relationship evolved over the next few weeks and we ended up doing everything except for having intercourse. "I'm saving that for marriage," she informed me. "Fine with me," I thought.

On a Saturday night her parents and sisters had gone to a movie. Regina and I took the opportunity to enjoy each other sexually on the couch in her basement. We had music playing and were engrossed in our activities, so we didn't hear the door open.

"That is horrible! It is a sin!" her father screamed. "A young lady does not act like that! Jeffrey, get out of my house! Stay away from my daughter!"

My relationship with Regina had officially ended. I stopped and stared at Marcie's house on the way home.

Seventy-Four

THE CHILLY SPRING WIND REFRESHED our bodies. The warm sun bathed our skin. It was a perfect day with mild temperatures that allowed us to wear shorts and tee-shirts. Ocean breezes cooled our perspiration. We were like excited puppies running up and down the court at the Park. It was the weekend and a best out of seven basketball tournament was being waged between two opposing teams. Sam, Robbie, and Craig Mowatt were grouped with me and we competed against four of their friends from Merrick. We had the radio on and sang as we locked horns and grappled for victory. *Come on baby light my fire! Come on baby light my fire! Try to set the night on FIRE!*

After more than two hours we were tied at three games apiece. We were leading by a score of twenty to nineteen in the seventh game. The first team to score twenty one points would emerge as the champion. I dribbled the ball up court, passed to Robbie, cut to the basket, and he passed back to me for a give and go. I caught it and scored the winning layup. "Game, set, match!" yelled Sam. We all shook hands and gathered around the cement water fountain.

"I got my Draft Card last week," lamented Robbie.

"Wow, it's off to Vietnam for you," said his friend Timmy.

"Nah, I'm going to college. I was accepted by Long Island University."

Everyone began to join the conversation. "They can get you when you graduate from college. Pauly graduated from Hofstra, was drafted, and six months later he's in 'Nam. He never came home."

"Yeah, Steve was drafted and he came back addicted to smack. He was all fucked up"

"This war makes no sense. People are dying for nothing."

"Well, I'm enlisting when I graduate," said Mike Hartner. "I want to serve my country."

Everyone proceeded to gang up on him.

"That's stupid. You're just helping the war continue."

"Millions of people are protesting the Draft and the War and you're gonna volunteer? Are you crazy?"

"My grandfather served in World War l, my father got wounded in World War ll, and I am going to serve my country too," said Mike.

"We have no business being there. It's not our fight."

"It's the Domino Theory. If one country falls to communism, it'll spread to all the surrounding countries and then eventually to us. We are fighting to protect democracy."

"I can't believe that you ate that bullshit sandwich. There's a civil war going on there and it has nothing to do with us."

"That's what the commie pothead hippies want you to believe. You're all brainwashed."

"You're the one who's brainwashed. This is LBJ's war, not ours."

"Our country needs us. America, love it or leave it!"

"We have the right to protest and to change things. America once had slaves. Would you have said 'America, love it or leave it' then?"

"There was a draft during the Civil War also. People our age have to fight for our country."

"The Civil War was about issues in our own country. Vietnam isn't. We need to protest, not enlist."

"I think that the biggest issue is that we get drafted when we're eighteen but we can't even vote until we're twenty one," I contributed.

"Let's all go home before this gets out of hand," said Timmy and we dispersed. A group of us went up to Mike and shook his hand.

"We don't agree with you but we respect your bravery. Good luck!"

The Draft and the Vietnam War suddenly loomed even larger.

Seventy-Five

BILL PETERSON AND I WERE smoking a joint in his backyard. It was July 1, 1967 and we were celebrating my sixteenth birthday. Earlier in the day I swallowed two valiums with my breakfast. Dr. Gittlestein had also given me a prescription and now I had a supply from him as well as from Dr. Birnbaum. Bill, as usual, was entertaining me with lascivious stories of his carnal liaisons.

"Did you ever screw Regina?" he asked.

"You can't screw a Catholic girl," I replied. "Her father caught us making out and went crazy."

"I fucked a Catholic girl," Bill countered. "I made her scream."

"How the hell do you do it? You're not that good looking, you don't play sports, you don't do well in school, you don't even have any musical talent."

"It's all in your attitude. I have self-confidence. I expect to get laid, and I do."

"You should write a fucking book," I said and we both convulsed with the silly, uncontrollable laughter of a stoned person.

"A fucking book!" We almost wet our pants.

After lunch I went to Bob's house to work out. "Now we're both sixteen and two years away from the Draft," he said.

"I probably would like the part of the Army where you exercise and run and bond with the other soldiers," I said. "I could never kill another kid just because he lived in another country, though."

"Yeah, I probably would let them shoot me before I shot them," said Bob.

When we finished working out, we went upstairs and decided to write down our favorite anti-war song lyrics.

Generals order their soldiers to kill, and to fight for a cause they've long ago forgotten, by Simon and Garfunkel.

How many deaths will it take 'til he knows, that too many people have died? by Bob Dylan.

Is there anybody here who thinks that following the orders takes away the blame? Is there anybody here who wouldn't mind a murder by another name? by Phil Ochs.

This continued until we had filled up over ten sheets of paper.

"I have been attempting to write a poem that is so profound that when people read it they would immediately recognize the futility of the war," I said. "I think that I am trying too hard."

I suddenly became very depressed. The Draft was like Eli. I felt the same hopeless and helpless sense of gloom. I shared my old poetry fragments with Bob.

Like battered leaves that cling to trees trying to survive a howling wind

I will break the wrists of hands that choke my throat and keep me in this hell

"Those are amazing," he said. "They really capture how I feel."

I was reminded of how complimentary Bob always was. I also realized that I wasn't alone.

Seventy-Six

I LOOKED IN THE MIRROR AND struggled to make the knot. I wanted the top and bottom parts to be hanging down at the same length. My hands were shaking and after about five or six attempts I asked Grandma to tie it for me. She had the ability to stand behind me and to make the necktie look perfect on the first attempt. She learned this skill while working at a haberdashery before she was married.

It was the middle of June and the temperature was over 80 degrees outside. I was wearing dark dress pants, black shoes, a long sleeved white shirt, and an impeccably knotted black necktie. I pedaled my bicycle and tried not to sweat. I had taken two valiums before I left.

I chained my bike to a pole outside of Bohack's Supermarket. Bohack's was on the corner of Newbridge and Merrick Road, kitty-cornered from our old hangout, Bart's. The grocery store just had its grand opening, the first one in South Bellmore, and I had filled out an application for part time work. I was scheduled for an interview with Mr. Caruso, the store manager. My mouth was dry and my armpits were wet as I sat and waited outside of his office. I avoided making eye contact with the shoppers who were wheeling their carts past me on the way to the checkout lines. I kept forcing myself to salivate.

A slim, dapper, gray haired man in a light blue suit came out of the office and extended his hand.

"Hi, Jeffrey, thank you for coming in. I'm Frank Caruso." He had a warm, friendly voice and I immediately felt at ease.

He told me to call him Frank, and asked me questions for more than ten minutes.

"I'm looking to hire some high school students to work around fifteen hours per week at minimum wage. The type of work would vary from week to week depending on what we need. How does that sound, son?"

"Great," I replied.

"Then come in next Saturday at 8AM and you'll do some more paperwork and we'll get you started."

"That was easy," I thought as I rushed home. I daydreamed about what I would do with all my extra money.

When I came in on Saturday, I was told to report to Harvey Moskowitz, the produce manager. "Make sure that you tell him your last name," said Frank.

"I'm Jeff Goldstein. Frank told me to see you."

An old, hunched over, unkempt looking man glared at me.

"You're a moron if you want to work in a grocery store. Go to school. Make something of yourself."

"I plan to go to college."

"Did I ask you? Keep your fucking mouth shut unless I ask you to talk."

I was told to carry crates of oranges out of the storeroom and to unload them onto the shelves. After about fifteen minutes Moskowitz came over and exploded.

"What the fuck are you doing? You're supposed to put the new oranges under the older ones, not on top of them. How fucking stupid can you be? Why do I always get the retarded ones?"

For the next three hours, I did nothing right. I heard the phrase, "fucking idiot" so often that it hung in the air even when he wasn't saying it. I debated in my mind whether or not the money was worth having to spend my time with another Eli.

Finally, my shift was over. "Nice working with you," I said. Harvey didn't even look up.

"How'd it go, son?" asked Frank.

"Not too well"

"Yeah, I heard Harvey yelling. I thought that maybe he'd like you since you're both from the same tribe."

I stared back with a blank look on my face.

"Jews, you're both Jews. Don't worry, son. Next time I'll assign you somewhere else."

I punched out my time card and decided to come back.

The next week I was given a white apron and a price stamper and told that I was going to be a stock boy. I spent the morning wiping the prices off of various cans and then stamping them with a new amount. In the afternoon I was given a box cutter and I opened cardboard cartons of canned vegetables, stamped the cost on the top, and stacked them on the shelves. Frank walked by several times and said, "Good work, son." The work was mindless and physical, and I enjoyed it.

With about two hours left in my shift, I was unloading cans of peas and noticed an envelope on the floor. It had nothing written on it and I opened it up. It contained ten one hundred dollar bills. One thousand dollars. I looked around and then stuck it in my apron. In another year I would be getting my license and this would be a great help in terms of buying a car, I thought. There was no way to identify who owned this money, so now it's mine, I reasoned. I kept on working, but began to feel that it was wrong to keep it. I walked over to Frank and told him about it.

"Thanks, son, you're doing the right thing. I'll put it in the safe and we'll see if anyone claims it."

As I was punching out at the end of the day, Frank walked over to me with a short white haired old lady. "This is the nice young man who found your money," he said to her. I was told that she had just withdrawn it from the bank and dropped the envelope while she was shopping.

"Thank you so much," she gushed. "I have a reward for you," she said as she place a dime in my hand. I stared at it as she walked away. Frank tried not to laugh as he saw the look on my face.

"You did the right thing, son."

I passed Bill on the way home and told him what happened. "You're a fucking idiot," he said. "You should have kept the money."

"*Fucking idiot* seems to be my description when it comes to supermarkets," I replied.

Seventy-Seven

"I've been waking up again with my insides churning. I am overwhelmed with the feeling that I've done something horrible. I feel evil."

"Have you been taking your valium?"

"Yes. Won't I get addicted?"

"You need to get the physical symptoms under control."

"I don't like being dependent on a drug."

"As I said, let's get your physical symptoms under control and then we'll look at diminishing your dosage. Tell me more about your feelings."

"I am convinced that I killed someone."

"Who?"

"Sheryl".

"Did you?"

"I know that I didn't in reality, but I have this uncontrollable feeling that I did. I see my Mother's face and I hear her voice telling me over and over again that I did. I have an incredible urge to kill myself."

"What about your father?"

"He starts to strangle me. I feel his hands around my throat and I can't breathe."

"Then what?"

"I feel an infinitely powerful rage. An immense tidal wave pounding on my guts. I feel like I am about to explode."

"Who is this rage directed at?"

"My parents. I want them to take back all the things they've said. I want to strangle my father for all the times he hit me. Then I feel guilty and I want to kill myself."

"Do you think that you might kill yourself?"

"I feel driven to but then I feel a strong urge to live. I want to have a life. I want to have the things that I always wanted."

"What are they?"

"I want to be loved. I want to give love and receive it back. I want my parents to love me, but I don't think that will ever happen."

"How do you feel talking about this?"

"I wish that I could stick my hand into my chest and pull out all these feelings. What if you just put me in a padded cell and I screamed and pounded the wall until all of these emotions were gone? Could I just scream them all out of me?"

"It doesn't work that way. They will always be there. Horrible things happened to you when you were a young boy and you didn't know how to process it. You formed emotions that are part of you. The more that you become aware of them, the more that you accept them, the more that you can control them. You have made remarkable progress already."

"I want to change even more."

"You will. It is a slow process."

I tried to assimilate everything on the way home. My mind searched for an analogy.

My negative emotions are like nails that were long ago driven into a young tree. The nails became embedded as the tree grew around them. My brain grew around the emotions. I can't change what the nails (emotions) are, but I can determine what the rest of my brain will be like.

I thought that I was finally grasping it. Dr. Birnbaum and I kept going over and over the same concepts as different events triggered the same reactions. It was happening so gradually, but I was changing, and felt a wave of optimism flow through my body.

Seventy-Eight

IN SEPTEMBER, 1967, I ENTERED my junior year at John F. Kennedy High School. "We're one year closer to graduating and one year closer to the Draft," Bob reminded me. Bob and I again had no classes together and a different lunch period.

At home we were told that Eli had married his girlfriend Anna and that they had a girl named Monica and a boy named David. Eli and his new family wanted to meet Keith, Michele and me. Mom agreed to allow a visit even though Eli still hadn't paid any child support. Mom, after the divorce, hired a detective who unsuccessfully had attempted to find Eli. Now Eli was contacting us.

"I can have him arrested, you know," said Mom.

"Why don't you?" I replied. "He deserves it."

"That still won't get us any money. You should see your father." Mom's facial expression didn't seem to match her words. I could see how much Eli hurt her, and was shocked that she agreed to let us see him.

"I really don't want to see him. Why are you agreeing to this?" I asked.

"You should have relationship with your father," she said.

"After what he's done to this family, I have no desire to see him," I said.

"I want you all to see him."

"I'd rather see him in jail." None of this made sense to me, but I reluctantly agreed to the meeting. Keith and Michele agreed to go too.

Mom drove us to the train station. Eli came and picked us

up in a green Rambler classic. He was by himself. I stared at him and tried to feel an emotion other than anger.

"Why haven't you tried to get in touch with us?" I asked.

"Your Mom would've had me arrested," he replied.

"You could have called. You just disappeared."

He just drove and ignored me. Whenever I had asked him a question that he didn't like, he pretended that I wasn't there.

"Where are you taking us?"

"To see your grandparents in Brooklyn."

"I haven't seen them since I was a little kid. They didn't even come to my Bar Mitzvah. Why all of a sudden do they want to see us?"

Again, no answer.

We drove into Brooklyn and parked in front of an old apartment building. I felt like we were descending into the depths of hell. I held Keith's and Michele's hands. I tried to remember what Eli's parents looked like. Then, all of a sudden, they descended on us and gave us self-conscious hugs. They seemed evil. They were smiling but in the manner that a witch would smile. I stared at them and tried to grasp the fact that we were biologically related. I wondered what they had done to make Eli turn out the way he did. I looked for clues as to how they could abandon their grandchildren. I thought that if I looked hard enough I might make some sense of the situation.

"Eli, look at Jeffrey. He's all skin and bones. Such a *skinny malink*!" said his mother. Her name was Hilda. She sounded hideous. Hideous Hilda.

"Doesn't the witch ever feed him," said Eli's father. His name was Ed. Evil Ed.

Anna then walked into the room. She had pale white skin and long straight jet black hair. She looked like Morticia from the TV show *The Adams Family*.

"Oh Eli, look at Jeffrey. He's so handsome, just like his father," she exclaimed. "Look at Keith and Michele. They're so cute!"

She talked like we weren't there. They looked at us as if we were exhibits at a museum.

Jeffrey Goldstein

"Come meet Monica and David," Anna said.

"One big, happy family," I thought. We all stared silently out of the window on the way home. When we arrived I ran up to my room and wrote:

The Monster

He slumps
Collapsed on his walker
Like a condemned brick
Building
Fighting
Struggling
To keep
Erect
Staring intently
With ancient, outstretched eyes
Poignantly imploring
"Please"
And I walk quicker
Looking away
Pretending
He
Doesn't exist

Seventy-Nine

THANKSGIVING VACATION WAS COMING UP. I was in the locker room changing my clothes after a late afternoon workout. As I pulled my t-shirt over my head, Ricky looked at my upper body and exclaimed, "Oh my God! Look at that six pack. If someone punched you as hard as they could in your stomach, you probably wouldn't even feel it."

"They'd definitely hurt their hand," I boasted.

Some of the other athletes overheard and walked over.

"Let me try."

"Yeah, I want to try. Let me punch you in the stomach."

"I'll let you kiss me on the ass. That's muscular, also," I replied.

"No, really. Let me punch you in the stomach."

"Wait a minute," I said. "If you really want to try, it will cost one dollar per punch."

"A fucking dollar!"

"You want to touch this fine specimen of a physique, it will cost you," I replied. "Who's first?"

"Let me try," said Neil. He then handed me a dollar. I balanced myself and flexed my abdominal muscles. He wound up and pounded me. I felt so powerful. Invincible. No one could hurt me.

"I smiled. "Like a flea bouncing off the wall. Who's next?"

A crowd had gathered. After seven boys had given me their money and punched me, Jay Flaherty came over. Jay was six foot five inches tall and weighed over two hundred fifty pounds. He was the center on the football team and by far the strongest kid in the school. The locker room became deadly quiet.

"Are you sure you want to go through with this?" Ricky asked.

"As long as he hits me in the right spot, I won't feel it". I grabbed a pen, and drew an "X" on the middle of my abs. "Jay, please don't miss," I said as I flexed.

"Wait," I said. "Let me stand with my back to the wall so I don't fall down."

Jay stared at my stomach, took several deep breaths, and waved his tremendous fist in the air. I looked at his face and his expression reminded me of Eli. I was enveloped by my determination. He was not going to hurt me. I felt the tension in the room as everyone stared with their mouths hanging open. I tightened my muscles as hard as I could, leaned back against the wall, and watched his fist rocket through the air and hit me like a cannon ball. I threw my hands up in the air and shouted, "Didn't feel a thing!" Everyone applauded.

I had collected 14 dollars and was about to go home when Alfie Gelfand asked for a turn.

"Alright, Alfie, you're the last one." I realized that Alfie was a little uncoordinated, so I pointed out the "X".

"Focus on the 'X', big guy," I said.

"Hey, everyone, Alfie's gonna try!" someone shouted and the crowd came back.

Alfie took three soft practice punches and danced around like a boxer.

"Muhammad Ali is about to knock out Sonny Liston," shouted Alfie as he threw jabs into the air and weaved back and forth. Everyone laughed. He spun around, exclaimed, "I am the greatest!" and propelled his fist right into my testicles. I collapsed onto the floor.

"Oh my God! Oh my God! I hit him in the balls!" Alfie exclaimed.

I writhed in pain, moaned, gagged and vomited into a bucket that someone brought over.

"Oh my God! Oh my God! I'm so sorry!" Alfie cried.

Coach Millhouse came into the locker room. "What's going on in here!" he demanded.

"Nothing, Coach," replied Jay. "Goldstein has an upset stomach. We'll help him get home."

A group of boys carried me to the Nurse's office. "What happened to him?" she asked.

Everyone looked around at each other, embarrassed to say anything. Finally Alfie blurted out, "I broke his nuts!"

"I'll go get the trainer," she said. I was doubled over in pain on the bed with Alfie holding my hand.

"I'm so sorry, little buddy. I am so sorry, little buddy."

"Who do you think you are? Gilligan?" asked Ricky.

"You better stop holding his hand or they'll think you're gay," said Sam.

The trainer finally came in and Alfie was still holding my hand.

"Everyone get out!" said Mr. Feinman, the sports trainer. He gently examined my private parts. There was no swelling and it only hurt in one spot.

"It looks like you're bruised, but there is no damage," he said. "If you're not feeling better by tomorrow, see a doctor. I've been hit harder playing football, so I wouldn't worry."

"Will I still be able to have kids?" I asked.

"All you want. Just wait until you're older."

That night Alfie called me. "Are you alright?"

"As good as new," I said. "Bring Marcie over and I'll show you."

"That's my boy!" laughed Alfie.

Eighty

THE VIETNAM WAR WAS AT its peak and the major topic on the news every day. Young people were becoming very outspoken and were protesting the Draft and the War.

Young people are speaking their minds
Getting so much resistance from behind, sang the Buffalo Springfield.

In school some teachers were allowing students to express their opinions during class discussions, while others were angry that students were even allowed to have opinions. My most irritated teacher was Mr. Whitley.

Mr. Whitley taught Advanced Trigonometry. He was tall, skinny, had big black glasses, greased back brown hair and always wore a suit and a scowl on his face. He was an excellent math teacher, but once or twice a week he began class with one of his tirades. He hated the young protesters and the fact that anyone would empower adolescents by listening to them. He regularly maligned the "liberal" teachers in the school who conducted "touchy-feely overly lenient" classes. One day he was especially annoyed.

"I am sick of hearing teenagers giving their opinions. None of you have lived long enough or are smart enough to have a viewpoint about anything. The only two topics that you have earned the right to talk about with any authority are acne and masturbation."

I turned to Marcie and whispered, "I bet that he masturbates more than all of us put together."

"Goldstein, do you have something to say?" he slowly and angrily whispered at me with a piercing gaze.

"I was just following your advice and giving my authoritative opinion about masturbation. I believe that it is a hard habit to break."

Everybody laughed until he glared at the class. There was silence as he walked up to me, stuck his nose in my face, gave me the evil eye, and softly spoke emphasizing each word, "Shut your malevolent mouth."

After the bell, as Ricky and I walked to English class, we decided to say as many euphemisms for masturbation as we could think of, in honor of Mr. Whitley.

"Jerk off."

"Choke the chicken."

"Beat the meat."

"Rub one out."

"Polish the sword."

Marcie was walking behind us. "You guys really are experts," she said.

"Yeah, because of her," I mumbled to Ricky.

Eighty-One

FRANK WAS HUGE. HE WAS well over six feet tall, had a short haircut, a big head and a wide, flabby body. He spoke in a deep resonant voice and I imagined that he was a good singer. Mom had been dating him for over a month and he wanted to meet the family. He had already spent time with Keith and Michele, and was now taking me for a ride in his car, a big black new model Cadillac.

"What classes are you taking in school? What do you want to do when you grow up?" He fired one question after another at me, and I liked it. An adult male was taking an interest in me and I felt important. I wasn't sure if he was just doing this as a way to get closer to Mom, but I didn't care. The topic turned to girls. No grown-up had ever brought up this topic to me before. I was fascinated.

"Girls will like you if you make them feel important. Really listen to them. Act interested. Give them compliments," said Frank as we continued to drive around in his car. "You're a good looking guy, but they're more attracted to a good personality. Have you had much experience with girls?"

"Have you?" I replied.

"Yeah, too personal," Frank responded. "Hey, would you like to drive?"

"I've never been behind the wheel before," I said.

"Nothing to it," he said. "I'll help you."

I participated in my first driving experience. It was exhilarating. Frank let me drive for almost one hour.

Afterwards, he asked, "What do you like to do for fun?"

"I love music, I play the guitar, and sports. I work out with weights to help me with sports."

"I work out, too," he said.

I looked at him incredulously. "You work out?"

"Underneath all of this blubber is an incredibly muscled physique. Would you like to be a guest at my gym and work out with me?"

"Sure."

That weekend Frank gave me another driving lesson, even though I wasn't seventeen years old yet and didn't have my learner's permit. Then we went to the Pequa Health Club on Merrick Road in Massapequa. There were Universal weight stations, rowing machines, exercise bikes, and various types of equipment that I had never seen before. Behind the gym was a full size quarter mile track. I was impressed.

After our work out, Frank asked, "How would you like to have a membership? Then you could use the equipment whenever you wanted to."

"I wouldn't be able to afford that," I said.

"It will be my gift to you."

I shook his hand. "That is extremely generous of you," I said. "Thank you!"

Mom was very happy when I told her. "Maybe good things are going to happen for us now," she said.

I was able to take the Merrick Road bus to the gym. It cost twenty five cents each way and only took about ten minutes. I started a routine in which I went once during the week after practice, and once on the weekend after work. Frank never seemed to go. The people who worked there knew me and greeted me each time I came.

I began to notice a middle-aged man who spent all of his time on an exercise bike. He pedaled very slowly and stared at the other men who were working out. He was completely bald on the top of his head and always wore loose gray sweat pants and a baggy gray sweatshirt. It was still obvious that he was very fat. Sometimes, he took unbelievably long showers. He'd be in the shower when I arrived and went to the locker room, and would still be there when I changed to go home over an hour later. If you made eye contact with him, he'd smile. I was thrilled to be using the gym and didn't want to jeopardize my membership, so I never asked anyone about him.

One weekend after a long, strenuous session lifting heavy weights, combined with a three mile run on the track, I enjoyed the hot water hitting my back as I stood relaxing in the shower. I was suddenly startled by a soft voice.

"Would you like to go to a movie with me?" asked the fat naked middle-aged man.

"What!?"

"Would you like to go to a movie? I'll pay."

I had no idea how to react. I ran out of the shower, got dried off, dressed as quickly as I could, and went home.

In Texas the football players always used the word "fag" in a derogatory way. Bob and I had discussed homosexuality abstractly, but we didn't think that we knew any real gays. After I arrived home I called Bob and told him about what had happened at the gym. Bob had a part time job at a movie theater and had a similar experience there. The manager there had offered to give him a blow job. He said to Bob, "Just close your eyes and you can imagine that I am whoever you want me to be. All you have to do is enjoy it."

"Wow, gay guys must really dig us," he said.

"Yeah, well, if this heterosexual thing doesn't work out, at least we'll have something to fall back on," I replied.

Eighty-Two

IT WAS ANOTHER "GRADING DAY" at school and we were bringing our mark cards to each class for our teachers to fill out. We received a numerical average for each class, plus a letter grade of "A" to "F" for our "attitude". You were on the "honor roll" if your numerical average was over a "90". If you had an "F" for any attitude grade, you were excluded from the "honor roll". I knew that I had earned high "90's" in everything, except for math where I had achieved a "100" on every homework, quiz and test.

My first class was chemistry, which everyone considered our most difficult. Mr. Szabado was our teacher. He spoke broken English but no one knew where he was from. He had jet black hair, always wore a sports jacket, and never smiled. He never talked about anything other than chemistry. No one ever misbehaved in his class because we all were trying so hard to understand him and the subject matter.

Mr. Szabado's salient feature was his chin. It jutted out from his face at a forty-five degree angle and it looked like he could open cans with it. The song, *The Mighty Quinn,* by Manfred Mann, had just become popular, and I began to call him, *The Mighty Chin.* On grading day, I organized some of the boys who were in chorus. When Szabado walked into the room they all sang, *You'll not seen nothing like the Mighty Chin.* He stopped walking, turned towards the singers and said, "Shut upper your mouths."

He sat at his desk getting ready to sign our cards. For the first time ever, he stood up and removed his jacket. Don noticed it first. He had numbers tattooed on his forearm.

"Holy shit! He was in a concentration camp!"

Everyone was extremely nice to him after that.

My next class was math. There was nothing that Mr. Whitley could do. I kept all my tests and homework assignments and they all had "100" written on top. Last marking period I had received an "85" on a homework paper because Whitley said that he couldn't read some of it and therefore it was incorrect.

"How do you know that it's wrong if you can't read it?" I inquired politely. I didn't get a good response. From that point on I wrote as neatly as possible. However, I acted as surly as I could in class. Whitely reminded me of Eli, and he was a trigger for my displaced hatred. But, he didn't intimidate me the way other Eli substitutes did, and I had no problem speaking in his class.

It was my turn to go up to Whitley's desk. He took my card, glared at me, turned and scribbled "100" in the grade box. I smirked. Then, he took out his red pen, wrote an "F" in the attitude box, and handed the card back.

"How can I earn a "100" average and get an "F" for attitude!?" I screamed.

"Maybe if you do some introspective soul searching you can figure that out," he replied.

"This will keep me off the honor roll!"

"There is nothing honorable about you, Goldstein," he replied. "Whose card is next?"

On the way out of class Marcie said, "What the fuck. How can you get a "100" and an 'F'?"

"This may be my greatest accomplishment," I said. Suddenly, I felt proud that I had made him so angry.

Eighty-Three

On Thursday, April 4, 1968, I was sitting on the Merrick Road bus heading home from the Pequa Health Club. The driver had the radio on and suddenly a news bulletin came on. An emotionally shaken voice announced the fact that Martin Luther King Jr. had been assassinated. The Reverend Dr. Martin Luther King Jr. was dead!

I softly cried. Just as I had memorized President Kennedy's inauguration address, I had learned many of the words to Dr. King's *I Have a Dream* speech. His voice filled my head.

I have a dream that one day the nation will rise up and live out the true meaning of its creed: "We hold these truths to be self-evident that all men are created equal.

I have a dream that my four little children will one day live in a nation where they will not be judged by the color of their skin, but by the content of their character.

As tears rolled down my face, I looked around the bus. Many people were crying. Then I noticed, everyone else on the bus, including the driver, was black. I was overcome by a wave of fear. I thought of the many race riots that were happening in the cities. I slumped down in my seat, and quickly exited at my stop.

Eighty-Four

Assassinations, RACE RIOTS, protests, body counts from Vietnam, social unrest, drugs, the generation gap, and the Draft. There was bedlam in the world. Barry McGuire reflected how we were feeling when he sang,
And you tell me over and over again my friend
You don't believe we're on the Eve of Destruction

I felt perpetually anxious and agitated. I tried to lessen my consumption of valium, but my panic attacks escalated at the lower doses. I wanted to be more proactive about improving my mental state and spent as much time as I could engrossing myself in music, sports, talking to my friends and working out.

Frank became a ray of hope for me. On weekends he took the whole family out to dinner. This was the only time that we all ate together. He never worked out with me, but he continued to talk to me, ask questions, and to show an interest in my life. My favorite activity with him was driving. I still didn't have my learner's permit and felt a sense of rebelliousness when I drove his big Cadillac. Our conversations were particularly open and enjoyable when it was just the two of us in his car.

On a day that I was feeling intense angst, I decided to go to the Pequa Health Club. I felt welcome and comfortable there and was looking forward to a vigorous session. Pat, one of the men who worked there, came into the locker room as I was about to change.

"We need to talk," he said. He seemed very uncomfortable.

"What's wrong?" I asked.

"I'm sorry to have to tell you this, but you can't come here anymore."

"What! Why not?"

"You're not a member."

"Frank said that he bought me a membership."

"He never did. We were letting you come here as his guest. His membership expired two months ago and he still hasn't renewed it. We've been letting you use the gym anyway, but the owner has cracked down and unless you pay, we can't let you in."

I felt like I was just hit in my balls again. "I can't be here anymore?" I stammered.

Pat put his hand on my shoulder and gave me a sympathetic look. "I'm sorry."

I was dumbfounded. I did not see this coming at all. I felt dazed as I rode the bus home. I told Grandma what had happened.

"Your Mom isn't seeing him anymore. He lied to her about everything. You don't even want to know," she said.

"He was a liar?" I asked.

"About everything."

Same old story, different father figure.

Eighty-Five

Bob discovered the author Alan Watts first. Watts was a British philosopher who wrote books about Eastern Philosophy. We began reading about Taoism and Buddhism and embarked on a quest to discover the meaning of life. The Beatles were travelling to India to study Transcendental Meditation with the Maharishi Mahesh Yogi, and many famous writers and musicians were openly discussing their use of psychedelic drugs like mescaline and LSD. Bob and I both yearned to understand and to transcend our lives and sometimes discussed these topics on the phone until two or three in the morning.

"Watts says that you need to look to find God in yourself."

"Reality is subjective. It is like looking at a Rorschach ink-blot test."

"The people who are fanatic about their religions and who try to proselytize, like the Catholics that we know, really have no faith at all."

On weekends we had more time to share what we had read and to compose our own theories. I took an opportunity to unveil my conceptualization of the "three levels of consciousness."

"The first level is when a person is totally enmeshed in the superficial part of life. They don't realize the meaningless of their mindless rituals. They don't understand that most of what they do is subjective and has no real importance," I explained.

"People running around like simple minded sheep," said Bob.

"Exactly," I said. "We all want to hold the hand of something that gives our life meaning."

"The third level is when a person is aware of enlightenment. He has knowledge of transcendence. He is truly connected to God or to the universe or to whatever exists. The goal until you reach this state is to live in the second level."

"How would you do that?" Bob asked.

"In the second level a person realizes that there is a third level that is comprised of true meaning. In this level of consciousness, he has the knowledge that most of life as we know it is meaningless and arbitrary. He would be aware, as Watts stated, that reality is subjective and he would create his own meaning. In the second level you refuse to be dragged into the purposeless games and you strive to create your own meaning as you move towards enlightenment," I said.

Bob sat, pondered, and drank it all in. "We really need to do acid sometime," he said.

Eighty-Six

My friends and I were all very cognizant of news and current events. The Draft and the Vietnam War were constant topics of discussion. We were in a presidential election year, 1968, and most of us were pulling for the latest Democratic hopeful, Robert F. Kennedy. President Johnson had announced that he was not going to run for re-election, and Kennedy was picking up momentum in the primaries. His platform included fighting for racial equality and ending the War. He was the beloved John F. Kennedy's younger brother. We thought that he had charisma and he offered us hope.

When Martin Luther King Jr. was murdered, Robert Kennedy gave an impassioned speech directed at the Blacks. He said that even though Blacks might feel tempted to be filled with hate and mistrust against White people, the country needed unity between the races. He talked about what it was like to have his own brother assassinated. He spoke his mind and it seemed like we shared the same values. The country was in a horrible state, and young people often asked, "What would it have been like if John F. Kennedy had still been president?" With Bobby Kennedy, maybe we could find out.

On Thursday, June 6 we all awoke to the devastating news. Bobby Kennedy was shot to death after winning the California primary. I again shed tears over another person's death. Dion's record soon became a big hit.

Caught in the Undertow

Has anybody here seen my old friend Bobby?
Can you tell me where he's gone?
I thought I saw him walking over the hill,
With Abraham, Martin and John

Jeffrey, age 17

Eighty-Seven

ON JULY 1, 1968, I turned seventeen, and within a week I passed the test and had my learner's permit.

"Where're you going?" I asked Mom whenever she left the house. "To the store? The doctor? Let me drive. I'll wait for you. Do Keith or Michele have to go anywhere? Does Grandma? Please, let me drive."

I couldn't get enough time behind the wheel. I felt pure joy. Exhilaration. A rush of power and a reprieve from all the negative emotions. When I was home, and Mom had somewhere to go, I insisted on driving.

"How'd you learn to drive so well?" she asked.

"I'm just a natural," I replied. I never told her about my lessons with Frank. I was determined to become an expert by the time school started and I was able to take Driver's Ed. We still owned the 1961 Chevy Impala that the Weiners had tried to repossess in Texas. The air conditioning had long since broken down, the body was scratched, and there were well over one hundred thousand miles on the odometer. But I loved this car. It was big and powerful and I beamed whenever I sat behind the wheel.

"You and I have both been through a lot," I thought as I looked at the white worn out body of the vehicle and recalled our life in Houston. I allowed myself to enjoy a sense of hope for the future.

With Mom by my side, I drove the family to the train station for our second visit with Eli. He was waiting for us in his green

Rambler Classic. I insisted on driving after Keith and Michele reluctantly slid into the back.

"I have my learner's permit and I've been practicing," I declared.

"Be very careful. It's a new car," Eli replied.

I felt him staring at me as I adjusted the seat and mirrors. We approached a traffic light on Sunrise Highway and it began to turn yellow. I sped up, then decided to stop before it turned red.

"Never hesitate when you're driving!" he screamed in my ear.

"You should have fucking hesitated before you beat me and yelled at me!" I thought.

I drove onto the Southern State Parkway as we proceeded to Brooklyn. It was my first time on the highway and the elation that I felt driving at sixty five miles per hour far outweighed the gloom that flowed through me from sitting next to Eli. I even mustered up the confidence to ask questions

"What do you do for a job now?" I inquired.

"I'm currently unemployed," he replied.

"What does Anna do?"

No answer.

"Are your parents meeting us today?"

"They're busy."

"Don't they want to see us?"

No answer.

"Where are we going?"

"To my apartment. Anna and the kids will all be there."

"*The kids!*" I thought.

Eli gave me directions and we arrived after about thirty minutes of driving. My good feelings soon disappeared.

"Oh, Eli, look at how big they're getting," shrieked Anna as we entered their living room. She still talked as if we weren't there. Keith and Michele went off with Monica and David while Eli and I silently watched the Yankee game on their little TV. Anna later served us cheeseburgers and French fries. The day went agonizingly slowly and finally Eli drove us home.

Jeffrey Goldstein

"Next time I come could you bring some wallet sized pictures of yourself?" he asked as we approached the Bellmore train station. His request made me feel sick to my stomach.

"I don't want there to be a next time," Keith whispered to me as we walked away.

"Me neither," I said.

"Me too," said Michele. "Monica was real mean to me."

"Well, she has to live with Eli," I said and smiled at Michele. When I got home, I wrote this poem:

I Want to be More

I want to be more than a picture in your wallet
I have survived your psychotic rage
I have broken away from your death grip
The hands that battered my childhood
The arms that refused to hug me
I have crawled out of your debris
I have transcended you
And I will not become just a picture in your wallet

Eighty-Eight

AT THE BEGINNING OF AUGUST we received a letter with our schedules for the upcoming school year. I was going to be a senior. I would soon be applying to colleges. I'd soon be able to take my road test and have the opportunity to receive my driver's license. I was also less than a year away from getting my Draft Card, but going to college would give me a deferment for four years. And most importantly, I was less than a year away from moving out of Bellmore to live in a college dormitory. I ran to Bob's house and we listened to music and fantasized about our futures.

"Yeah, if there is a future," Bob said.

"Just think, since we've been little there's been the Cuban Missile Crisis, President Kennedy was killed, Bobby Kennedy was killed, Martin Luther King was killed, Malcolm X was killed, there's the Cold War, the Vietnam War is escalating, Blacks are rioting, we might be drafted, and we still don't even have our licenses," I said.

"I wish that we had a fallout shelter."

"Let's just have as much fun as we can while we can."

"Maybe we should be like Al and drop out of school and move to California."

"Then we could get drafted. I want to go to college, anyway. Once we get our licenses it will be a lot easier to have fun."

Having spending money was essential in terms of having freedom and fun, and I was able to work more than thirty hours a week at Bohack's during the summer. I had climbed the ladder and was now a cashier. The cashiers earned the most money of all the part time workers. I made an effort to talk to all the customers who went through my line and many of them told Frank about how polite and friendly I was. Frank liked to use the males to do the heavy, physical work, and the feedback from the shoppers helped me maintain my position as a checkout person.

"I can't believe how expensive all the meats have become," complained a short, gray haired lady as I rang up her purchases.

"It must be difficult to afford everything on a fixed income," I replied.

"Luckily I have my social security," she said. "It's still not easy."

"My mom's a teacher and we're having trouble, too," I said.

I commiserated with many of the customers who went through my line about the high cost of food. The clientele at Bohack's consisted mostly of the poorer and elderly residents from the older sections of Bellmore. The wealthier residents went to a bigger supermarket in Merrick called Waldbaum's, which is where Mom shopped. She went there because Bohack's did not sell kosher meats. Ever since Grandma moved in with us we kept a kosher home.

One night after work I heard Mom complaining to Grandma about finances.

"I'm working two jobs and we still don't have enough to live on," Mom said. "And Eli gives us *bubkas*."

I felt a responsibility to help the family. "You know," I interjected, "if you come through my line at Bohack's, I'll save you money."

"How could you do that?" she asked.

"I won't ring everything up. I'll bag stuff without charging you," I said.

"They don't have kosher meats."

"Buy everything but the meat."

The next week Mom, Grandma, Keith and Michele all came to my line. I pretended that I didn't know them and rang up only about seventy five percent of what they put in front of me. We never talked about it. They came back a few times and then the girl at the register next to me was fired on the spot, in front of the whole store. She had been doing the same thing with her friend's groceries.

"I must have made a mistake," she pleaded. "I didn't do it on purpose."

"We've been watching and you've failed to ring up food several times. You're lucky we're not having you arrested," Frank replied. "Don't ever come back to this store!"

I went home and told Mom that she should do all her shopping somewhere else from now on.

Eighty-Nine

I WAS SITTING IN HOMEROOM on the first day of my last year at Kennedy High School. Marcie still sat next to me and we compared schedules. She and I had many of the same classes together. We were both scheduled for Political Science the first semester, and Sociology the second semester, two social studies electives that I had been waiting to take. Marcie was also in my Physics, Calculus, and College English classes. In addition, I was enrolled in fourth year Latin, and, best of all, Driver's Ed. each day during first period. At the completion of Driver's Ed. in January I would be allowed to take my road test. I was one semester away from having my license.

Many classmates commented on my longer hair and sideburns. The coaches had relaxed the rules in football and we were allowed to grow our hair, as long as it didn't come down past the bottom of our helmet. My hair grew thick and bushy like an afro, so it easily stayed in my helmet, and I kept my sideburns trimmed so that they fit the code for facial hair. I needed glasses for driving and had purchased wire rimmed frames similar to John Lennon's. I wore my bell bottomed pants, multi-colored shirt, and truly felt like a hippie.

"Looking groovy," said Marcie. I blushed as she looked at me.

I eagerly rushed through the crowds in the corridor and found a seat in the first row for Driver's Ed. The teacher's name was Mr. Finley. I was amazed at his resemblance to Eli. Mr. Finley had a crew cut, a scowl on his face, anger emanated from his eyes, and he was the embodiment of arrogance. He spoke with a thick, gruff New York City accent.

"I have recently retired from the Marines. I served my country during World War Two, The Korean War, and did three tours of duty in 'Nam. I will not take any crap from anyone."

He looked around the room like a shark searching the waters for blood. I felt like I did when Eli was about to hit me. I bled first and he smelled it. He must have seen the terrified look on my face. He walked up to me and yelled, "Who the hell are you? You look like a Negro woman with sideburns!"

I could tell that people wanted to laugh but they were afraid to.

The class finally ended. "Why are there so many Eli's in the world?" I thought as I scurried from the room.

My next class was Political Science. I sat next to Marcie.

"How was Driver's Ed.?" Marcie asked.

"I don't know. I think that the teacher is my father," I said. Marcie reacted with a totally perplexed look, and then laughed, probably thinking that I meant to be funny.

Mr. Dubroff was a short, chubby, bald man with big thick glasses in black frames. He wore a wrinkled brown suit and a gaudy bright necktie. He told us that he lived politics. He practically glowed as he talked about his role as the president of the teacher's union, followed by stories about when he worked on John F. Kennedy's presidential campaign, and then enthusiastically explained what we were going to do in his class. He wanted us to have intelligent, lively discussions about issues such as the Draft, the War, racism, feminism, and politics.

"You all need to be able to make informed decisions in a democracy. 'Not to decide, is to decide.' What does that mean?"

My hand shot up. "If a person doesn't make their own decision, they are deciding to let someone else make it for them," I said. "Edmund Burke said that all that it takes for the triumph of evil is for a few good men to do nothing."

"Excellent," he said. "The course will culminate with a Mock Congress that will combine you with all the other seniors taking this class. You each will be assigned the role of a real

Congressman and you will research that person and write, act and talk in accordance with his or her beliefs. We will have debates, committee meetings and votes on bills. You will experience politics first hand."

I almost floated out of the room. We were going to do all the activities that I loved; debating, analyzing current events, and learning about how the government worked; with a teacher that enabled me to feel self-confident. This would be an opportunity for me to develop my speaking skills before I went to college. I knew that there would be no hands around my throat in this class. Then I chided myself. "Why can't my mind work like this with an asshole like Finley? I fucking hate you, Eli!"

Ninety

It was 6:30 in the morning. The alarm clock buzzed. I rolled over and tried to get out of bed. Waves of nausea rippled through my body. Lethargy and depression dulled my senses. I tried to concentrate.

"What day is today?" I thought. "Oh yeah, I have Finley in the classroom first period."

"Mom, I feel really sick. I need a note saying that I was late to school because of an upset stomach."

"Again," she said. "Maybe you need to see the doctor."

"I'll be alright. I'll only be missing a study hall anyway," I lied. "I must be eating too much food before I go to bed. You know that I'm trying to gain weight."

After Mom left for work, I got dressed and walked the two miles to school. I arrived just in time for second period with Mr. Dubroff. I enthusiastically participated in the class discussion analyzing the relationship between the Bill of Rights and the Draft. Marcie was always very outspoken and we usually had contrary opinions. My lively debates with Marcie felt almost sexual to me and the rest of the students were inclined to watch and to be entertained. Sometimes I knew a fact that Marcie had no counter argument for and I received applause from the other students. I practically glowed as I looked at the expressions on their faces. I yearned to feel this way more often.

Later that day, I threw a chest pass that shot past three opposing players and hit the hands of my teammate Steve as he jumped up and converted a layup. Then we all ran into the locker room, quickly changed back into our school clothes, and hurried to our next class. We were coming from the senior lounge. The seniors who were on the honor roll had the privilege of being in the lounge during lunch or study halls. We had the use of a small auxiliary gym. It contained a basketball court, ping pong tables, guitars, and a stereo system. It was our responsibility to keep it clean and to keep anyone out who didn't belong. Most days I gulped down my lunch and then spent the rest of my time playing basketball while we enjoyed the music. The seniors took turns bringing in albums by the Beatles, the Stones, the Doors, the Grateful Dead, Jimi Hendrix, the Jefferson Airplane, the Who, Bob Dylan, or the musician du jour.

Every few days, I spent my time playing guitar with Ronnie and Randy. One day at the beginning of October, we were playing *All you Need is Love* by the Beatles, while Debbie sang with us. As our guitars harmonized behind the sound of Debbie's melodic voice, I reflected on my days playing the violin in the orchestra. I luxuriated in my serenity. The senior lounge was an oasis and I imagined that college would be the same way. "There is no Eli in this world," I thought. My reverie was suddenly shattered by his venomous voice.

"You didn't show up to class again, Goldstein! If you don't give your oral report, you will fail, and I will make sure that you never get your license!" Finley spun around and slithered away with his words still hanging in the air.

"Wow, he really likes *you*," said Debbie.

Ninety-One

THREE DAYS DURING THE WEEK we practiced in the Driver's Ed. car. I had to show up for these classes or I would be ineligible to get credit for the course. Auto insurance was extremely high for teenaged male drivers on Long Island and passing Driver's Ed. entitled you to receive a sizeable discount. Our practice vehicles were all new model Fords which were supplied by the local dealership in Bellmore. My car contained four senior boys, including me, and Finley. The instructor always sat in the front seat by a dual brake. He then had the ability to slow down or to stop the car, or to yell into the driver's ear.

"I'm glad that we have one girl in the car to go along with the boys, Goldstein."

"You look like an old lady and you drive like one, too."

"If the brakes fail you can always stop the car with your sideburns."

Finley was constantly taunting me and I was too choked off to ever say anything.

"Think you're too good to talk to any of us, huh, Goldstein." He always brought a paper cup in the car with him and spit tobacco juice in it while we drove.

I became friends with Ronnie Lefkowitz, one of the other boys in the car. "Why don't you ever talk back to him? You're smarter than he is and definitely funnier."

I'd always change the subject. I refused to let Finley's derisions affect the way that I drove and I didn't want any of my friends to know how he affecting me.

"You could get Finley in trouble if you told the Principal or guidance counselor about how he puts you down. I'd back you up," said Ronnie. "He'd get in trouble just for chewing tobacco."

"I'm not a narc," I said. Ronnie then would laugh and repeat some of Finley's insults. His favorite was, "Goldstein, you can stop the car with your sideburns." I just smiled.

Finley did became a topic with Dr. Birnbaum, however.

"How do you feel when your teacher talks to you that way?"

"Like I'm struggling for air. I feel like I'm being strangled and I'm helpless."

"Who is strangling you?"

"My father."

"How does that make you feel?"

"When I was younger, one of my friends had a big dog that was taken away from a family that had kicked it and abused it. If anyone yelled around the dog, the dog would cower and whimper and start to shake. His tail, which was almost always wagging, would become rigid. He'd stand in one spot and he'd refuse to move. That's how I feel."

"What was your reaction to the dog?"

"I hugged him until he loosened up and relaxed, and then I started to cry."

"Who do you want to hug you?"

"My mother and my father."

"What exactly causes you to feel like that dog?"

"When an adult is yelling at me with angry emotions in their voice. When they have a condemning look in their eyes. When I feel like they hate me. The worst part is the look on their face."

"What do you think is really happening in your head?"

"I am hearing my mother say, 'You should be dead'. I am feeling my father hit me. I am feeling scared, guilty, and helpless. I don't want to be alive."

"You have to keep working at being aware of this. Your

teacher is not your mother or father. You are not a helpless little boy anymore."

"I get overwhelmed with these emotions before I can think."

"I know that it's overwhelming. Your brain and your body were changed by your horrible circumstances. A switch gets turned on by certain stressors and you almost instinctively have a specific reaction. Just think of all the progress that you have made so far. Focus on that and on how you will continue to move forward."

Ninety-Two

"Finley is not my parent. He's just a mean, stupid man. He cannot hurt me. I am not a little boy." I filled my head with thoughts that would counteract my dysfunctional feelings. I had to show up to give my oral report or I would fail Driver's Ed. I spent the bus ride to school slouched back in my seat with my eyes closed and pretending that I was sleeping so that no one would talk to me. I needed to focus on what I was going to say in my presentation and on not being inundated with negative thoughts.

I ignored everyone in homeroom. "Hey, are you ok?" Marcie asked. I remained in my trance. My stomach was in an upheaval. I ran into the boy's room on the way to class and vomited. I washed my face and resolutely walked into his room.

"Well, well, look who's finally shown up. Do you have the balls to give your report today, Miss Goldstein?"

"Just tell me when it's my turn," I said. There were only three students who still hadn't gone. I was sure that I would be called on first, but Finley chose a girl. I didn't even hear her speak as I remained focused on what I was going to say.

Next he called on Alfie. I was going to have to wait even longer. I took deep breaths and tried to calm down. The sweat rained down from my head and I fought off the waves of nausea. I watched Alfie and was amazed at his calmness. He looked as if he was having a conversation with his best friend in his living room. Alfie smiled, told jokes, was interesting, and connected with everyone in the room. "That's the way I will be someday," I thought.

I suddenly realized that Alfie had been talking for over ten minutes. I didn't want the period to end before I had a chance to go. It would be agonizing to have to wait until next class. I caught Alfie's eye, put my palms up and mouthed the words, "Come on!" He finally brought it to a close. There were ten minutes left.

"Alright Goldstein. Let's see if you can do this," challenged Finley.

I meandered, almost unconsciously, to the front of the room. I took several deep breaths, cleared my throat, and avoided making eye contact with Finley. I stared at the back wall and went into auto-pilot. Words crept out of my mouth. I had no idea what I was saying, but kept talking and staring at the back of the classroom. I somehow became aware of Alfie smiling at me and felt myself smiling back. I intermittently wiped the perspiration from my forehead and dried my hands on the back of my pants. Reasonably sure that I had said what I had prepared, I stopped talking and the class applauded. I marched triumphantly back to my seat and stared at Finley.

"Fuck you! Fuck you! Fuck you!" I thought. He sat at his desk, looked down, did paper work and didn't say anything else until the bell rang.

"Hey, good job," said Alfie as he slapped me on the back on the way out of class.

Ninety-Three

I WAS PULSATING WITH EXCITEMENT. I had been waiting for this to happen for such a long time, and now there I was, sitting in Mrs. Brody's office. I was meeting with my guidance counselor to discuss the process of applying to colleges. I had read through dozens of catalogues and brochures and felt exhilarated from just skimming through all the course descriptions. I smiled while thumbing through all the inviting pictures of beautiful campuses and coeds. It was as if I was about to apply for entry into heaven, and I met all the requirements.

Mrs. Brody's face lit up as she told me about my financial situation.

"Jeffrey, based on your test score, you have earned a New York State Regents Scholarship and you will also receive a College Incentive Award if you go to school in New York. Also, based on your grades and participation in sports, you will almost certainly receive a scholarship from the high school at the awards ceremony. You are in excellent shape financially and could attend any state school tuition free and with most of your room and board paid for."

"In terms of state schools, I am interested in Stony Brook and Binghamton," I said.

"To be considered at either of those universities, you need to have a total academic average higher than 90 percent, and a total score on your SAT's higher than 1200. Looking at your record, you obviously have exceeded those requirements."

"What if I want to go to a school in another state?"

"You wouldn't receive any of the New York State money,

but with your record, I am sure that you'd meet the requirements for other scholarships."

"I am also interested in Columbia University in New York City."

"Columbia is an Ivy League school and is very expensive. You would be eligible for all the New York state money and probably could get more aid and scholarships to help with the costs. Do you know what you plan to major in?"

"I like English and social studies, and I also know that I want to do something where I am working with people. I plan to take a big variety of courses and see what happens."

"Good idea. I see that you do equally well in all of your subjects. In terms of choosing a college, I recommend visiting the schools that you are interested in, attending a few classes, and staying overnight in a dorm. See what the atmosphere feels like to you."

"I would love to do that. Thank you for all the help."

I walked away smiling. I was going to go to college! At night I went to Bob's house.

"I'll be able to take the courses that I want, I'll be living away from home, there'll be beautiful girls, I'll be safe from the Draft, there'll be beautiful girls, and it won't cost much money. It's going to be amazing!" I gushed.

"I want to major in psychology," replied Bob. "I want to study the philosophy of the mind."

"Where are you applying to?" I asked.

"St. John's University."

"Are you crazy? That's a Catholic school! You'd never fit in there."

"My parents have zero money to give me, and with my grades I can go there for free. I want to put my money into buying a nice car."

"So you're going to live at home and commute?"

"My Grandmother is moving out of the apartment above our house and I'm going to live there. I'll have total privacy."

As I went home my disappointment in Bob's decision soon faded from my consciousness as I again focused on the realization that I was going to be living somewhere else next year.

Ninety-Four

As A RESULT OF COACH Millhouse's efforts, senior athletes were now allowed to use the weight room during their senior lounge time. In Millhouse speak, *allowed to* meant *required to*. He apparently didn't want us spending our free time having fun if we could be working out. I decided to lift with some of the other football players on Tuesdays and Thursdays, and was still able to play basketball or guitar on the other days.

The first Tuesday that I was in the weight room, eight of us became involved in a "military press" contest. We all started out with a 100 pound barbell, and when a person failed in his attempt to complete the lift, he was out of the contest. We kept increasing the amount in 5 pound increments. Everyone stayed in until we reached 120 pounds. At 130 pounds, there were four people left. When we increased to 150 pounds, Stan and I were the only two left. My previous personal record had been 160 pounds. We both completed our attempts at 170 pounds, and when we reached 175 pounds, Stan had the weights halfway up, and then dropped them. My heart was racing and my adrenaline was pumping as I pushed the 175 pounds over my head. I won the contest.

"I'll try 180 pounds," I said.

I was all pumped up and felt energized from the crowd of spectators. As I struggled to straighten out my arms, my brain filled with images of all the monsters in my life. There were Mom's horrible words, Moskowitz the produce manager at Bohack's, and I even envisioned the monster in the drain from Brooklyn. I was crushing them all as the barbell slowly rose up into the air. As I completed the lift I drove the weights through Eli's angry face.

"Once more," I said. They loaded 185 pounds onto the barbell.

"This would be a school record!" Alfie exclaimed. "Wait until I get my camera ready so that I can have a picture for the school newspaper."

I took several deep breaths, balanced myself, grabbed the barbell, strained, flexed every muscle in my body, grunted, and slowly willed the barbell up into the air as I pictured Finley swallowing his tobacco. I extended my arms above my head, triumphantly held up the 185 pounds as Alfie snapped the photograph, and then exhaled as I dropped the weights and watched them bounce on the mat. The picture ran in the *Cougar Crier* later that week with the caption "Jeffrey Goldstein presses 185 pounds under great pressure."

The next day after the newspaper came out, Finley called on me at the beginning of first period class.

"Hey, Goldstein, you think you're really strong, don't you?"

I didn't know how to answer and said nothing.

"Why don't you come on up here and arm wrestle me? Let's see how strong you really are."

Finley outweighed me by over forty pounds and he was much taller with longer arms. He had spent years in the military and allegedly had a black belt in karate. I had no expectations that I could compete with him at anything physical.

"Come on up here. Let's see what you've got," he challenged.

The class was silent. Finally, Alfie blurted out, "You're super strong, Goldstein. Don't back down!"

Finley was leaning forward with his elbow on the table in front of the room. His forearm was extended upwards and his big hand was open and waiting to grip mine.

I reluctantly ambled up to the front, went to the other side of the table, steadied myself and prepared for battle. His big hand swallowed mine and he squeezed it with a vice-like grip. I looked at him as he transformed into Eli.

"Your forearm is twice as long as his!" someone shouted at Finley.

"Yeah, but look at how big his biceps are," Finley retorted. "Ready, let's go!"

It felt as if he was squeezing the life out of my fingers. I managed to fight back as hard as I could and held my arm up for almost a minute. Then violently, he slammed the back of my hand onto the table. He wiped the sweat from his hands into his pockets, adjusted his necktie, walked to the middle of the room, and began teaching. He acted as if nothing had happened.

As the bell rang, I snuck out of the room feeling that once again, Eli had won.

Ninety-Five

"What would you like to talk about today?"

"Dr. Birnbaum," I replied, "you have helped me tremendously and I am very grateful. But, I feel like I want to do something different at this point. I want to make even more progress before I leave for college."

"What exactly do you want to happen?"

"I have been reading about behaviorism and cognitive behavioral therapy," I said. "I want to approach my challenges from a different perspective. I want to try some different philosophies. Can you help me get an appointment with a behavioral therapist?"

Dr. Birnbaum was very supportive of my decision and he referred me to Dr. Samuel Levine. Dr. Levine was part of the same practice and he had an office next door to Dr. Birnbaum's. A week later I had my first session.

Unlike my first meeting with Dr. Birnbaum, I came into Dr. Levine's office feeling very calm and optimistic. He was much younger than Dr. Birnbaum and spoke with an energetic voice. He had long, curly brown hair, a bushy brown beard, wore silver wire-rimmed glasses, and was casually dressed in a bright, colorful, patterned shirt. His first words were, "Please call me Sam."

"I've read your file and Dr. Birnbaum and I discussed your case," he said. "I know all about your history, so it won't be necessary for you to talk about all of that again. If you are willing, we will use a type of treatment called 'Rational Emotive Therapy'. We are going to focus on the link between your thoughts and your emotions, and their effect on your behavior. The goal is for you to replace your irrational, dysfunctional thoughts with rational ones. How does this sound so far?"

"Intriguing," I replied.

"One of our fundamental premises is that we don't need to continually revisit your past. Just because something once strongly affected your life, it doesn't have to affect it forever. Your present is your past of tomorrow and changing your present will help you to have a better future."

"Don't I need to continue to analyze the events that lead to my problems?" I asked.

"You by now are well aware of these events. We believe that you were indoctrinated into having self-defeating reactions to certain stimuli, and these tendencies grew stronger and were reinforced as you grew older. Circumstances occur, but your perceptions, attitudes and internal sentences are what affect you emotionally. For you to change, you must first change your thoughts and reactions to your experiences. We need to help you develop a better, more self-helping functional set of constructs. This probably sounds very abstract to you right now."

"I think that it makes sense. I am just wondering about my emotions. Sometimes they seem to have a life of their own. How is it possible to turn them off?"

"Do they control you all the time? Do you always respond to similar circumstances in the same way?"

"No. Some of the time I am in control and can be the way I want to be. It's just that when the most powerful emotions arise, I feel overwhelmed."

"Our belief is that every time you have an emotional reaction, the feelings are preceded by a series of thoughts. This process is usually an unconscious one. When you control the thoughts, you determine the ensuing emotions. It's a matter of cause and effect. You have the ability to control this chain of events. With practice, you can choose how you feel. You have been conditioned to embrace being overwhelmed in a negative way. If you develop an awareness of what you're doing, you can learn to form a new pattern. You already have been changing the negative constructs. What do you think about all of this?"

"I understand the concept of what you're saying. I am having difficulty picturing what the process would be like."

Sam gave me a book by Dr. Ellis entitled *Rational Living*, and a chart to fill out. The chart had the title, *Using Rational Thoughts to Overcome Irrational Discomfort*. It was divided into three sections. The first column had a heading called "Description of Situation," the second said "Irrational Thoughts" and the third one was titled "New Rational Thoughts". It all seemed very overwhelming and intimidating.

"Read as much of this book as you can before next week," he said. "Also, when a situation occurs that causes you to feel emotional distress, write a brief description of the event on the chart. Then become very introspective and write down the irrational, dysfunctional thoughts that cause your negative emotions. The final step is to apply your logic and to create thoughts that will help you diminish or replace the inhibiting emotions. We will discuss this chart each week and explore ways of controlling your undesirable reactions."

My first reaction when I left was, "Wow, he's given me homework." But the more I thought about it, the more encouraged and hopeful I felt. I read the book for almost three hours after I got home, and then called Bob to explain it to him.

It fits in with many of the Greek philosophers," he said. "Your life is what your thoughts make it."

"Yeah," I said. "You are what you think."

Ninety-Six

"Do THE THING YOU FEAR and the fear disappears," was a quote attributed to Eleanor Roosevelt. Sam shared this thought with me during one of our sessions over Thanksgiving vacation. I attempted to exemplify this concept when school resumed on Monday.

"What's the implied speed limit in a village if no speed limit is posted?" asked Finley in first period Driver's Ed.

I raised my hand and blurted out, "Thirty miles an hour," before anyone else could speak.

Finley glared at me and then asked the class, "What happens if a police officer clocks you exceeding the speed limit while you are driving in the passing lane and overtaking a slower moving vehicle in the right hand lane?"

"You get a speeding ticket anyway," I exclaimed.

By the end of the class, I actually began to feel relaxed. Ronnie and Alfie joked around with me on the way to the next class.

"Remember when he said that you looked like a Negro woman with sideburns?" asked Ronnie.

We all laughed.

"I've never seen a teacher arm wrestle with a student before," said Alfie. "I thought that the veins on your head were going to pop. You should have let him punch you in the stomach, instead."

"Yeah, that worked out real well when you did it," I said. "Finley probably would have missed my stomach on purpose."

Later in the day I went to Physics class. Mr. Reiger was

the teacher, and he held us all accountable by asking random students to answer tough questions, and requiring us to solve difficult problems based on the homework. If a student made a mistake, or wasn't prepared for class, he was merciless with his criticism. I forced myself to volunteer to solve a problem on the blackboard, even though everyone hated being in this position. If you didn't do everything perfectly, he exploded with vitriol, while everyone watched you squirm. I remembered the Eleanor Roosevelt quote and became calm and focused. I exhaled as I nailed the problem.

In English, I agreed to memorize and to recite a poem in front of the class. I chose *A Dream Deferred* by Langston Hughes. The beginning of the poem says,
What happens to a dream deferred?
Does it dry up
Like a raisin in the sun?
I reminded myself that I had a dream for myself. I wanted to have the ability to speak freely and easily without feeling choked up. I was determined to have this capability around anyone. I did not want to be diminished by Eli, Finley, or any other asshole who verbally abused me. I didn't want my dream to be put off. I recited the poem with all the confidence and poise that I could muster.

Even though I was acting differently, it still was a struggle to change my irrational thoughts into rational ones. My negative emotions would insidiously manifest themselves. During our sessions, Sam reminded me that I was the only person who knew what was going on inside of me. Others could only see my behaviors and I was definitely acting more confidently. He encouraged me to persevere in my efforts to control my thoughts, and to act and to think as the person that I wanted to be.

I never talked to him about my medication. I was still using valium, but stuck to the minimum dose. Whenever I attempted to stop completely, I started having intense anxiety attacks. I had several renewals left from Dr. Birnbaum's prescription and promised myself that I would stop taking the pills as soon as my supply was depleted.

Ninety-Seven

I DECIDED TO FOLLOW MY GUIDANCE counselor's advice and to go on a college visit. My friend Rich Katz was now a freshman at Stony Brook. In high school, Rich was part of a group that included Skinny Vinny. When Rich and his friends were seniors at Kennedy, and I was a junior, they invited me to join them when they drove to Nunley's in Baldwin to play miniature golf, or to go roller skating at the rink in Levittown. The roller skating rink was next door to Jahn's, an ice cream parlor, and we'd all have sundaes before driving back to Bellmore. Rich and his friends were the straightest people that I knew. When I was with them, it seemed as if we were living in the 1950's and part of the TV show *Leave it to Beaver*.

Rich was extremely intelligent but had very strict parents and had lived a sheltered life. He dressed, looked, acted, and moved like a middle-aged man. He had a very affable personality, however, and laughed very easily. I enjoyed playing records for him in my room and watching his reaction. With the rock music blaring, he allowed his repressed emotions to come to life. When I played the first side of the Doors *Light My Fire* album, he shed his mature man persona and danced around the room in an unrestrained jubilation. I tried unsuccessfully to get him to smoke pot. However, he always wanted to hear my newest records. Sometimes the other members of his group would join us and sit there with their jaws hanging when I told stories, most of them true, of my drug experiences and romantic escapades with girls. I always presented myself as the coolest person in the room.

Rich had become radicalized in college. He looked the same, but was very politically aware and spoke with a socialist ideology. I called him up to ask if I could visit and spend a few nights in his dorm. He happily obliged, with the stipulation that I bring a few of my newest albums. I put some Janis Joplin and Jimi Hendrix into my bag. Rich came home on a Thursday night to get some winter clothes, and I drove back with him to campus. I would miss school on Friday, but a college visit was a legal excuse to miss school for seniors.

Rich lived in a suite that contained three bedrooms, a bathroom and a living room. I would be able to sleep on the couch. Rich's dorm was named Frederick Douglass College and it was one of five dormitories in a group called Tabler Quad. There were five quads spread out around the Stony Brook campus. Each quad had its own student cafeteria. We ate a late dinner in Rich's cafeteria when we arrived on Thursday.

Even though it was late, there were still many students hanging around after dinner. Rock music emanated from speakers in the ceiling while coeds laughed and had lively conversations at the various tables. Rich spotted David Adcock and waved him over. David was tall and skinny with shoulder length dark brown hair that was partially tied back into a ponytail.

"You and David have something in common," Rich said. "You both know more about music than anyone I've ever met."

"Well, Jeff, let's see if you are worthy of that description," said David. "I like to play a game where I say a line from a Dylan song and the other person then has to say the next line. If he gets it right, he tries to stump me. So, here's your line:

My friends from the prison, they ask unto me, how good, how good does it feel to be free

"What comes next?"

I replied,

And I answer them most mysteriously, are birds free from the chains of the skyway?

"That's from *Ballad in Plain D*," I said. "It's one of my favorite lines."

"Impressive," he said. "Dylan is a fucking genius. He should win the Pulitzer Prize."

We continued trying to stump each other for the next ten minutes while Rich watched and laughed.

After dinner we returned to Douglass College and passed a big group of males and females excitedly playing a board game in the hall. They proudly told us about how they invented a way to transform *Monopoly* into a drinking game. Mugs and half full pitchers of beer sat on the tables. The smoky smell of incense and grass drifted out from under several suite doors as we made our way back to Rich's room. A beautiful half naked blonde haired girl walked past us as we opened the door. I stayed up most of the night talking to Rich's suitemates.

On Friday morning I accompanied Rich to his first class. He was taking Twentieth Century American History in the Lecture Center, a brand new modern looking concrete building. Dr. Trask, the professor, passionately lectured about why Woodrow Wilson was the greatest modern American president.

"If Congress had accepted Wilson's ideas, there never would have been a Second World War," he animatedly opined.

"This is fascinating," I told Rich.

"We go to a lecture twice a week, and then one day a week we have discussions in a small group with a teaching assistant," explained Rich. "They're called recitations."

After class, Rich walked me around the whole campus. He showed me the other academic buildings, dorms and the Student Union building. "This is where they hold small concerts and lectures." He explained. "It also has a café, several places to eat, lounges, and bowling alleys." We then entered the Athletic Center. He pointed out the workout rooms, the countless sets of weights, the exercise equipment, the pool and the many basketball courts.

"Any student can use the gym whenever he wants. It is always open. You can play basketball or workout at 4AM if you want to," he said.

Friday night we attended a concert in the gym. We enjoyed

a psychedelic band from San Francisco named *Quicksilver Messenger Service*.

"We get free concerts and free movies every weekend. The Grateful Dead were here last week and Blood, Sweat and Tears are performing next weekend. Many of the groups who play in the City come here also"

On Saturday I played basketball in the gym with several people from Rich's dorm, read in the library while Rich did some research for a history report, met more people in the cafeteria and played guitar with other members of the suite. We watched a group of students at a rally in the middle of campus singing songs and giving fiery speeches. Everyone that I met was interesting and fun to be with.

On Sunday, Mom and her latest boyfriend Hal came to take me home. First, we took a stroll around the campus.

"Everyone here looks like a hippie!" Mom exclaimed.

"Yeah, isn't it great!" I replied. I knew that I was going to commit to Stony Brook. It was as if everything there was created just for me.

Ninety-Eight

"NEXT WEEK WE BEGIN OUR Mock Congress," Mr. Dubroff announced. "Each of you will be assigned to play the role of an actual member of the House of Representatives. Your job for the rest of this week will be to find out everything that you can about your new persona. You will study the bills that they introduced and familiarize yourself with their voting record. You will adopt your Congressman's political philosophy and ideology. Your ultimate goal is to think, speak, and act in the same way your person would. As we move forward, each of you will be required to introduce, and work for the passage of two separate bills. These pieces of proposed legislation must be congruent with your legislator's philosophy."

"How will you decide which particular Congressman each of us is assigned?" asked Debbie.

"I will do it randomly."

"Do we have to try to look like our person?" asked Donald.

"Definitely," joked Mr. Dubroff. "In your case, Donald, I will make sure that you are a Congress *woman* so that we can all see you in a dress."

After spending a few days in the library, we began introducing and debating bills in committees in our class. The Congress was scheduled to conclude with all three political science classes combining for all day sessions in the auditorium. We had permission to miss our other classes on those days.

I was assigned the role of a very liberal Democratic representative from the San Francisco area, and Marcie was a very conservative Republican from Louisiana. We had antithetical points of view and found ourselves on the opposing sides of almost all the issues. The idea of arguing with Marcie was intoxicating.

The most contentious debate occurred when Marcie introduced a bill that would in effect eliminate welfare in the United States.

"The government run welfare state has created a culture of dependency and indolence," she argued. "Welfare is a disincentive for people to work. Unmarried, young, indigent woman get pregnant and have babies because they know that the government will take care of them. Then, these children born into relief families, are more likely to live on public assistance when they grow up. They never learn to be self-sufficient. The hard-working, responsible American citizens are forced to give up large portions of their paychecks to support and subsidize people who won't work."

"The welfare system was established in the 1930's under President Roosevelt to help the families that were devastated by the Great Depression," I replied. "It is true that the current system is imperfect and needs reforms. However, if it is eliminated, millions of innocent children will be adversely affected. Many people are born into situations and circumstances beyond their control and are working as hard as they can to improve their lives. Our government can't just turn its back on them."

"If people need help, then private charities and neighborhoods should pick up the slack," said Marcie. "The government programs have grown to the point where they are enabling people to be lazy. Because this safety net exists, young women, for example, can have babies knowing that they can live on government aid. These girls would have to think twice about having children out of wedlock if the government wasn't there to subsidize their irresponsibility."

We continued to argue back and forth and eventually others joined the discussion and spoke from their Congressman's point of view. Marcie gave very cogent rebuttals to all of the other opinions. After class I approached Marcie.

"You're doing an incredible job," I said. "It must be difficult to take a side that you don't agree with."

"I am giving my real opinions," she said. "I despise welfare."

I was flabbergasted. I assumed that she had the same liberal beliefs that I did.

"Don't you think that many people have the deck stacked against them?" I asked. "A black kid born in a poor, inner city ghetto will have a much more difficult chance of succeeding than we do as whites born in the suburbs and going to a good school. Millions of innocent children would probably die without some sort of government assistance. And it's not their fault that they were born into a racist, prejudiced, unequal society."

"Then maybe they should die out," she replied. "Remember learning about natural selection? No one helped the dinosaurs. There is no welfare system for weak animals that can't survive on their own in the jungle. Why should we help people who don't have the intelligence, skills or attributes necessary to survive in modern society?"

"Because we humans have compassion and empathy. Every person has worth and dignity. Should we just throw all the retarded babies off of a cliff like they did in Sparta?"

"The world is a tough place and we all have to fight to be successful. I'm not saying that we should throw anyone off of a cliff. I believe that if I work hard and become successful, then it isn't fair for the government to take my money away and redistribute it to people who haven't earned it."

Marcie now seemed like a racist to me. I couldn't believe how smug and insensitive she appeared. As I walked away, however, I realized the source of my passion for defending welfare. It was tied into my feelings that someone should have helped me when I was being abused. Still, I had lost my attraction for Marcie. "I guess I'll have to start fantasizing about someone else," I thought.

Ninety-Nine

SHE GLOWED WITH AN ALLURING warmth. She seemed to be smiling, even when she wasn't. Her name was Audrey and she operated the checkout line cash register next to mine at Bohack's. Her presence was enhanced by the fact that she had a gorgeous face and sexy body. I looked at her as often as I could while I was ringing up groceries and excitedly noticed that she often looked back at me. Audrey was a year younger than I was and a junior at Kennedy. We only saw each other at work.

Audrey and I were often the only two cashiers on Sunday evenings as we both manned our registers until closing time. I took advantage of the opportunity for us to be alone by waiting outside with her until her mom arrived from South Merrick to take her home. Audrey seemed to be very well read and intelligent and our conversations were free flowing and comfortable.

"What's your opinion about the welfare system?" I asked one Sunday night.

"Why are you asking me that?" she replied.

"We had a big debate about that topic in my political science class and I'm curious about other people's opinions."

"Well, I don't like the fact that I lose a big chunk of my paycheck, and all the taxes that are deducted, but there are obviously many people who would die if we didn't help them."

"Would you date a black man?" I asked.

"What a question! Why, are you black?" she laughed.

"Well, Finley, my driver's ed. teacher did say that I look like a 'negro woman,'" I said as I made quotation marks with my fingers.

"You do have quite the afro going, although I've never seen a woman with sideburns and muscles like that."

"You didn't answer my question. Would you date a black man?"

"Honestly, I would date anyone that I liked, if he truly liked me."

"I truly like you. Do you want to go on a date?"

"Ask me again when you get your license."

"I have my road test in February. Just two more weeks!"

Audrey waved good-bye as she opened the door to her mom's car.

Two weeks later I sat in the car waiting to take my test for my driver's license. I was in Freeport, the most difficult location, but the place that had the earliest openings. There were several one way streets in Freeport and you were required to parallel park on both the right and left sides of the street. I had persuaded Mom to take me out practicing almost every day. We drove around looking for places to park and I progressed to the point where I could easily maneuver the vehicle into any space. I was feeling very confident as I sat and waited.

Finally the man from the DMV entered my car. He had a crew cut and his looks and demeanor reminded me of Eli and Finley. I suddenly felt panicked, but forced myself to slow down my breathing, and to fill my head with positive thoughts. I focused on my driving as I followed his directions. I performed a perfect three point turn. He said nothing while he wrote on his clipboard. I executed a parallel park on the right. My car ended up equidistant from the vehicles in front and behind me with my wheels two inches from the curb. He told me to do a parallel park on the left between a small sports car and a big pickup truck. The big difference in size between the front and rear vehicles made it difficult to judge my distance from the curb. I concentrated and parked flawlessly. When we were finished, I knew that I had easily passed.

The first phone call I made was to Audrey. She said yes! Saturday night she would be sitting next to me in my car! I was officially a licensed driver and I had a date with a sexy girl!

One-Hundred

ON SATURDAY I SPENT THE whole morning washing, waxing and vacuuming the Chevy. It had never looked so good. In the afternoon, it started to rain, and by evening, it was sleeting and snowing. Our date was at 7:00, and after dinner, the precipitation finally stopped.

"The roads are terrible," Mom said. "I don't think that you should drive tonight."

"I'll be alright," I replied. "You know that I'm a good driver."

"You don't have experience on roads like this. Wait until another night."

"I'll be careful. How can I get experienced if I don't drive? It's going to be winter for a while. I'm not going to wait until spring"

"It's too icy. Wait until the roads are better."

"Listen to your Mother," Grandma chimed in.

I persisted until she finally gave in and I grabbed the keys. I drove to Audrey's house with a big smile on my face. When I arrived, I made small talk with her parents, promised to drive safely, and assured them that I would bring Audrey home early. I held her hand as we walked to the car.

A block away from her house stood a stop sign. As we approached it, I talked about how the car had come from Houston, Texas. "It's an amazing car. It has unbelievable acceleration," I said. "Check this out!"

I looked both ways and then sped away from the intersection. Suddenly, I hit a patch of ice. The car went into an uncontrollable skid and started to fishtail. I tried to straighten it out by steering in the same direction as the skid, like we learned in driver's ed., but we were now doing 180's. We gained speed as the car wildly glided down the street, as if it had a will of its own. I glanced over at Audrey. She had her feet up and pressed against the dashboard. There was a look of terror on her face. My insane vehicle, without warning, then shot up a driveway and violently crashed into a small car parked in a garage. The innocent little sports car hit the front wall of the garage, bounced back, and hit my front bumper. It then crumpled like an accordion as a rake fell on it.

"Are you okay?" I asked Audrey.

"I'm fine but I'm going home," she said as she opened the door and walked away.

I looked at my Chevy. There was a slight indentation in the front bumper. I looked the other way. The car in the garage was totaled. A man came running out of the house. He screamed in horror as he surveyed the damage to his car.

"I just bought a new, expensive Fiat and I parked it in the garage to keep it safe! Look what you did to it! You destroyed it in my own garage!" He came towards me and I ran away as he chased me around the house. He slipped and fell on some ice just as the police arrived.

Eventually Mom and her boyfriend Hal arrived. She screamed at me the whole way home. At home, Grandma joined in. I kept my mouth shut.

"All teenagers are eventually going to be in an accident," Hal said to Mom later that night. "Fortunately, Jeffrey had one where no one was hurt. If he learns from this, then at least he now has his accident out of the way."

Mom listened to him and was calmed down by the end of the weekend. She had planned to buy a new car anyway, and we made a deal. I was going to pay her $200 for the Chevy and I vowed to drive more cautiously. The car would stay in her name to keep the insurance rates down.

The biggest challenge I now faced was the ridicule that I

anticipated receiving on Monday at school. I decided to take the same approach that I had in the past and to joke about it.

Ricky was first. "How do you fucking total someone's car while it's parked in his garage?"

"He should have closed the garage door," I laughed.

"Goldstein, you're amazing," mocked Sam. "I couldn't do that if I tried."

"Well, I have driving skills. I hate those foreign cars and wanted to destroy his. If he had an American car like mine, it probably wouldn't even have a scratch."

Soon everyone was focused on a new topic. I still had to face Audrey at work on the weekend. I didn't have enough courage to call her.

The next Sunday I occasionally glanced at her as we rang up the customers' groceries. She avoided making eye contact. I approached her after work.

"I am so sorry," I said. "I was reckless and I put you in danger. Please accept my apology. I really like you."

She finally looked at me. "Please don't do anything that stupid again. I want to be able to feel safe in your car."

"You can. I promise."

The next Saturday night Audrey was sitting next to me in my car as Bob and his girlfriend Olivia sat with their arms around each other in the back. I had installed a tape deck and we sang at the top of our lungs as Jerry Garcia and the Grateful Dead poured over us. It was only 40 degrees but the windows were wide open as I sped at 75 miles an hour along the ocean highway on the south shore of Long Island. My left hand was on the steering wheel and I grabbed Audrey's hand with my right one. She placed her hand on my knee as we inhaled the cold salty air. Being careful was not on the agenda that night.

One-Hundred One

Lysergic ACID DIETHYLAMIDE. LSD. Timothy Leary, a psychologist, became famous conducting experiments with psychedelics at Harvard University and publicly advocated their use. "Turn on, tune in, drop out!" was the ubiquitous slogan. The Beatles famously dropped acid. "Turn off your mind, relax and float downstream," sang John Lennon in the song *Tomorrow Never Knows*. Popular writers, including Ken Kesey, Tom Wolfe, and Allen Watts, had spoken of their *trips* .Rock bands openly praised the effects of hallucinogenic drugs. "Feed your head!" urged Grace Slick of the Jefferson Airplane. Tripping seemed to be a rite of passage for my generation.

Ronnie Lefkowitz had dropped acid. I met Ronnie in driver's ed. and sometimes sat with him at lunch. Ronnie had a severe case of acne and long, greasy hair that came down past his shoulders. He was unkempt, wore scruffy looking clothes, and radiated a disgusting body odor. He was highly intelligent but refused to apply any effort to his school work. This was 1969 and the supposed *Age of Aquarius* and *Era of Peace, Love and Understanding*, but kids like Ronnie were still ostracized. I assumed that he was too much of a *hippie* to care about how he looked and I enjoyed talking to him because he saw the world differently from my other friends.

"You've got to do acid with me sometime soon," he urged.

Now both Bob and Ronnie were trying to sell me on LSD.

"My head's too messed up to handle that shit. I keep hearing about people's bad trips. My life's been painful enough as it is."

Caught in the Undertow

"Your life couldn't be any more miserable than mine. Acid helps you get past the bullshit."

"I have been talking about tripping with my friend Bob. If we decide to, I'll definitely tell you. You are the only person I know who's experienced."

"There's a pool hall in Baldwin that I go to on weekends. That's where I get my acid. I take a tab and play some eight ball while I hallucinate and expand my consciousness. Let's go on Saturday."

"Alright, I'll pick you up and check it out. Where do you live?"

"On Bedford Avenue."

"There are no houses there. Only stores."

"We live above the drug store."

On Saturday night, Ronnie invited me upstairs to an apartment, which I never knew existed. His family lived in a tiny, one room walk-up, and when I first entered, I was overpowered by an unidentifiable stench. It was sparsely furnished with items that appeared to be stolen from a junkyard. Ronnie's father was slumped on a tattered sofa and was staring at a small black and white portable TV while deeply inhaling a cigarette. He didn't even notice me. Ronnie's older brother was sprawled out on a cot listening to loud music through big headphones. He also had a cigarette in his mouth. Ronnie's mother quietly smiled at me as she moved a pot back and forth on a stove. She had deep, black circles under her eyes and looked like she hadn't slept in a month. A filthy, hairy dog limped up to me and sniffed my shoes.

"Welcome to my world," Ronnie said.

"What does your father do?" I asked Ronnie as we drove away.

"He's a janitor at some factory in Hempstead."

"Why do you live in Bellmore, then?"

"They wanted me to go to a good school. That's done me a lot of good."

Ronnie dropped a tab of acid as we drove to Freeport. We spent the next few hours shooting pool and discussing life.

Ronnie did most of the talking. He was obviously hallucinating and shared many nonsensical ideas. He moved back and forth from lucidity to absurdity. Sometimes he seemed to break from reality, but then would come back and engage me. After about three hours he took some barbiturates to help him come back from his trip.

"It's over," he said. "Time to go home."

On the way back I asked him what his brother did.

"He was in college but screwed up and flunked out. He was drafted and goes to basic training next week."

"Are you going to college?" I asked. "You're one of the smartest people I know."

"I've had enough of school. It has nothing to offer me. As soon as I graduate I'm off to Canada."

"What about your family?" I asked. "If you go there, you can never come home.

"The hell with them. My father smacks me around when he gets angry, my brother joins in, and my ma just watches. I don't care if I never see any of them again. Fuck 'em."

As I drove home, his words echoed in my head. "Fuck 'em."

I had some horrible experiences with my family but I would never desert them. I wanted them to be a part of my life. Eventually, I wanted a wife and children of my own, and to be surrounded by love. I longed for the feeling of being connected, not alienated. There was rock music playing in my car but my mind wandered to the musicals that Grandma had taken me to in the City when I was younger. A song from *Carousel* played in my head. I cried as I recalled the lyric.

> *When the children are asleep we'll sit and dream*
> *The things that every other dad and mother dream*
> *We'll think what fun we have had and be glad that it all came true*
> *When today is a long time ago*
> *You'll still hear me say that the best dream I know is you*

One-Hundred Two

THE RICH ARE THE SAME as you and me. They just have more money. I had heard someone say that in a movie. My friends from South Merrick, especially Shawn, Marshall and Dave, were very rich. Everything about them fascinated me. I was one of the few "poor" kids that they allowed into their world. The Merrick boys reminded me of Barry and Bruce in Texas. My friendship with them gave me the opportunity to be at the Astrodome on opening day to see the Yankees.

As I walked through Marshall's front door, the contrasts between our lives hit me in the face. I drove a 1961 Chevy that had over 150,000 miles on the odometer. Their parents bought them 1969 high- end sports cars. They all had passports and had travelled to Europe and Asia. They went on expensive ski vacations in the winter and golfed at exclusive country clubs in the summer. Their huge houses were mansions compared to my home. Their families had maids and cooks who prepared exotic foods that you couldn't buy at Bohack's. They ate dinner on mahogany tables using real silverware. Their well-groomed French poodles and pure bred cocker spaniels luxuriously rested on plush, velvet couches and strutted across oriental Persian rugs. The teenagers smoked Turkish hashish and stole brandy and cognac from oak liquor cabinets. Professional landscapers nurtured their lush, green lawns and gardeners groomed their Bonsai plants.

Their legendary poker games on Friday nights were often discussed at school. Only a very exclusive group of kids were allowed to attend. I had been invited several times, and now that

I had a car, I was finally able to participate. I had played poker with my other friends and we bet nickels and dimes. The most anyone ever won or lost was ten to fifteen dollars. The South Merrick group started the betting at one dollar and increased it to fives and tens. I showed up at Marshall's house with one hundred dollars. Other kids came with more than a thousand dollars. Larry Lanpheer, whose father was allegedly a millionaire, arrived with his pockets overflowing with fifty dollar bills. He was drinking directly from a bottle of whiskey. He played recklessly and was known to lose over one thousand dollars at a time.

"Doesn't it bother you to give away so much money?" I asked.

"I believe in Epicurus. Eat, drink and be merry for tomorrow we may die. If the nuclear missiles don't get us, the pollution will," he replied as he drank some more whiskey.

The competition began as eight of us sat around an actual poker table. We ate pretzels, drank various forms of alcohol, and passed around joints. The deck circulated in a clock-wise direction and the dealer chose the game. We played differing permutations of stud poker, draw poker, high/low, blackjack, and other creative betting games. Everyone spoke as obscenely as possible, with the word *fucking* or *motherfucking* being the primary adjective.

After about five rounds, it was my turn to deal again, and I chose Acey Duecy. Everyone starts out by putting ten dollars into the pot. Each person is then dealt two cards face up, and then bets against the pot whether a third dealt card will fall numerically in between the first two. The minimum bet was five dollars and you could bet the amount of the whole pot. The game was over when someone won the whole pot.

After we had gone around the table four times, Larry was dealt an ace and a picture card, the biggest spread. I always counted the cards in my head, and I knew that there were three aces still left in the deck, and several picture cards.

"I bet the pot," Larry declared.

I counted the money. "There's three hundred fifty dollars," I said. "You sure that's your bet?"

"Go pot!'" Larry screamed.

I hesitated, then dealt him an ace.

"You lose!" everyone shouted. He slowly counted out the money and put it on the table.

The next round I had a three and a ten and bet two hundred dollars. I won. It was the biggest wager I had ever made. Each time we got to Larry, he bet pot, and lost. There was now over three thousand dollars in the kitty. Finally, with over five thousand dollars at stake, Marshall bet the pot and won. I passed the deal over to Dave. Larry pulled more money out of another pocket and started on his second bottle of whiskey.

As I drove back to my world, at four in the morning, I realized that being rich didn't necessarily prevent you from being screwed up.

One-Hundred Three

Bᴏʙ ᴀɴᴅ ɪ ᴡᴇʀᴇ sɪᴛᴛɪɴɢ in my room and listening to the Beatles album *Sgt. Pepper's Lonely Hearts Club Band*. We paid special attention to *Lucy in the Sky With Diamonds*.

Picture yourself in a boat on a river, with tangerine trees and marmalade skies

Somebody calls you, you answer quite slowly, a girl with kaleidoscope eyes

Cellophane flowers of yellow and green, towering over your head

Look for the girl with the sun in her eyes, and she's gone

Lucy in the sky with diamonds

"That song is definitely about an acid trip," Bob said. "Lucy in the Sky with Diamonds. That stands for LSD."

"John Lennon said that he got the title from a picture that his five year old son drew at school and the lyric is about the different images in the picture," I replied.

"Bullshit," said Bob. "Just look at the cover of the album. It's all about acid."

"Well, the Beatles all do admit that they have tripped. Maybe the album would be censored if they revealed the drug connection," I said.

"I am ready to drop some acid. Al has had several trips and I want to see what it's like," Bob declared.

"Ronnie Lefkowitz can get some. I'll ask him."

I purchased three tabs of *Sunshine* from Ronnie at school and hid them in the back of my glove compartment. I picked up Bob and Al on Saturday night and we drove to the Greek Diner on Merrick Road. The diner was open all night and Bob,

Al and I had spent hours there talking about life, death, God and philosophy. We sat at a table and ate dessert with the acid under my wallet in my pocket.

"I figured out the perfect way to describe God," I said. "No matter how you look at it, 'God is a creation of Himself'. I defy you to contradict that statement!"

"Wow," Bob contemplated, "God *is* a creation of Himself."

"If there is an almighty, omniscient, omnipresent, religious model of a God; He is God because He decided that He was God. He created Himself. If there is no God, and God is a concept that was contrived by humans, then man is God, and again God is a creation of Himself. No matter how you conceive of God, my statement stands; God is a creation of Himself."

"Incredible," said Al. "That line belongs in a Dylan song. Are you sure that you weren't tripping when you wrote that?"

"God is a creation of Himself. God is a creation of Himself." We all repeated it like a mantra.

"Did you bring the acid?" Bob asked.

"I've got three tabs of *Sunshine* in my pocket," I said. "I'll save mine for another time so that I can stay straight and drive, and take care of you guys."

In reality, I was afraid. I wanted to see what tripping was like, but the intensity of my childhood emotions terrified me. I couldn't be sure what might happen if they were all unleashed at once.

Without any warning, we looked up and saw Paul Baldwin standing by our table. "I haven't spoken to you since elementary school," I said. "What's happening?"

"I overheard you talking about acid. I want to try it."

Bob and Al burst out laughing. "Have you ever tripped before?" I asked. "Have you done any other drugs?"

"No, my parents would kill me," said Paul. "But I really want to do acid."

"Bob and Al were practically rolling on the floor. "I don't even know what these pills are like," I said. "We've never done them before."

"I don't care," responded Paul. "Let me buy one."

I held one in my hand and he grabbed it and immediately swallowed the whole pill in one gulp.

As Bob and Al laughed even harder, I said, "We can't leave him here alone. Let's just wait awhile and see what happens."

Al slid over into the booth. Paul sat, and we all stared at him waiting for something to happen. After about ten minutes, his face began to emanate terror. "Oh my God, I'm freaking out!" he cried. "I'm freaking out!"

Bob and Al again were overcome with hysterics. "I'm having a bad trip! I'm freaking out!" The more Paul screamed, the harder Bob and Al cackled.

"Is there anyone who can come and get you?" I asked Paul.

"I'm really freaking out," was his only response. I walked Paul over to the phone booth, found the sticker that read, "Drug Hotline," and dialed the number. "I've got a friend here who is having a bad trip," I said. "I'll put him on the phone."

We watched Paul calm down as he interacted with the voice on the phone. I poked my head in and he promised to call his parents.

"Where's our acid?" demanded Bob.

"You're not going to freak out on me, too?" I asked.

"We're not Paul Baldwin," said Bob and they threw the pills into their mouths.

We drove around aimlessly and talked about God and religion as we waited for their trips to start. Gradually, images of their hallucinations began to slide into the conversation.

"Your car keeps getting bigger and smaller!" Al screamed.

"Yeah, let's get out of it before it explodes," warned Bob. I yelled at them to wait until I stopped.

We ended up sitting on a bench in a dark, closed park. As they vividly chronicled the ever changing images swirling around their heads, I began to harmoniously share their experience. I was absorbed in a dream-like state and was comforted by the pulsating objects and shifting colors. I was falling into a peaceful, calming, kaleidoscopic world that was suddenly shattered by explosions. I realized that Bob was roaring, "They're after me! They're gonna kill me! They're everywhere!"

"Who?" I asked.

"Don't you see them!? Look! Over there! No, over there! They're after me!"

"There's no one there," I said, but Bob was no longer hearing me. Al sat and smiled and whispered about his hallucinations.

Bob became louder. I had never heard him scream this loud. Afraid of attracting attention, I guided them into my car and drove to my house. Bob's rants escalated.

"They're after me, damnit! They're gonna kill me!" Bob paced around my den. I made him drink some gin and tonic, hoping that it would calm him down, but he continued to get louder.

"What's going on down there?" Mom shouted. "Get them to stop or I'm going to call the police."

Al had now joined in but was laughing as he repeated Bob's paranoiac ravings. Suddenly, Bob began yelling that he was Jesus Christ. Then, he became God.

I took them outside. The neighborhood was asleep as I walked them down the deserted sidewalks. The louder they bellowed, the faster I walked. Bob would be livid if I took him to a hospital. His mother would never let him out of the house again. Walking it off was the only option.

The sun was rising by the time they both calmed down. "What do you remember?" I asked.

"Everything," said Al. "It was beautiful."

"It was awesome!" said Bob.

I took Al home and then Bob and I sat in the car outside his house. I wanted to make sure that he was totally over his trip before I let him go inside.

I slept until noon and then called Bob. "I definitely want to do that again," he said. I knew that this wasn't a path that I wanted to go down and felt unsettled by the fact that Bob and I were again making different decisions.

One-Hundred Four

It was Wednesday morning in April. I just swallowed my last valium tablet. My supply was now depleted and my renewals had all run out. I could easily get another prescription from Dr. Gittlestein, but while Bob had become more involved with drugs, my goal was to be valium free. Graduation was less than two months away and I was determined to leave high school liberated from my dependency. Sam Levine, my behavior therapist, had taught me several relaxation techniques and we were continually working on changing my destructive thoughts. I was confident that I had the tools to overcome any difficulties that might arise from quitting "cold turkey".

On Wednesday night, I sat on my bedroom floor in a lotus position, and practiced yoga breathing techniques. I slept soundly and woke up feeling triumphant. I was one day and night closer to being drug free. I had no symptoms on Thursday, and again performed yoga and breathing routines at bedtime to relax. I was peaceful and serene as I fell into a sound sleep.

At 2AM my eyes shot open. My breathing was rapid and shallow, and I was soaked in sweat. A switch in my viscera got turned on and a tidal wave of toxic fluid continuously crashed against my chest. I was drowning and violently struggling for air.

"Shit, I will not go through this again," I thought. I desperately endeavored to fill my head with positive and calming thoughts, but Jim Morrison and the Doors were replacing my words with their song, *The End*.

Caught in the Undertow

This is the end, my only friend, the end, of our elaborate plans, the end

Of everything that stands, the end, no safety or surprise, the end

I quickly walked in circles around the living room. I was crying, incredulous, and not willing to accept the reality of what was transpiring. "I will not give in to this," I said to myself. "And I will never take valium again."

It was 3:30. I forced myself to go back to bed. My arms and legs were so restless and fidgety that I couldn't stay in one position for more than five seconds. My muscles were all in spasms. The tension was excruciating. I went outside to the backyard and screamed. Further attempts to go to bed became futile, so I got dressed and jogged around the dark, sleeping neighborhood. I hoped that I could out run the monsters. The monster who lived in the bathtub drain in Brooklyn. The monster undertow who sucked me into the ocean. The monster named Eli who was trying to kill me. The monster who told me that I didn't deserve to live after Sheryl died. I wanted to exorcise them, to free myself from all these demons. But they all seemed to be overtaking me. Was this the end? I was overcome with a sense of doom.

The sun was coming up. Cars began to drive down the streets. I smelled breakfast coming out of kitchen windows. I went home and took a long shower, and went to school.

"Are you okay?"

"You look sick."

"What happened to you?"

"I had a rough night," was my only reply. I gradually calmed down and meandered through the fog of my day. Evening finally arrived. I fell asleep on the couch while watching TV.

Bob called. I forgot that I had promised to play poker with him and his friends at Jan's house. Theo and Pat met us there. I used to sit with this group at lunch in ninth grade, but hadn't had much interaction with any of them since. They had talked me into writing a poem to mock Seahag. I sometimes thought about her.

Jan lived in a newly painted, two bedroom, single story

house in the old section of Bellmore. We dealt the cards around the kitchen table and played for pennies. I thought about the games in South Merrick and wondered what the rich kids would think if they saw the stakes here. My heart was still racing, but I kept telling myself that I had everything under control.

Gradually, my chest ached more and more, and my heart felt like it was about to explode. I tried to hide my discomfort but my erratic breathing gave me away. The other kids periodically glanced at me, trying hard not to stare. I attempted to push myself past the intense discomfort. Then the thought entered my head that maybe I was really having a heart attack from the physical effects of valium withdrawal. All of my symptoms abruptly escalated.

"Holy shit, are you freaking out? Did you do acid?" Theo exclaimed.

"No, but I'm really sick. I need to go to the hospital," I moaned.

Theo and Paul drove me to Meadowbrook Hospital using my car. This was the place where Sheryl died, where Grandpa died, and where I had almost died. "What drugs did you take?" asked a doctor.

"Nothing," I said.

"If you're honest with us, we can help you quicker," he replied.

I told him about the valium. They did a series of tests and finally a doctor sat down and talked to me.

"Valium is an addictive drug," he explained. "You have been taking it for years and now you are in withdrawal. You can't talk yourself out of your body's reaction. You are having severe physical symptoms that must be treated medically."

"I don't want to take any more drugs," I said.

"I admire your determination, but you have to deal with the physical effects. You need to discuss this with your doctor."

"He'll just want me to take valium again. He was the one who kept increasing my dosage."

"Okay, what I can do is give you a less potent form of the

Caught in the Undertow

drug and have you gradually lower the dosage until your body adjusts. You can be weaned from it within about a month. A nurse will be back with a week's supply, written instructions, and a prescription. I do urge you to follow up with your family physician."

Mom and her friend Marsha came to pick me up at the hospital. She was extremely sympathetic when she heard about my experience.

"Where's your car?" she asked.

I found out that Theo and Paul had driven it up and down the streets of Bellmore at very high speeds. They used up most of my tank of gas and eventually received tickets for speeding and for running a stop sign. My anger at them was overshadowed by my jubilation. I was finally going to rid my body of valium.

One-Hundred Five

GRADUATION WAS LESS THAN TWO weeks away. Mom and Grandma were accompanying me to the Senior Awards Assembly. Grandma was wearing a fancy dress, lipstick and gold earrings. While looking at her, I thought about when I was younger, and recalled our trips into New York City to see Broadway plays. The high school's auditorium was filled with hundreds of well-dressed graduating seniors and their proud families. We students sat in the front rows, for easy access to the stage when our names were announced, and the glowing family members scrambled for seats behind us. The room was buzzing with the sound of indistinguishable, concurrent conversations as we all glanced at the programs and saw the lengthy list of scheduled awards. The administration had sent invitations to the honorees, but no one knew which award they would be receiving. All we knew was that we would be presented with some sort of cash scholarship for college.

As the presentation of the scholarships began, I tried to predict the one that was earmarked for me. The Teacher's Association Award was coming up. Mr. Dubroff was the president of the Teacher's Union and I knew that he liked me. He had complimented me many times for my ability to "logically and cogently present opinions and points of view." I actively participated in his class and he went out of his way to praise me. I also thought about all the occasions in which I could not speak in classes. I remembered Eli's words blaring in my head and the embarrassment that I felt hearing the sound of my own voice. I recalled vomiting before giving my oral report in

Finley's class, and felt proud that I struggled through so many difficult situations.

The Teacher's Award, however, went to Eric Meyers. He was very active in school politics, the star of the Debate Team, and the president of Student Council.

The Social Studies Scholarship was next. I had earned a 98 on the American History Regents, had taken the most difficult social studies electives, and had always excelled in those courses. But the award was given to Barry Brownstein, the chairman of At Your Service, a student volunteer organization. I looked at the list again and wondered which one I would receive.

I thought that the English Award might be a possibility. I had achieved a 98 on the English Regents, one of the highest scores in my grade, and won accolades for my writing, but the honor went to the editor of the school newspaper.

Everyone knew that Albert Frankenstein, the valedictorian, would be the recipient of all the math and science scholarships. His name was announced, as predicted, for all three of those awards.

The different honors for athletics were about to be bestowed. My high school sports career was my biggest disappointment as a student. My participation on school teams had always followed the same pattern. I felt free, athletic, and confident with my friends and at practice. I always made the team, but fell apart when the coaches yelled at me. I became the helpless little boy being abused by Eli. I felt as if they were about to hit me, like Eli did, and I felt choked off and threatened. I was able to overcome this feeling everywhere except with my coaches. I knew what was going on in my head, but still hadn't developed the ability to overcome my reflexive, dysfunctional physical reaction to being screamed at.

I had to fight back tears as a memory from my junior year flooded my consciousness. I had earned the starting spot, against some intense competition, as centerfielder on the varsity baseball team, only to lose it after some bad performances during games. I fought valiantly to gain my spot back. At practice, I caught any ball hit to the outfield, and I drove hard line drives to all the deepest parts of our stadium. I moved and ran with total poise and self-confidence. The coach put me back in as starter and batted me in the leadoff position. During an important game, I dropped two fly balls, and struck out three times. The more the coach yelled at me, the worse I performed, and finally I was benched again. Eli's hands were around my throat. I was devastated.

As I sat and listened to the athletes' names being called, I filled my head with positive thoughts, using the method that Dr. Sam had taught me. I had made all the teams that I had tried out for. I had improved my skills. I thought about going to Stony Brook next year and the competitive intramural sports program that they had. I was confident that I could make the teams for football, basketball and softball. Also, I had learned about the different drills that are used at practices, and I knew that I was going to coach someday. I was going to be an encouraging, inspiring, uplifting mentor, like Mr. Hill, my little league coach. My disappointments would become remnants of a distant past.

The presenters informed the audience that the Scholar/Athlete Awards were about to be presented. The three males and the three females who had the highest academic averages and had been on varsity sports teams would be the recipients. My name was the first one announced. As I glided up to the stage, I drank in the sound of the applause. I heard several students shouting, "Way to go, Goldstein!" "Good job!" "Congratulations!" I heard others whistling.

Mr. Whitley, the math teacher who gave me a "100" and an "F" for attitude, was my presenter. He was on the student awards committee. As he handed me an envelope, he shook my hand, looked me in the eyes, smiled, and whispered, "You represent everything that is wrong with today's youth. If it were up to me, I'd be handing you your Draft Notice, not an award!"

I smiled back and said, "You have been such a role model for me. You represent everything that I never want to be. Thank you, sir."

I sat down and looked at the certificate and the check in my envelope. It was made out to "The State University of New York at Stony Brook." I smiled as some of the students patted me on the back.

Towards the end of the evening a group of students burst through the rear doors and chanted, "What do we want? Peace! When do we want it? Now!' They were led by Mick Kaufman, our school "radical hippie," as he described himself. His real name was Mitchell, but he called himself Mick, after Mick Jagger. Mick had a round, hairy face and resembled Jerry Garcia. He had the courage to protest and to speak out, and many students and teachers highly respected him.

A group of teachers ushered the protesters out of the auditorium as many of us stood and raised our arms with our fingers in a peace sign. Several students and parents booed. Mr. Whitley stood on the edge of the stage and shook his head.

A few days later I registered for the Draft and received my Draft Card. I was classified ll-S, and given a student deferment.

One-Hundred Six

I DROVE MY CAR AWAY FROM John F. Kennedy High School for the last time. It was a warm, sunny afternoon and I was now a high school graduate. I went to Wantagh Park and drove to the far end of the road. I sat on a bench and stared at the ocean. I lit up a celebratory, cherry flavored Tiparillo cigar and inhaled the smoke. Alfie had passed these out after the ceremony. Mitch was distributing joints, but I hadn't done any drugs since becoming valium free.

Most of my friends were having graduation parties at different times over the course of the weekend. Many of them had handed me invitations and I ignored all of them. There was no party planned by my family. Eli hadn't even shown up at my ceremony.

I purposely sat alone at the park. It was profoundly obvious that there was a gaping void in my life. A cavernous emptiness and sadness. I needed to be alone.

A week ago, I had driven to the cemetery, to Sheryl's grave. I stared at her tombstone. I realized that she was a little girl. Only five years old. I asked, "Did you suffer? Were you in pain? Were you scared? Did you ask for me?" Do you know that I love you?" Her image filled my head and there was tranquility. I knew that I needed to forgive Mom. Sheryl wanted that. And I needed to move forward.

I took a clipboard out of my car, sat back on the bench, inhaled the ocean air, and wrote a letter to my sister.

Caught in the Undertow

To Sheryl Robin Goldstein

When we were little kids, I could not have imagined living my life without you. Even when we were fighting or angry at each other, I knew that we were connected and encircled by love. There was an intimacy that we both knew existed. I cherished our late night discussions. We'd meet in the hall outside our bedrooms. Just you and me. Everyone else was asleep. I picture you going to Kindergarten, and the pride that I felt when I saw you at school. "That's my little sister," I'd say.

Now, I think about you, and gaze at your pictures. You are all dressed up and smiling. I imagine us growing up together. Sharing our lives. Having deep discussions late at night. Arguing like a brother and sister, but smiling inside. You would have clapped the loudest when they called my name at Graduation. You would have visited me at college, and I would have told everybody, "That's my little sister!"

I cry when I realize that you are not here. I smile when I think of you and our time together.

I love you little sister!
Your big brother,
Jeffrey

Epilogue

In winter
As trees stand bare
Their plumage fallen to the earth
Piled up withered and dead
A lone brown, brittle leaf
Clings to a naked branch
Flapping in a biting wind

What will become of it
When new buds grow and prosper
In spring

Jeffrey Goldstein

THE SUMMER AFTER I GRADUATED from Kennedy High School was defined for me by two major events. On July 20, 1969, the United States achieved the first manned landing on the moon. Grandma and I sat and watched, transfixed by the images on the TV. Grandma was full of awe and amazement. "I can't believe that I am alive to see this," she kept repeating. I felt honored to be sharing these moments with her. The woman, who as a young girl embarked on a long, arduous journey on a ship across the ocean to America, was now watching a spaceship travel across the heavens to the moon. I was experiencing the past melding into the future and it seemed as if anything was possible.

The second event also occurred In July when I started driving a cab for the Bellmore Taxi Company. I worked for them each summer while in college and for a while after I graduated from Stony Brook. A taxi driver was able to earn a large amount of money, 40% of all the fares plus tips, and in Bellmore it was a highly coveted part time job. Mom, a staunch Democrat, joined the local Republican club so that I could get the job. "That doesn't mean that I can't still vote for the Democrats," she said. "What political party does your family belong to?" was the first question that I was asked at the interview with the taxi owners, and despite my long hair, I gave the correct answer and was offered summer employment.

I volunteered to drive the night shift, from 6PM until around 2AM, and received a valuable education. I developed my people skills by interacting with customers that I wouldn't have met under normal circumstances. I drove prostitutes, transsexuals, drug addicts, some celebrities, self-confessed criminals, as well as suburban commuters to their destinations. I spent hours talking to, listening to and learning from my diverse group of passengers.

One shift, at midnight, I picked up a fare at the Jones Beach Hotel Bar. He was very overweight, had long unwashed hair, and a scruffy beard. He stared at me with droopy blood shot eyes and then his face lit up. "Jeffrey Goldstein! How the fuck are you? Remember me, we went to school together."

As I stared back it dawned on me that he was Bob Conroy. The "hood" bully from junior high school. "Nice to see you, Bob. Where can I take you?"

"What the hell are you doing driving a taxi? You were so fucking smart!"

"I'm going to college. This is a summer job."

"Well make sure you do something with your life. Don't end up like me." He gave me a five dollar tip.

I went to Stony Brook in September with a significant amount of money from my commissions and tips. The night before my first class I was in bed by ten o'clock. I had a dreaded 8AM class the next morning and didn't want to be late. I had arrived on campus three days earlier, checked the list of required textbooks, and purchased all of my supplies at the campus book store. Everything that I needed for my first day was sitting on my desk and I was totally prepared for all my classes. I had spent the morning walking around the grounds and finding all of the academic buildings where I had classes.

The incoming freshmen had been spread out and assigned to all the different dorms. I was placed in the oldest building, Gray Dormitory, and living in a small two person room. Everyone else on my hall was a junior or senior. My roommate, a senior named Mike Parmley, had not yet arrived, and no one seemed to know who he was. I was hoping that he'd never arrive and I'd end up with a single.

At 3AM, I heard someone unlocking the door. A tall figure, reeking of marijuana, wearing a fur lined, hooded, winter parka, burst into the room. "Hey, man, I'm your roommate."

I rubbed my eyes and gawked at him.

"Why the hell are you in bed? Let's smoke a joint and get to know each other," He said.

"I have an eight o'clock class."

"Fuck that! It's all bullshit. They just want to brainwash you."

"Why are you dressed like that?"

"I was working up in Alaska over the summer. Made a shit load of money. Here, this is the best grass you're ever gonna smoke."

"Don't you have any classes?"

"I'm just here to stay out of the Draft."

We eventually reached an understanding and both "did our own things". His name for me was, "Brainwashed Boy," and I called him, "Eskimo." I ended up doing all of my schoolwork in the library. "Eskimo" ended up leaving in March and stuck me with a $550 bill for long distance calls that he made on our room phone.

During freshman orientation I met Rob, who became my

closest friend that year. I now had two Roberts as best friends. Rob and I roomed together the next three years.

In September I also met Laura Lynn Carey, who came from Kentucky. She became the most significant female in my life, mainly because of the sexual education that I received from her. She was totally uninhibited, and we couldn't get enough of each other. I spent several nights a week sleeping in her bed and avoiding the contact high that I received from spending the night in my room.

I enjoyed my academic experiences, but slowly gave in to the many distractions of being on a college campus. I found myself skipping classes and missing assignments. Laura and I had been drifting apart, and finally, after a bitter argument, we broke up at the end of the semester. The same day my grade report arrived: English-A, Psychology 101-B, Sociology 101-C, Statistics-D, and Physical Science-C. My cumulative average was 2.4 out of 4.0. I should have seen it coming, but I was devastated. I had never received such poor grades.

I ignominiously returned home for the semester break. My childhood feelings were awakened and I was depressed and suicidal. This time, I was able to talk to Mom. She listened and was supportive. She had evolved, and I now had a supportive mother. We never yelled at each other again

When I returned to school, I became more focused on my school work. I made a schedule and set aside times to study and do assignments, and still had plenty of opportunities to enjoy all the social amenities of college life.

During the summer, I spent much of my free time with Bob. He'd regularly pick me up after my nightly taxi shift and we'd go to various college bars attempting to pick up girls. Some nights, when we were unsuccessful, we'd sit in his car in front of my house and talk until sunrise. Books were a major topic of discussion. We were both enthralled by a book called, *A Clockwork Orange,* a dystopian novel about an ultra-violent teenaged boy and a controversial psychological procedure that was inflicted upon him. We both read it several times. Bob had become a heavy smoker, at one point he consumed more than three packs a day, and I often left his car dizzy from all the smoke.

One hot night at the end of July I was driving my taxi down Bellmore Avenue at 2AM. I had just dropped off the last fare of my shift and had all the windows open. The streets were normally empty this time of night but I heard an engine running and looked over at a car stopped by the side of the road. I slowed down, and suddenly, the car pulled out and cut in front of me at a right angle. I couldn't stop and crashed into its side and spun it around. The police quickly arrived and discovered a very drunk, young girl passed out behind the driver's wheel. It was obvious that she had cut me off and that I had been driving under the speed limit. No one was hurt, and my taxi just had a dented front bumper. The police came back with me to the taxi stand to fill out a report.

Anthony Pavones owned the cab that I was driving. He was an inveterate gambler and was often visited by scary looking thugs demanding money. It turned out that he had no insurance on the cab, he had not renewed the medallion, and the vehicle had not been inspected. Anthony was arrested. I later visited him, feeling horrible about what had happened, and he shook my hand. "It's not your fault," he said. "This was bound to happen sooner or later. I'm just a fuck-up. You're going to be someone, someday." Anthony became another example of someone who had made awful choices and who unwittingly motivated me to make good ones.

Back at Stony Brook, I continued to experience personal growth and academic success. Sometimes, certain people or events would trigger an onslaught of my dysfunctional childhood emotions, and I took advantage of the student counselling services. They introduced me to Transactional Analysis, and other proactive, empowering approaches for improvement. In addition, I read books about Eastern religion and philosophy. I was becoming more and more in control of my emotions and reactions to events. I never had to endure another panic attack.

Jeffrey Goldstein

My last three years in college, I lived in a suite with Rob as my roommate, and our friends Dennis and Howie in another room. The third room had various occupants, including my high school friend Sam Mowatt, who had attended Nassau Community College, and then transferred to Stony Brook. Junior year I declared myself a social science major, specializing in psychology, sociology and American history, and planned to apply to law school.

At the beginning of my senior year, I impulsively decided to student teach during the second semester. Sam had decided to become a teacher, and, even though I had never considered it before, it sounded like fun. I had never taken any education courses, so I had to convince the coordinating professor, Dr. Seifman, that I was serious about teaching before I could be accepted into the program. I realized that I still had a fear of public speaking, and remembered the quote, "Do the thing you fear, and the fear disappears." I forced myself to raise my hand, and I answered questions and gave opinions in every class. In my Adolescent Sociology class, I volunteered to present an optional report. My assignment was to explain the effects of the 1950's Beatnik subculture on the Hippies of the 1960's.

I delivered my research in front of a group of more than forty students, the professor and a group of teaching assistants. As I spoke, I somehow compelled myself to look at the faces of my audience. I noticed their engrossed expressions when I said something interesting, their smiles when I said something humorous, and their engaged body language when I became animated and enthusiastic. All my self-consciousness melted away as I began to feel important and in control. They were all attentive and listening to me. I was getting the approval of all of these people at the same time. As I focused on the listeners, I became free flowing and dynamic. I could be myself without any inhibitions. Eli's hands were finally gone from my throat.

I chose to student teach at Brentwood High School. Brentwood was about twenty miles from campus, and was one of the few inner city type schools on Long Island. I knew that I would have the most rewarding experience there. Brentwood's population was predominantly non-white, and they were so overcrowded that they operated on a split session. I was assigned to the morning set of classes and had to wake up by 5AM, so that I could be there by 6:30 AM.

As soon as I entered my first classroom, I knew that I wanted to be a teacher. This was the type of environment that I felt comfortable in. I was immediately able to connect to the students. I felt an empathy towards them that enabled me to grow up and to mature, and to forget about my own inadequacies. I spent my free time during the day interacting with the students, listening, talking and giving advice. I knew exactly how to act. It was easy. I simply became the adult that I wish had been there for me when I was a kid. I sincerely cared about the students and was genuinely interested in them. It took very little effort to be positive and enthusiastic. On my last day, my cooperating teacher told me, "Wow, you seem to be a natural at this." In my evaluation at the end of the semester, Dr. Seifman, who had initially been reluctant to let me student teach, said, "I believe that you will develop the ability to teach anybody, anything." I concluded that it was worth getting up at 5AM every day.

Everyone else in my suite graduated in May, but I had to come back for a fifth year and take education classes to get my certification. During the summer, I got my job back driving a taxi, and spent time with Bob. We both were writing a great deal of poetry and decided to print a book of our best work. We named it, *And I Complacently Smile*, the title of one of my poems. Bob had a serious girlfriend named Claudia, who eventually became his wife, and we printed copies at her father's office. I wrote an interview of myself for the beginning of the book, and we wrote a glowing review of the poems for the back cover. We attempted to sell copies to anyone that we met. Our sales pitch was, "We're going to be famous writers someday, and you can buy a copy of our first publication for only five dollars. Think of it as an investment. When we are established poets, it will be worth a fortune, like having a copy of the first ever recording of the Beatles." We sold dozens of copies.

I returned to Stony Brook in September and lived in a new

suite with a group of friends who were a year younger. The first week of school I travelled around campus with a box filled with copies of my book and visited old girlfriends. They were easier to sell to than the boys that I knew. On a Wednesday, I went to Lois's suite, a girlfriend from my junior year. I had just finished my sales pitch, had sold six copies, and was flirting with a group of Lois's friends. Suddenly, a new girl walked out of the bathroom. She was wearing a bathrobe and her wet hair was wrapped in a towel.

"Meet Gretchen," Lois said. "She is a visiting student from St. Lawrence University and will be living in our suite."

Gretchen smiled and I was smitten. The next day I came back and gave her a copy of my book for free. I emphasized the fact that this was the only copy that I had given away. That weekend we went on our first date and saw an "X" rated movie called, *The Last Tango in Paris*, a controversial film starring Marlon Brando. When we were together, I felt as if I had known her all my life. Our relationship quickly moved forward. We travelled to Montego Bay, Jamaica for winter break. We couldn't afford to stay in a hotel, so we went backpacking and slept in a tent on the beach. As we spent all our time together, I realized that I was in love. The summer of 1974, after I graduated, we lived together in the basement of a house in Hempstead, Long Island. I drove a taxi and Gretchen worked at a Friendly's Restaurant and for the newspaper. One night in August, I proposed marriage to her. She said yes.

In September, 1974, Gretchen went back to Stony Brook for her senior year, while I continued to drive a taxi. On June 7, 1975, we got married using vows and a ceremony that I wrote. The wedding took place outdoors in a field in Pompey, New York, near Syracuse, where her parents lived and she grew up. We decided to settle down in Central New York.

Gretchen and I have been happily married since then. We have two amazing sons. Gregory was born on April 11, 1980, and Justin was born on February 18, 1983. My Grandma was alive to meet both of them. I now have what I had always wanted, to be a part of a loving family. Greg and his wife Hannah blessed us all with our first grandchild, Reid, on November 26, 2012. In July, 2013, Greg, Hannah, Reid, Justin, and his girlfriend, Kerry all surprised Gretchen by meeting us in Montego Bay, Jamaica. Forty years after Gretchen and I made the trip in college, we had the joy of spending time there with our family.

I also had the honor of spending thirty six rewarding years as a high school teacher and coach, and I am now working as a Dale Carnegie instructor.

My childhood dreams have all been fulfilled. I got on my horse and I rode, and I escaped the undertow.

Bob riding motorcycle

Gretchen at Stony Brook

Jeff and Gretchen at Stony Brook

Jeff and Gretchen at house in Bellmore

Jeff senior at Stony Brook

Mom's Epilogue

As I look back, I realize how much Mom has progressed, and I admire her resiliency and determination. She lost her daughter, a few months later lost her father, and had a dysfunctional husband. Eli uprooted the family and took us to Houston, where he abandoned us. He returned, only to abandon us again on Long Island, and Mom became the breadwinner for the family. She taught school, tutored, and dealt with the enormity of the stress from our situation.

The best part of Mom's progress was the way she grew into the role of a Grandmother. When Greg was born, she immediately made the trip to upstate New York, and I watched the look of love and pride on her face as she held our first born child. She was then one of the first people to visit and to hold Justin. Each time that she held one of my boys, she was *k'velen*, bursting with happiness.

Mom, as my sons grew up, developed into an adoring Grandma. Visiting her home on Long Island became a highlight of their school and summer vacations. She took Greg and Justin to spend time in her third grade class, to museums, aquariums, and to play in parks. They developed a warm, affectionate relationship, and they still love going to see their now 88 year old Grandma.

Mom also made a point of being positive and friendly to Greg's wife, Hannah, and to Justin's girlfriend, Kerry. They both also love *Grandma*. And now, watching the total joy and elation that Mom exudes when she interacts with Reid, it is obvious that I really *do* have the family that I always wanted.

Mom also found a way to escape the undertow.

Credits

Page 146
Fort Worth, Dallas or Houston
Written by John D. Loudermilk,
performed by George Hamilton IV

Page 267
Like A Rolling Stone
Written and performed by Bob Dylan

Page 274
Light My Fire
Written and performed by The Doors

Page 277
Scarborough Fair/Canticle
Written and performed by Paul Simon and Art Garfunkel

Blowing in the Wind
Written and performed by Bob Dylan

Is There Anybody Here?
Written and performed by Phil Ochs

Page 290
For What It's Worth
Written by Stephen Stills, performed by Buffalo Springfield

Jeffrey Goldstein

Page 295
The Mighty Quinn
Written by Bob Dylan, performed by Manfred Mann

Page 299
Eve of Destruction
Written by P.F. Sloan, performed by Barry McGuire

Page 303
Abraham, Martin and John
Written by Dick Holler, performed by Dion

Page 331
Ballad in Plain D
Written and performed by Bob Dylan

Page 342
Tomorrow Never Knows
Written by John and Paul McCartney,
performed by The Beatles

Page 344
When the Children are Asleep from *Carousel*
Lyrics by Oscar Hammerstein II, music by Richard Rogers

Page 348
Lucy in the Sky With Diamonds
Written by John Lennon and Paul McCartney,
performed by The Beatles

Page 353
The End
Written and performed by The Doors

CPSIA information can be obtained at www.ICGtesting.com
Printed in the USA
LVOW06s1506110614

389606LV00001B/212/P